E. W. Gough

The royal Hourse Book

E. W. Gough

The royal Hourse Book

ISBN/EAN: 9783337728021

Printed in Europe, USA, Canada, Australia, Japan

Cover: Foto ©ninafisch / pixelio.de

More available books at **www.hansebooks.com**

THE ROYAL HORSE BOOK.

"CENTAUR;"

OR,

THE "TURN OUT,"

A Practical Treatise on the (Humane) Management of Horses, either in Harness, Saddle, or Stable; with Hints respecting the Harness-Room, Coach-House, &c.,

BY

E. W. GOUGH.

(THIRD—AND POPULAR—EDITION.)

HENRY THACKER & CO.,
NEW STREET SQUARE, FLEET STREET, LONDON, E.C.

1885.

COPYRIGHT.] [ALL RIGHTS RESERVED

CONTENTS.

	PAGE.
PREFACE TO THIRD EDITION	9
THE "CENTAUR"	13
THE ARGUMENT	15
DEDICATION AND ADDRESS TO SIR C. FORSTER, Bart., M.P.	17, 18
INTRODUCTION TO FIRST EDITION	19
PRELIMINARY REMARKS	21
THE "THOROUGH GROOM"	23
SELECTING THE HORSE ...	26
CLASSIFICATION OF HORSES	30
STANDARD MEASURE, AND PRINCIPAL POINTS OF THE HORSE	31
RULE FOR JUDGING THE AGE OF THE HORSE	32
PURCHASING OR ORDERING THE HARNESS	39
FITTING THE HARNESS	44
TO ATTACH THE HORSE TO THE VEHICLE	58
DRIVING	63
MEMOS. NOT TO BE FORGOTTEN IN CONNECTION WITH THE HARNESS	71
UNHARNESSING AND CLEANING	72
THE VEHICLE	80
JIBBING	86
RIDING	89
THE STABLE AND STABLE FITTINGS	101
DOCKING AND NICKING	123
CART, FARM, AND PIT GEARS; SHOEING AND ROUGHING	125
EFFECT OF MUSIC UPON THE HORSE	133
NATURAL CLEANLINESS OF THE HORSE	136
WONDERFUL HORSES	138
WILD HORSES	140
HORSEY PHRASES, SLANG TERMS, AND RACY REMARKS...	141
HORSE SHOWS AND MAY-DAY CELEBRATIONS	147
THE FREE REGISTRY SYSTEM	150
SADDLERS' SHOPS	153
SADDLERS' GUIDE	154
A FEW NECESSARY HINTS AND RECEIPTS	176
VARIETIES OF THE HORSE	179
IRON HORSES: CYCLES	183
A CHAPTER OF ACCIDENTS	186
SHAKESPEARE A HORSEMAN	204
TESTIMONIALS, &c.	212
CONCLUSION, EXPLANATION OF TITLE	225
CHAPTER OF SPECIALITIES	227

LIST OF ILLUSTRATIONS.

THE CENTAUR.

MUTUAL FEELING—FEAR AND SURPRISE.

ANATOMY OF THE HORSE.

EASE AND COMFORT.

PLEASURE AND ACTION.

A SCREW LOOSE.

BITS, POULTICE BOOTS, MUZZLES, &c.

THE TEETH AND FEET.

THE AUTHOR'S CENTAUR.

INDEX TO ADVERTISERS.

ATKINSON & PHILIPSON	Carriage and Harness Manufacturers.
BARNSBY, J. A.	Saddle Manufacturer.
BOWDEN, F. H.	Henry's Hippacca.
BOWN, WILLIAM	Horse Clippers.
BRECKNELL, TURNER, & SONS	Saddle Soap.
BUNCH, BENJ., & SONS	Iron & Steel.
CLARE, JOSEPH	Currier.
DAWES, F.	Horse Cloths, &c.
DAY, SON, & HEWITT	Horse Keeper's Medicine Chest.
DOULTON, & CO.	Blue Brick Pavings for Stables, Sanitary Appliances, &c.
EGLINGTON, F.	Bits, Snaffles, Stirrups, &c.
ELD, GEORGE	Hames, Traces, &c.
GOUGH & CO.	Harness, Saddles, Saddle Bars, &c.
HAMBLET, J.	Terra Metallic Pavings for Stables.
HANFORD, JAMES	"The Golden Embrocation" or "Cure All."
HART, ARTHUR	"Saddlery Webs" and "Cavalry Braces."
HASSALL & SINGLETON	Stable Fittings, &c.
HAWKINS, J. H., & CO.	Bits, Stirrups, Spurs, &c.
HINKLEY, WALTERS, & CO.	Hinkley's Liniment.
HUMBER & CO.	Bicycles and Tricycles.
JAMIESON & CO.	Harness Composition.
LISTER, R. A., & CO.	The Beaufort Hunt Mill.
LONDON & PROVINCIAL	Horse and Carriage Insurance Co.
LONDON RUBBER CO.	Waterproof, Driving, and Riding Coats, &c.
MYERS, T.	Royal Cattle Spice.
PLANT, W. & J.	Horse Clippers.
POND'S EXTRACT CO.	Pond's Extract, Veterinary Remedy.
ROPER, R., SON & CO.	Jem Cook's Alterative and Condition Powders.
SPRATT'S PATENT	Forage Biscuits, "Locarium," &c.
SWINDEN & SONS	Watches for Hunting and Shooting.
THACKER, HENRY, & CO.	Inks, Pens, Glu-ene, &c.
TONKS, J., & CO.	Curriers.
URCH & CO.,	Saddlery, Harness, &c.
VENABLES, THOMAS	Coach and Gig Harness, Furniture, &c.
WILKINSON, W. B. & CO.	Stable Floors, Stable Yards, &c.

PREFACE
TO THIRD EDITION OF "CENTAUR."

> "All tongues speak of him, and the bleared sights
> Are spectacled to see him; your prattling nurse
> Into a rapture lets the baby cry,
> While she chats him: the kitchen malkin pins
> Her richest lockram 'bout her reechy neck,
> Clambering the walls to eye him; stalls, bulks, windows,
> Are smothered up, leads fill'd and ridges horsed
> With variable complexions; all agreeing
> In earnestness to see him."—SHAKESPEARE.
> *Coriolanus*, ACT II, SCENE I.

ENCOURAGED by the intense curiosity and excitement which greeted the appearance of this work in 1878, and the extensive sale of the second issue, together with its still increasing popularity—which, indeed, has far surpassed his most sanguine expectations—the Author is induced to publish another edition, and in order to bring the work within the reach of everyone interested in the care and management of horses, he has decided to issue the book in a cheaper form. In arriving at this decision the writer is actuated by a sincere desire to diffuse practical knowledge among people who have horses, either of their own, or are entrusted with the care of those of others, as will enable them to obtain the greatest amount of work at the least cost, and with the greatest amount of ease and comfort to the animals themselves.

There can be no doubt that in many cases—

> "Evil is wrought from want of thought
> As well as want of heart,"

and that much of the cruelty inflicted upon the horse is the result of ignorance rather than intention on the part of the attendant; therefore, it was with the view to removing this ignorance or carelessness that the Author was constrained to publish this work originally, and the very encouraging and numerous letters and testimonials he has received from all parts of the world are convincing proofs that his humble endeavours have not been in vain, but, on the contrary, that they have been productive of much practical good; and he trusts that by this popular or cheap edition of his work many persons who could not afford to purchase the higher-priced book may now be enabled to procure a copy, and permanently profit by the perusal and study of its contents. If a man can only succeed in convincing a horse that he is its friend, and has no intention of rough usage, or to hurt it, then the horse will do anything for such a man; and the Author's object is to show his readers how to win and retain the ready confidence of the horse, and, at the same time, to preserve its health, and keep it and the "turn out" generally in proper condition; which means ease and comfort for the driver, as well as the probability of greater freedom from accident.

Although the present edition is much lower in price than the preceding editions, yet it will be found to contain the same original matter and many lines added, in harmony with the times. It has also been carefully revised, and recent discoveries and reliable opinions touched upon. One novel feature in the present edition, and one which will be found both edifying and amusing, is the introduction of what might be aptly termed a "Shakesperian chapter" on the horse and its belongings.

The fact is well known that the "Great bard of Avon"—who wrote "Not for an age, but for all time"—was a careful student of both Nature and Art; and many of the quotations in the chapter referred to will prove how carefully and correctly he had studied the character of this noble animal the horse; and how thoroughly he understood all that was necessary to its comfort and convenience.

The interest and value of this work will be further enhanced by the addition of a chapter devoted to useful inventions and practical discoveries, so that persons in want of articles connected with the horse may see where he can be supplied; and, where the Author has had an opportunity of testing any speciality, he will give his unbiased judgment of its merits for the guidance of his readers, who may rely upon the opinions expressed, as they will be given only after a careful and painstaking examination or thorough testing of the articles, as the case may be. It is intended that, either now or at a future time, this department shall form a standard register or book of reference to the advertisements shown at the end of the work, which shall consist only of specialities of genuine merit and real utility to which intending purchasers can with confidence turn. Referring to the one continuous stream of praises and complimentary encomiums passed upon the previous editions of this work, the Author would here mention one brief opinion sent by a gentleman who prides himself upon the number and value of his horses. He says: "Your book, 'CENTAUR,' is a real life saver, and a copy of it ought to be chained to every stable door."

It is gratifying to find that an effort is being made to encourage the carters and others employed by the Railway Companies and other large proprietors to treat their horses with systematic kindness, and to keep the stables and harness in proper order. This is a step in the right direction, and one which this work will render an easy task for those who make themselves acquainted with its directions and arguments.

In adding a chapter on cycles, the Author thinks such observations peculiarly adapted to the times in which we live, and to the present issue of "CENTAUR." Since the first edition of the work appeared, bicycles and tricycles have made immense strides in perfection of manufacture, and have indeed become a permanent institution of the road; so much so, that now in all our rides and drives, with horse, carriage, or team, the modern machine has to be bargained for, and its noiseless approach claims special observance of the "Rule of the Road," which applies as strictly to one as to the other, the bicycle being no longer a toy, but a recognised and welcome motive-power, and in thorough harmony with the requirements of this fass and go-a-head age; therefore the Author would call the particular attention of horsemen and cyclists alike to the rules and laws laid down for the general guidance and public safety, for

> The rule of the road is a paradox quite,
> As the drivers they jog it along;
> If you keep to the left you are sure to go right,
> But if you keep to the right you are wrong.

While venturing to place before the public another edition of "CENTAUR" (which the Author believes to be a requirement and a want), he would take this opportunity of tendering his thanks for the extensive patronage and good feeling bestowed upon his former editions.

The Author thinks that perhaps the best proof of the popularity of his work, is the number and variety of piratical imitations, and persistant borrowers of his registered title, and the frequent use of the word "Centaur" in connection with inventions and periodicals which have no bearing whatever upon the subject treated of in the original, and which undoubtedly furnishes a monster illustration of the old adage, that—

"Imitation is the most complete flattery."

PARK HALL HOUSE,
    WALSALL,
        May 1st, 1884.

THE "CENTAUR."

"O Circe! O mother of spite,
Speak the last of that curse and imprison me quite,
In the husk of a brute; that no pity may name
The man that I was, that no kindred may claim—
The monster that hunters shun in their flight,
The men in their horror, the women in fright."

ENTAURI (-orum), that is, the Bull Killers, were an ancient race, inhabiting Mount Pelion in Thessaly. They lead a wild and savage life, and are hence called "savage beasts" in Homer (who lived 1,000 years before Christ). In later accounts they were represented as half horses and half men, and are said to have been the offspring of Ixion and a cloud. The Centaurs are celebrated in ancient story for their fight with the Lapithæ, which arose at the marriage feast of Pirithous. This fight is sometimes placed in connexion with a combat of Hercules with the Centaurs. It ended by the Centaurs being expelled from their country, and taking refuge on Mount Pindus, on the frontiers of Epirus. Chiron is the most celebrated among the Centaurs. We know that hunting the bull on horseback was a national custom in Thessaly, and that the Thessalians were celebrated riders. Hence may have arisen the fable that the Centaurs were half men and half horses, just as the native Americans, when they first saw a Spaniard on horseback, believed horse and man to be one being. The Centaurs are frequently represented in ancient works of art, and generally as men from the head to the loins, while the remainder of the body is that of a horse with its four feet and tail.

Chiron, the wisest and justest of the Centaurs, son of Cronos (Saturn) and Philyra, lived on Mount Pelion. He was instructed by Appollo and Diana, and was renowned for his skill in hunting, medicine, music, gymnastics, and the art of prophecy. All the most ancient heroes of Grecian story are described as the pupils of Chiron in these arts. He saved Peleus from the other Centaurs, who were on the point of killing him, and he also restored to him the sword which Acastus had concealed. Hercules, too, was his friend; one of the poisoned arrows of Hercules struck Chiron, who, although immortal, would not live any longer, and gave his immortality to Prometheus. Zeus placed Chiron among the stars as Sagittarius.

Ixion—Zeus (Jupiter) created a phantom resembling Hera, and by it Ixion became the father of a Centaur.

While Pirithous was celebrating his marriage with Hippodamia, the intoxicated Centaur Eurytion, or Eurytus, carried her off, and this act occasioned the celebrated fight, in which the Centaurs were defeated.

"THE CENTAURS, or BULL KILLERS.

"Those strange beings, half man, half horse, which we see represented in works of art, are the Centaurs. Such creatures seem impossible in nature, yet the ancient Greeks firmly believed in their existence. It is not hard to discover what gave them the idea of such monsters.

"Centaur, does not mean 'half man, half horse,' but 'bull killer;' a being half a horse would more properly be called a Hippocentaur. In the oldest Greek stories about the Centaurs they are spoken of as a savage race, inhabiting the woods and mountains of Thessaly, a country famous for wild bulls, which the natives hunted on horseback.

"Now, there was a time when the horse, now so useful in most parts of the world, was a wild, untamed animal; and the people who first brought it to subjection, broke it in and rode upon it, would be looked upon as wonderful beings by the men of those tribes, who had perhaps never seen a horse. To them the horse and his rider would appear to be one animal, especially when seen at a distance, and from the back view, so that the horse's head was not visible. Indeed, this really occurred when the Spaniards invaded Mexico. The natives had never seen a horse in their lives, and when they saw the extraordinary animal leaping and bounding, with an armed figure apparantly growing out of its back, they were terrified at the monster, and it was not till they had seen the Spaniards dismount from their horses that they would believe they were separate from their steeds, and only men after all!"—*Chatterbox.*

THE ARGUMENT.

"A horse!
A horse!
My kingdom for a horse"!

IN the above quotation, as in many other sentences of the great dramatist, there is more philosophy than at first meets the eye. No doubt if Richard, when the tide of battle turned against him at Bosworth Field, could have procured such a steed as that which carried the renowned Dick Turpin to York, he might, like Turpin, have effected his flight to that city, and there, as he was highly esteemed, he might not only have escaped from his adversary, but have raised such an army among his northern retainers, by whom he was sincerely beloved, as would have turned the tide of war in his favour; but for want of a horse he was overtaken and slain. No doubt the Egyptians, who were the first to use the horse for military purposes, won many of their tributary kingdoms by means of their cavalry. One legend says that the success of the Spaniards in Peru was in no small degree owing to their cavalry, as the natives, who thought the horse and his rider were one animal,* became alarmed, and fled at the very sight of the cavalry. It is, therefore, no exaggeration to say that kingdoms have been won and lost by means of the horse. King Robert Bruce, through a little strategy and the fleetness of his horse, escaped the machinations of the traitor Comyn, and saved his life, and afterwards won the crown and kingdom of Scotland. A friend of Bruce's—who was residing at the Court of Edward, King of England—ascertained that a plot had been concocted to murder Bruce in his castle at Lochmaben; and fearing to send any written communication, lest it should be intercepted, forwarded to Bruce a pair of spurs and a purse of gold. Bruce knew that the spurs meant flight, and the purse means for his journey; but the ground was covered with snow, and if he were to fly, the conspirators could easily trace him. He,

---
* Centaur.

however, got the blacksmith to invert his horse's shoes, so that by the prints of the horse's feet upon the snow, it appeared Bruce had returned to his castle instead of having just left it. The ruse succeeded admirably, and Bruce escaped to Dumfries, a town about eight miles from his castle, where he met the chief conspirator and slew him. At the Battle of Bannockburn, Bruce's horse rendered him valuable service in several of the hand-to-hand encounters in which he was on that day engaged. Many instances are on record of monarchs and others being saved through the swiftness, courage, or ingenuity of the horse. Thus we are told, 1st Book of Kings, 20th chapter, and 20th verse—That " every one slew his man, and the Syrians fled, and Israel pursued them, and Ben-hadad, the King of Syria, escaped on an horse."

The horse has, from the time of the Egyptians to the present day, been intimately associated with man in all his undertakings; a book, therefore which will practically treat of "The Horse and its immediate surroundings" cannot fail to be both interesting and useful, and such the Author trusts this his work will prove.

RESPECTFULLY DEDICATED

(By Special Permission)

TO

SIR CHARLES FORSTER, BART., M.P.,

BY

THE AUTHOR.

ADDRESS

TO

SIR CHARLES FORSTER, BART., M.P.

My Dear Sir,

ALSALL, your native town, being the great emporium of Saddlery, where that, and the kindred trade of Harness manufacturing, are carried on in all their various departments, and everything used in connection with the Horse, either for civil or military purposes, is produced in the highest state of perfection; and you having for over a quarter of a century been the faithful representative of Walsall in Parliament, I know of no one to whom this work could be more appropriately dedicated, or one so deserving as yourself of this humble tribute of respect.

The work, which aims at being a thoroughly practical treatise on the Horse and its Rider, will be found to contain such instructions as will, if strictly carried out, enable those entrusted with the care of that most useful and faithful companion of man—the Horse—to secure its comfort, preserve its health, prolong its years, and increase its usefulness. Information will also be found in this work which will enable parties requiring horses for business or pleasure to select those best suited to the purposes for which they are intended.

Such a work may therefore be looked upon as an effort to introduce a more rational and humane system of treatment for that noble animal, and knowing that your sympathies are sincerely with all movements having for their object the amelioration of the condition of the human subject, or that of the lower animals, I sincerely hope this humble effort to secure better care for the horse, more comfort and safety for those in charge, and greater satisfaction to the owner, may meet with your approval.

Your humble and obedient Servant,
EDWARD W. GOUGH.

Park Hall House,
May 1st, 1878.

INTRODUCTION
TO FIRST EDITION.

" To advise and not dictate."

IN obedience to the urgent wishes of my numerous patrons and friends, I have the pleasure of submitting, in Book Form, that system of treatment relative to the care of the Horse and its belongings, which I have throughout my life's experience and engagements, (at home and abroad,) in connection with my business, always practised and upheld; and which system, when advised verbally, has met with such general appreciation.

Dating, as I have the honour to do, from a most important midland town—indeed I may say the very seat of the harness trade and every article connected with my subject—it will not, I trust, be considered egotistical if I pride myself in being the proprietor of one of the principal General Saddlery and Harness Manufactories in that town, and venture to put before my readers this work and " *Great Want*," in the shape of instructions and suggestions to those about to *set up* a " Turn out," which may be applied to useful account in many cases by those already in possession of that necessity, or luxury, as the case may be.

The Author's hope and belief is, that the contents of this book will be appreciated by all interested in the Horse, emanating as it does from one who is, and has been from his youth, directly connected with the subject in hand, and whose sole object is, and whose wish and ambition has always been, to alleviate the risks and labours of the horse owners, and the two frequent administration of unnecessary punishment to the noblest of animals and man's universal favourite.

At the same time, the writer is fully conscious of the fact that this ground has, in various forms, been trodden before; but he has never found the *one real want*, namely, a little less Theoretical and a little more Practical writing upon this very important subject.*

In the work undertaken I shall endeavour to place before my readers, actual experience and results, in "plain, simple, and unvarnished language," being fully confident of the good-will and indulgence which shall be shown towards me in this my first "*Turn out.*"

I am,
Your obedient Servant,
E. W. GOUGH.

Park Hall House,
Walsall,
May 1st, 1878.

---

* It is said that the practical man cannot be a literary man. Should this apply somewhat to the present publication, the Author will rejoice, providing his one aim is attained, namely, more thoughtful care for, and less inattention to, the Horse and its surroundings.

PRELIMINARY REMARKS.

"Knowledge is the wing, &c."

IN this pushing and go-a-head age the ambition to possess a "turn out" is very great, and, when that is attained, the frequent crying evil is want of system and method, and more particularly, kindness and patience, in the care and treatment of the principal comprising it, namely, the Horse. A thorough knowledge of that noble animal's real use will tend to prevent it from being abused, as it very often is, and would gain its confidence and obedience at all times.

It is a well-known and acknowledged fact amongst experienced owners, stud grooms, and coachmen generally, that a quicker and more marked improvement is made in the condition and general health and temper of the Horse, and more work can be got out of it with kindly and judicious treatment and permanent system, than by carelessness and bustling.

Corn without consideration is useless, and it is a grievous truth that many whose business commands the constant use of the Horse, who have, more or less, from their early days been in possession of one, are generally more careless and reckless, and exhibit greater ignorance, than others whose experience is more limited; and, it is often found that great want of thought and persistence is shewn by some proprietors and horse-owners towards those whom they employ, and whose duty it is to care for the steeds—intrusting them sometimes to totally ignorant and inexperienced persons, not only in the stable and in the field, but in the public thoroughfares, thus endangering the lives of not only the horse and driver, but the public generally.

If owners of horses, however small the stud, would be more careful and strict, or systematic, in seeing for themselves that their "turn out" is not neglected or abused, and if drivers would exercise more patience, adapting themselves steadily to circumstances, and displaying less disposition to flourish, particularly in towns and crowded thoroughfares, with restive animals, the general risks would be greatly if not altogether diminished, and less work would be found for the police and members of the Society for the Prevention of Cruelty to Animals. Experience frequently tells us that the Horse is systematically illtreated, illcared for, and abused by some, when kindness, moderate attention, and thoughtful consideration would cost less trouble and bring about quicker and more satisfactory results. The whip is introduced where a kind word or gentle pat on the neck would be effective in producing prompt obedience; a curse is used where the simple mention of the horse's name would be sufficient; filth and dirt are allowed to accumulate where cleanliness is absolutely necessary; ventilation is grossly neglected; bad grooming, irregular feeding, impure water, and many other things from which the Horse is a sensitive sufferer are the result of carelessness and want of thought as a rule, but in some instances they are the wilful offspring of idleness and deceit. The harness and vehicles, like the horse, can be easily neglected, and allowed to suffer and rot from dirt, want of oil, and regular washing and cleaning, thus entailing expense, great risk and dissatisfaction, which might be avoided without much labour or inconvenient effort.

In this work the writer does not purpose giving an elaborate display of high-flown terms, but will simply adhere to plain language not directly intended for owners of large establishments,—although its contents may be perused by all to advantage. Neither would he encroach upon the sphere of the "vet.," the farrier, or horse-breaker, knowing at the same time that they will understand and appreciate the purport and meaning of his good intentions, in putting before those immediately concerned, in plain English book form, without effort at embellishment, a few condensed articles shewing the simple system that should be laid down by all owners, large and small, and whether they set up a temporary or permanent turn out. The Author's experiences being those of a life time, at home and in foreign countries —under ground and upon the surface—justifies him in feeling fully confident that the following suggestions and lines for the general good, will be looked upon in the usual appreciative light, and every indulgence extended for oversights or technical errors that may arise, whether it be on the part of the Author, or otherwise.

THE "THOROUGH GROOM."

"Achievement is command."

THE "Thorough Groom" is the man that takes a pride in his steed, and that alone is the test, whether it be the paid servant or the owner of the horse; it being equally important that the master should do his duty, when he undertakes it, as well as the man. The business of horse-keeping should not be skimmed over or carelessly treated by the employer or his employés. Thought must be taken not to be prompted to adopt *all* the complicated and expensive experiments that are frequently suggested and advertised, and which in some cases do not mean economy or improvement, but anxiety and reduction in the market value of the horse and its surroundings.

Is it not a real pleasure to see the very easy and systematic manner in which the thoughtful and cheerful groom goes about his work, and the perfect understanding that exists between man and horse. "Mutual feeling" and obedience are brought about by nothing so easily as regular habits on the part of the groom—doing everything in the right way and at the proper time—no noise, no irritation, but constant rule and steady firmness makes the obedient and thriving horse; and it must be noted that early rising is the first sign of a genuine groom.

If the inexperienced owner cannot or does not care to avail himself of the services of a thoroughly practical groom, he should pay an occasional visit to some of the good studs in his locality, where he will always find example, and advice can be given which will tend greatly to aid him in the amateur regulations of his own stable, and make that which has previously been to him a toil, a really healthy pleasure. One of the most important principles of good grooming and driving is good temper—an irritable man not only irritates himself but all around him.

The writer's business engagements frequently call him into the mines, and it is always a very pleasurable sight to see the wonderful control exercised over the strong, well-corned animals there to be found, from year's end to year's end, and which so seldom see day-light that they become restive at the appearance of strangers, and blind and almost mad if drawn up into the light of day. The amount of work these horses are capable of doing, and the good condition in which they are invariably kept, is a striking example to many above ground, especially when it is considered that they are principally controlled or driven by mere lads. Of course there are properly qualified persons appointed to superintend the horses, and look after their food, health, &c., and it must be admitted that the general appearance of underground horses reflects great credit upon those concerned, and speaks volumes in favour of the system adopted and thoroughly practised in some collieries.

The stables in connection with the Cannock Chase Colliery Company's Mines, and many others in that district, would surprise most persons accustomed to horses and stable routine on the surface. Down the one pit alone the writer has seen as many as 150 horses—all fat and happy—seemingly far more contented than many to be seen in our streets, which alone is the result of the excellent rules laid down by the managers, and adhered to by the horse-keepers. Everything caculated to contribute to their comfort and safety, or, in other words, for the welfare of all concerned below is well considered; special attention is given to gas lighting, whitewashing, ventilation, and cleanliness.

The dray horses of the Midland Railway Company are particularly noticeable for their clean and sleek condition. Regular attention appears to be paid to the harness—it being always kept thoroughly supple and sound. The contented manner in which the horses stand in the public streets (in all weathers), for loading and unloading the drays and wagons, and without winkers* in the bridles; and the frequent conversation and even caresses that at times may be seen passing between man and horse, is a pleasing and instructive example to thousands of carters and drivers of other teams.

A good system is adopted by Messrs. Allsopp & Sons, the eminent brewers of Burton-on-Trent, towards their horses, which, like others belonging to several noted firms in that locality, and in Liverpool and Manchester and other large cities, affords ample proof of what horses can learn and will do under proper treatment.

---

* In some parts they are called blinkers.

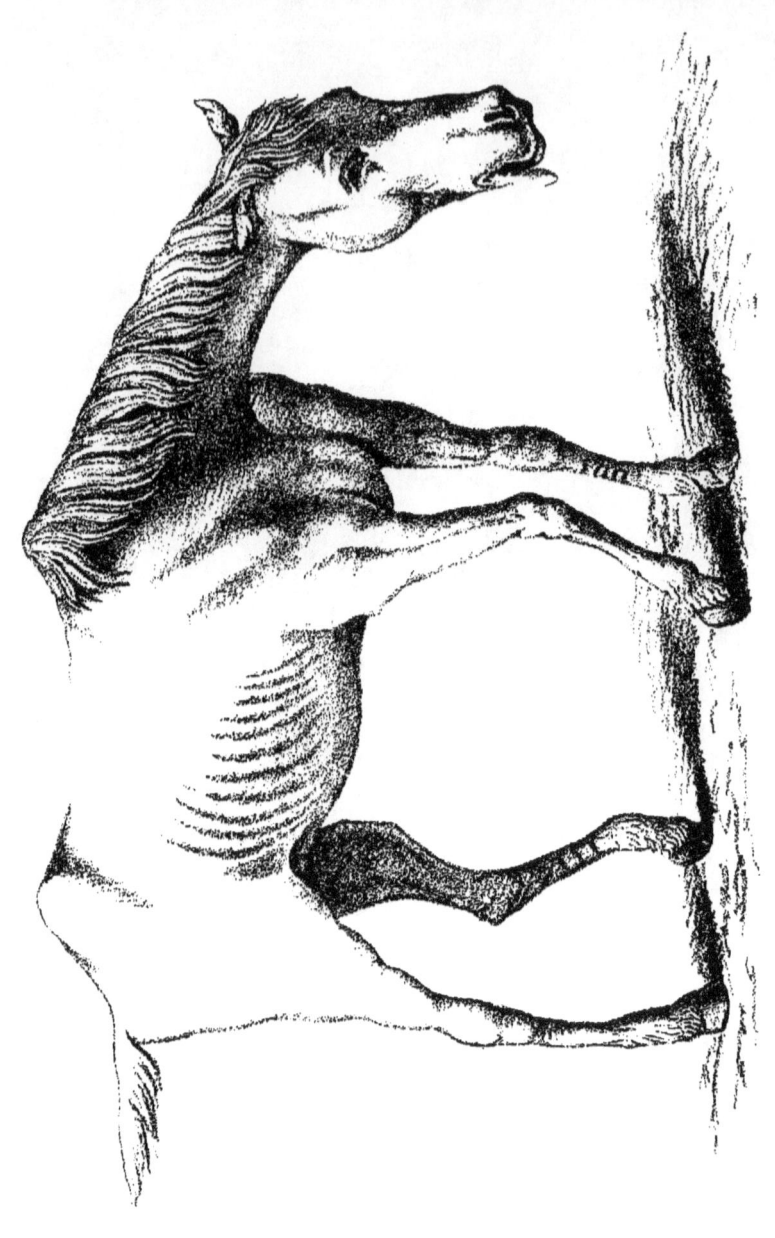

The "thorough groom" should by all means be a sober man, and punctual early riser, and should strive by cleanliness, straightforwardness, smartness, and truthfulness, to gain and maintain the confidence of his employer; and by kindness and steady firmness he will easily obtain control over, and continued obedience from, the animal or animals under his care.

It is a well-known fact that comparatively young horse have been reduced nearly to the decrepitude of old age by the barbarous treatment and ill-feeling of those who should be considered and looked upon as their zealous protectors.

How often have we seen and do we see the over-loaded animal staggering and struggling along, to all appearance more dead than alive;* with limbs bowed, the feet neglected, battered, and distorted; its under lip fallen; the cavity above the eye deepened, and numerous other signs of premature decay † which are brought on by abuse and negligence alone, and all of which can be, and are, warded off by the care, kindness, and genuine attention of the "thorough groom."

"Men in thoughtlessness cruel actions do,
Which on reflection oftimes deeply rue."

---

* "A SCREW LOOSE."—*(See Illustration.)*

† GROWN aged, used up, and turned out of the shed,
Lame, spavined, and wind-galled, but yet with some blood,
While knowing postillions his pedigree trace,
Say his dam won that sweepstake, his sire won that race;
And what matches *he* won do the ostlers count o'er,
As they loiter their time at some hedge alehouse door;
While the harness sore gall and the spurs his side goad,
And the high mettled racer's a hack on the road;
Till at length having laboured, toiled early and late
Worn out by degrees, he plods on to his fate.
Blind, old, lean, and feeble, he treads round a mill,
And draws sand 'till the sand of his hour glass stands still.

SELECTING THE HORSE.

―

"Let your wisdom be your guide."

IN choosing your steed it is as well to remember the genuine old saying—that a good horse is never a bad colour—but in setting up the first "Turn Out" there are often many difficulties to surmount in this respect, it being the wish or desire on the part of the purchaser, or those of his family or friends whom he may consult, that the horse *shall* be some particular colour; and the height, age, make, and price is carefully laid down; in fact the undertaking is gone into with such apparant nicety, and made of so serious a moment, that certain precise items are ultimately determined upon, and thereby it almost becomes an absolute necessity that the speculator shall be *measured* for his wants, e're he can be (to use the old trade term) carefully or successfully fitted. Newspapers are frequently looked over with the object of meeting with some advertisement of an animal calculated to answer the exact purpose, and after considerable searching, a horse is found that will propably suit in every respect, and a journey is made for the special purpose of purchasing. On arriving at the address given, it is invariably discovered that an omission has been made in the notice, viz., that the horse has been *down;* or, is *aged;* perhaps too young; a mere baby, and, like a cub bear, has all its troubles before it ; or, has once run away; is a kicker; crib biter; not quiet in harness or with children ; is given to shying ; requires a lot of whip, or is vicious tempered ; in fact, the probability of numerous faults or shortcomings are likely to be found, unless the would-be purchaser has had some previous correspondence with the advertiser before waiting upon him. The excuse, then, to get out of the business is invariably the price, or some sort of unsatisfactory termination is invented on one side or the other for the purpose of closing

the matter, which, considering the expense and loss of time incurred, means double preliminary cost. The writer's advice is, should the purchaser be inexperienced in horses, prejudice as to colour, and other trivialities should be somewhat modified at least; and if, on confidential enquiries having been made, the desired speciality cannot be found or heard of among one's friends, a respectable, well-known, old established horse dealer should be consulted, who will soon learn your wants and requirements, and prompt satisfaction will thus be ensured, and the special benefit of the option of exchanging the horse after reasonable time has elapsed, thus saving considerable anxiety and loss, besides risk and responsibility.

If a friend supplies the animal, the offer of a trial should by all means be taken immediate advantage of, the ribbons being handled by the purchaser (if he has had experience) in the presence of the seller. Back money, and other horsey phrases should never be mentioned in commencing the deal.

Special care must be taken by the inexperienced in buying at *Fairs or Public Markets*. The saying must be remembered that—"They can see you coming." A queer sort of gentry are known to exist at these institutions by being on the "look out," and are never to be found after the bargain is concluded. In fact their name is "Vanish." *Money makes the mare to go*, but it is often the case in spending money too conspicuously, that the only *goer* in the business is the *seller;* and the rule is for the inexperienced horse buyer never to visit an auction alone, which advice the writer has heard from the lips of an old-standing conscientious auctioneer.

Under any circumstances, if the horse is required for immediate work do not buy a young one; and it must be remembered that if the animal must grow into money, it is absolutely necessary to keep clear of an aged one. If the horse has once been down, or fallen upon its knees whilst being driven, it is very likely to come down again; and the same rule applies to its running away, or what is commonly known as bolting. Shying is not a very serious matter in the hands of an experienced whip. In any case, if the purchase be a high-priced one, a veterinary inspection is necessary, and a warranty the general rule and only safe satisfaction.

FORM OF WARRANTY.

Walsall,_____18

RECEIVED of Mr. A. B., the sum of £
for a (Bay Gelding),
(warranted five years old and no more), sound in every respect, quiet to ride and drive, and free from vice.

£_____   Receipt Stamp only
                        requisite.

Warranty must be upon the sale; if it be made afterwards, it must be reduced to writing, otherwise it will not be binding on the Vendor. A warranty of soundness may be defined, in an enlarged sense, an assurance from constitutional defects; but in its practical import is construed so as to exclude every defect by which the animal is rendered less fit for present use and enjoyment; the horse is not on that account to be held unsound, still less if the purchaser be informed of it, and admits the exception into the terms of the contract. The agreement for the sale of horses has been held to be an agreement "relating to the sale of goods," within the Statute of Frauds; therefore, a written receipt for the price, containing the warranty or other condition of sale, is admissable in evidence, stamped with a common receipt stamp, without an agreement stamp, and is the usual mode in which the contract is made and proved. A verbal representation of the seller to a buyer of a horse in the course of dealing, that he "may depend upon it the horse is perfectly quiet, and free from vice," is a warranty; or that he "could warrant." If the seller says at the time of the sale "I never warrant, but the horse is sound as far as I know;" this is a qualified warranty, and the purchaser may maintain an action if he can show that the horse was unsound to the knowledge of the seller.

Should the seller shew an extreme anxiety to hurry the sale, or display the slightest irritability of temper or impatience at the purchaser's enquiries and examinations, the business with him is better concluded at once, and the horse left in his possession; forcing the sale, by the aid of displays of temper and sometimes insult, such as, "what do you know about a horse," is an evident sign that "all is not right above board." In selecting your horse, the first consideration should be the class or character of work intended for it to do; the size, make, and proportion of the horse, should be at all times in exact harmony with the weight expected to be moved with ease. As regards the colour, dark horses are mostly preferred; light coloured horses are generally, it is said, more weak and nervous tempered; mares are not, as a rule, selected or chosen on account of their being at times of uncertain disposition, but the writer has no choice in that particular respect, having as much confidence in and affection for the mare as the horse.

Piebald or skewbald horses are not in much demand, excepting for public exhibitions and public displays, because of their conspicuous colour and marks.

It is at all times advisable, particularly where quality and figure is at stake, to hand the steed over to a breaker for the first drive or so, as may be deemed necessary, he having thorough experience, and special vehicles and harness for any emergency, which precaution alone will be calculated to save a multitude of after discoveries, risks and inconveniences, and give confidence to the speculator, and a better appreciation of the value, and probable after comfort for the horse. At the same time it will not be considered out of place for all concerned in horse bargaining to endeavour to endorse the Shakesperian line, viz. :—

"Truth loves open dealing."

CLASSIFICATION OF HORSES.

THE COLT.—The male under 3 years old.

THE FILLY.—The female under 3 years old.

THE SHETLAND PONY.—Is the smallest, and comes from the highlands of Scotland.

THE WELSH PONY.—Larger than the Shetland.

THE NORWEGIAN PONY.—Larger than the Welsh Pony, and commands heavier prices, being very handsome and docile.

THE PONY.—Is less than thirteen hands.

THE GALLOWAY.—Is about thirteen hands, and named after Galloway in Scotland.

THE COB.—Is stoutly built, between the horse and the pony.

THE HACKNEY.—Is about fifteen hands, useful for almost every purpose, the hunting field, the farm, and private turn out; in fact, is the farmer's and gentleman's servant of all work.

THE DRAUGHT HORSE, OR CART HORSE.—Averages sixteen hands.

THE DRAY HORSE.—Is the heaviest and most ponderous of his race, being intended for slow heavy work; weight is the principal feature in the breeding of these useful animals. Lastly—

THE BLOOD HORSE, OR THOROUGH BRED.—Of which nothing need be said, more than it is perfection, and as beautiful as a picture.

"Pleasure and action make the hours seem short."

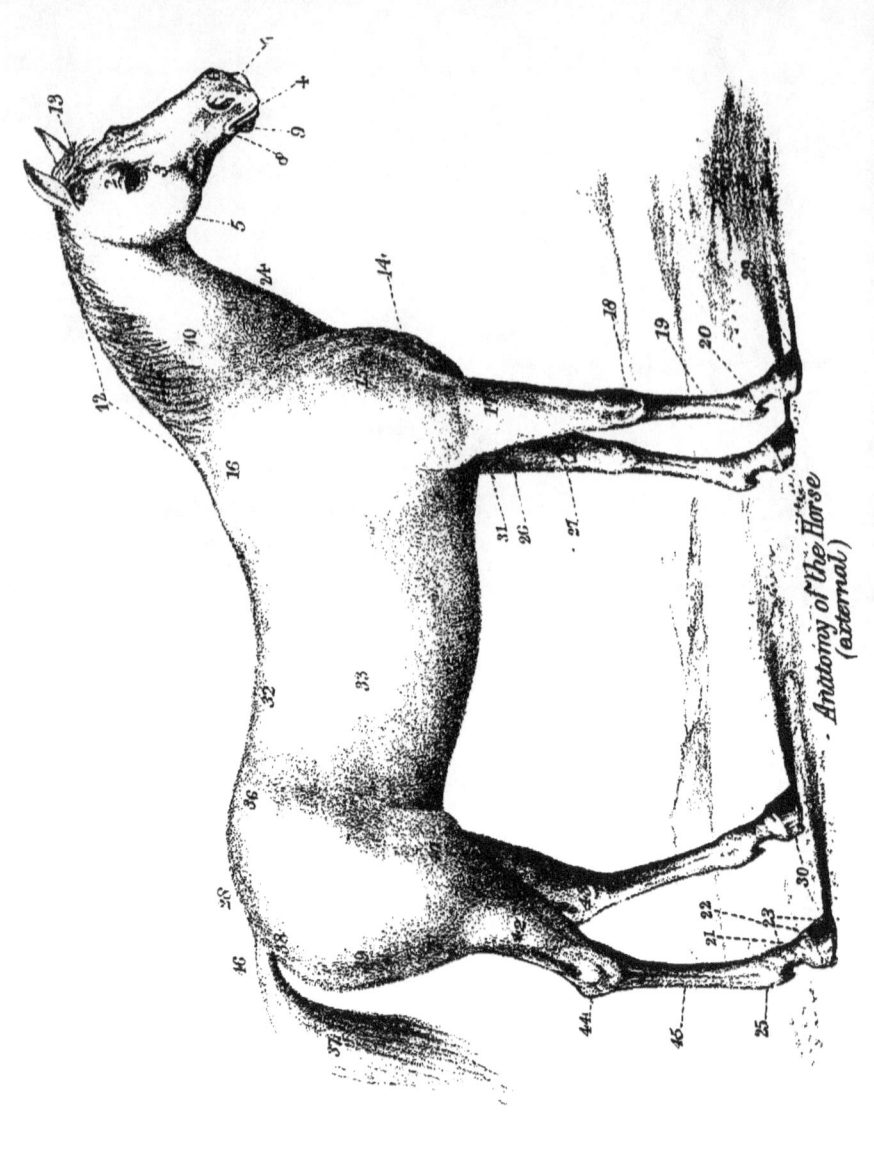

EXPLANATION OF ILLUSTRATION.

ANATOMY OF THE HORSE.

1. Forehead.
2. Cavity above the eyes.
3. Temples.
4. Lips.
5. Jaw.
6. Nostrils.
7. Tip of the nose.
8. Beard.
9. Chin.
10. Neck.
11. Throat.
12. Mane.
13. Fore top.
14. Chest.
15. Shoulders.
16. Withers.
17. Arm.
18. Knee.
19. Shank.
20. Fetlock joint.
21. Pastern.
22. Coronet.
23. Hoof.
24. Wind pipe.
25. Back sinews, or main tendons.
26. Plate vein.
27. Chesnut.
28. Croup.
29. Toe.
30. Heel.
31. Elbow.
32. Reins.
33. Ribs.
34. Flanks.
35. Belly.
36. Fillets.
37. Tail.
38. Rump.
39. Buttocks.
40. Stifle.
41. Haunches.
42. Thigh.
43. Hock.
44. Point of the hock.
45. Cannon.
46. Dock.

STANDARD MEASURE, AND PRINCIPAL POINTS OF THE HORSE.

"HAND" is 4 in.; the height is taken from the sole of the foot to the top of the withers, by which standard all horses are measured.

The principal points of the horse are:—

THE CHEST,
    THE BACK,
        THE SHOULDER,
            THE ARM,
THE KNEE,
    THE TEETH,
        THE FOOT,
            THE EYE.

RULE FOR JUDGING THE AGE OF THE HORSE.

" Corruption wins not more than Honesty."

TO form something like a correct idea of the age of the horse, and at the same time to test the veracity of the salesman, it is usual to first ask the question—How old is it? then to look for yourself, not only at the mouth, but the eyes, and the legs, and in fact, to carefully scrutinize and examine the animal all over; at the same time asking the owner a few questions as to its health, habits, capabilities, &c. Many an aged horse has been doctored, or to use the term, "faked up," and hurridly palmed off upon the unwary or over-anxious buyer, who has set his mind upon that particular steed, for a younger one; and it is not unusual for a young horse, shewing a good mouth, to prove dull, heavy, and sluggish, after a little regular work, and to wear a languid and listless aspect, which results from frequent overdoses of the whip, kicks, and physic, freely and constantly administered to the poor animal that has been worked too early in life, and neglected and badly cared for both in the stable and out of doors. It is an easy matter in purchasing a useful aged horse, to determine whether it has been over-worked, systematically physiced, or properly cared for in good hands. Some owners do not consider a horse equal to a fair day's work until it is five years old, and that it does not gain its full power of strength until it arrives at seven; the universal system is, never under any circumstances to give a young horse a full load, or to risk a long day in bad weather.

THE TEETH.

The teeth of a horse are hard bones placed in sockets in a horse's jaw, which serve not only to facilitate the nourishment, but likewise to distinguish the age. A horse has forty teeth, including the tusks. The teeth are of a substance much harder than any of the other bones, which is absolutely necessary, considering their office is to break and cut and grind. That part of them which stands above the gums is smooth, and free from any covering, but all within the sockets of the jaws is more rough, and covered with a thin membrane of exquisite sense.

The age of a horse should be judged from various points of his anatomy. If the hoof be smooth, moist, hollow, and well-sounding, it is a sign of youth; on the contrary, if rugged, and as it were seamed, one seam over another, and withal dry, foul, and rusty, it is a mark of old age.

The tail, say the stem, close to the buttock, grip it between the finger and thumb, and if a joint be felt to stick out more than the rest, the size of a nut, the horse is under ten, but if the joints are all plain he may be fifteen.

The eyes being round, full and bright, the pits that are above them filled, level and smooth, even with the temples, and no wrinkles to be seen either under or over, are marks of youth.

The skin being plucked up in any part between the finger and thumb, and let go again, if it return suddenly to its place, and without shewing wrinkles, then the animal may be believed to be young.

It is possible by nice judgment to age a horse by looking at his legs and palate. As the animal grows old, the roof of his mouth becomes leaner and drier towards the middle, and the ridges, which in young horses are pretty high and plump, diminish as they increase in years, so that in very old horses the roof of the mouth is nothing but skin and bone.

The simple rule for telling the age is by examining the teeth. There are six permanent nippers or front teeth in the lower jaw; the two front teeth are understood to be cut at ages varying from two to three years, and the teeth each side the middle ones from three and a half to four years. Between four and a half and five years introduces the corner pair and the male tusks. The horse is known as aged at eight, when the marks in the corner nippers are effaced. They are worn out at six in the two centre teeth, and at seven in the next pair.

The trick used to make false marks in a horse's mouth, by hollowing the tooth with a graver, and burning a mark with a small hot iron, may be easily discovered; because those who are acquainted with the true marks, will perceive the cheat by the roundness and bluntness of the tushes, by the colour of the false mark, which is generally blacker and more impressed than the true mark, and by many other visible tokens which denote the advanced age of a horse. After a horse has passed his eighth year, and sometimes at seven, nothing actually certain is reckoned to be decided by the mouth. Some horses have but indifferent mouths when they are young, and soon lose their mark; others have good mouths for a long time; the teeth being white, even, and regular, sometimes till they are sixteen and upwards, with many other marks of freshness and vigour. But when a horse comes to be very old, the fact may be discovered by several indications, the constant attendants of age, viz. :— his gums wear away, and leave his teeth long and naked at the roots; the teeth also grow yellow, and sometimes brownish. The bars of the mouth, which in a young horse are always fleshy, and form so many distinct ridges, in an old horse are lean, dry and smooth. The eye pits in a young horse (except those said to come off old stallions) are generally filled up with flesh, and look plump and smooth, whereas they are sunk and hollow in an old horse, which gives him a ghastly and melancholy aspect.

Horses have been known to live for thirty and forty years, but, from over-exertion and ill-usage frequently die, or are slaughtered, before they reach ten.

To give the growth and decay of a horse's mouth. The first year he has his foal teeth, which are only grinders and gatherers; the second, the four foremost change, and appear browner and bigger than the rest; the third year he changes the teeth next to these, leaving no apparent foal teeth, but two on each side above and two below; the fourth year, the teeth next to these are changed, and no foaling teeth are left, but one on each side above and below; at five, his foremost teeth are all changed, and the tushes on each side are complete; those which come in the places of the last foaling teeth being hollow, and having a little black speck in the midst, which is called the "mark in a horse's mouth;" this continues till eight years of age; at six, he puts out new tushes, near which appears a little circle of young flesh at the bottom of the tush, the tushes withal being small, white, short and sharp; at seven, the teeth are all at their growth, and the mark in the mouth appears very plain; at eight, all his teeth are full, smooth and plain, and the mark scarce

THE TEETH.

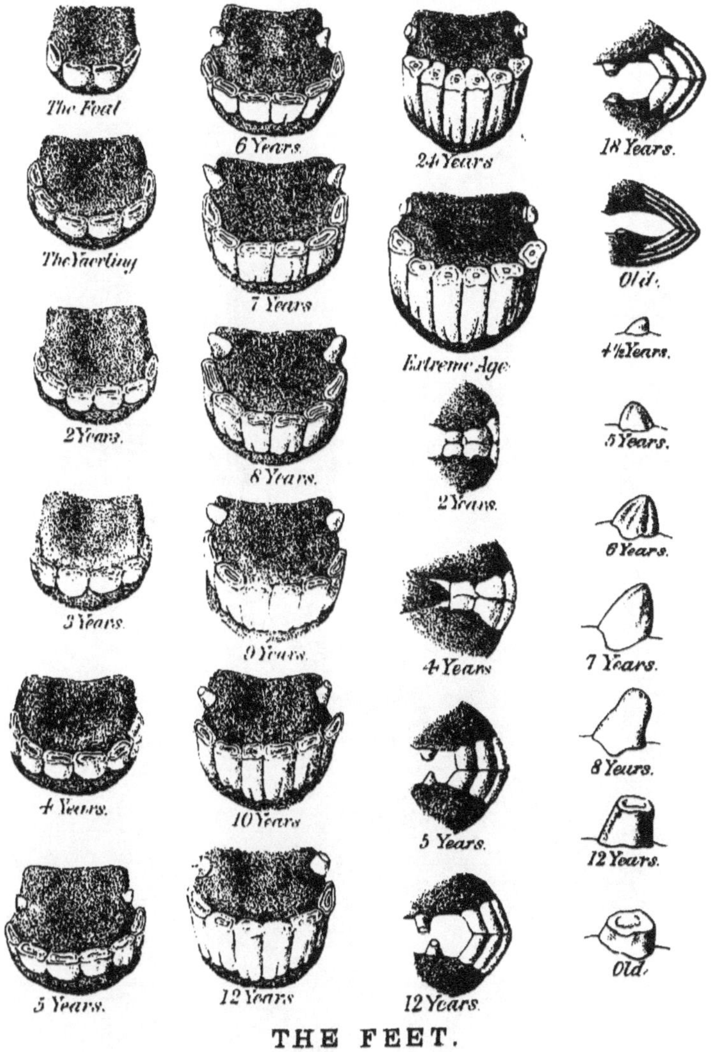

THE FEET.

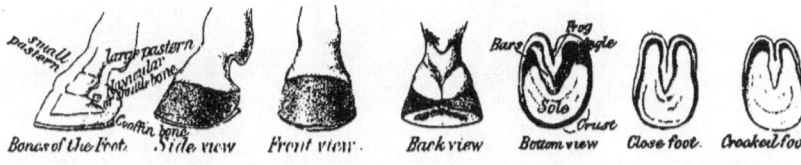

discernable, the tushes looking yellowish; at nine, the foremost teeth appear longer, yellower, and fouler than before, and the tushes become bluntish; at ten, no holes are felt on the inside of the upper tushes, which till then are sensible; add that the temples begin to be crooked and hollow; at eleven, his teeth are very long, yellow, black, and foul, but he will cut even, and his teeth stand directly opposite to one another; at twelve, the upper teeth hang over the nether; at thirteen, the tushes are worn close, if he has been much ridden, otherwise they will be black, foul, and long.

THE FEET.

We would here refer the reader to our illustration, " Teeth and Feet." Respecting the latter, we received some time ago from the R. S. P. C. A., a very useful and instructive pamphlet, entitled, "The Horse's Foot," which should be read by all who have to do with horses, and which we here give for the good of the cause, and of the horse in particular:—

" To most persons, the foot of the horse appears to be only a roundish hard lump of horn, on which an iron shoe is nailed to prevent its being worn away by the roads. Such persons may perhaps hear with astonishment that it is a complex and elaborate instrument, perfectly adapted to the work it is intended to perform, and that our artificial assistance, far from preserving, often cripples, and very frequently totally ruins it.

"The real foot of the horse, is enclosed in a horny case called the *hoof*; the outside rim of this casing forms what is called the *crust* or *wall*. The fore-part is about half an inch thick, becoming thinner towards the back. It extends round towards the heel, and then curves sharply inwards.

"The ends which incline inwards are called *the bars*. In the natural state of the foot they are quite prominent and visible; but in a horse which has been frequently shod they are often nearly obliterated, as, often, the farrier, by a mistaken and very faulty system, cuts them almost entirely away. The mischievous effects of this practice will be seen when we come to consider the uses of the hoof. In the middle and hinder part of the foot is an elastic horny substance called the *frog*, which occupies about a quarter of the sole. It forms a soft and yielding cushion on which the horse's foot partly rests, being thus relieved from the shock of the hard hoof on the ground. This important part is, in too many instances, pared away by the ignorant and prejudiced farrier, who follows what he has been taught by those as unskilful as himself.

"The part of the foot which has a plane surface, which is opposed to the ground, and extends from the frog to the outside or wall of the hoof, is called the *sole*. It is horny and hard, yet not solid, but somewhat elastic.

"In the hinder part of the foot, where the two ends of the frog terminate, are the *heels;* and these also are of the same horny character.*

"Immediately inside the hoof, in the fore part and sides, is the bone of the foot, properly so called, or the *coffin bone*, as it is termed. It fills the fore part of the hoof, and is of a light and spongy formation, being filled with numerous blood vessels, through which the circulation of this extreme part of the body is carried on, without any danger of their stoppage by means of the pressure to which they are continually subjected; the substance of the bone not only allowing the blood vessels to pass freely through, but protecting them from every obstruction. Around this bone are a great number of elastic prominent ridges of a membranous nature, which fit exactly between similar leaves or ridges on the inner part of the hoof. The end for which they are so placed is to modify and soften the shock to which the horse's foot is naturally subjected on passing over the rough ground he has constantly to traverse, and also to attach the hoof to the bone. At its summit, in front, is fixed the large extensor tendon of the foot.

"Fitting into this bone, at the top, is another called the *small pastern bone*, to which is joined another strong tendon, that regulates the use of the foot. On its upper surface it forms a cube-like hollow, and receives the end of the *large pastern bone;* while below and behind is a small movable piece named the *navicular bone*, which seems to have for its object the steadying and strengthening of the action of the powerful flexor tendon that is inserted into the sole of the coffin bone.

"If the foot were a flat and unyielding mass, the danger of slipping would be, in many instances, very great. But in-

---

* AUTHOR'S NOTE.—This not being a medical work we shall not attempt a full description of the internal structure of the foot; but our illustration will give a general idea.

stead of this, it has a prominent edge all round, which takes a firm hold of the ground and obviates the difficulty. Further, this hoof is somewhat elastic, and on the weight of the horse being fully thrown upon it, allows the inner soft cushion or frog to descend, and press firmly and tightly on the earth. Thus two ends are wonderfully and completely attained; firmness in the tread, insuring the horse's safety, and a regularity of pressure, which obviates the jarring that would be so painful and prejudicial.

"When the animal is in a state of nature, its hoof is strong enough to need no artificial protection; but on the hard and stony roads common in all civilized countries, it has been found necessary to fit something to the foot, to protect it from the great wear and tear which is unavoidably incurred. For this purpose nothing has been found so effectual as what is termed *shoeing*, or affixing a thin plate of iron round the outer hard and horny edge of the hoof—a practice known in Britain during the time of the Romans. When done with judgment, the proper action of the foot goes on nearly as usual; but if injudiciously performed, the action of the horse is impeded, lameness is caused, and temporary or permanent diseases are brought on.

"Many persons, from an idea of saving time, desire the smith to come and shoe their horses, instead of sending them to the forge. This should never be done. For when the workman is by his fire, if the shoe should not quite fit (as is nearly certain to be the case) he can easily heat and alter it; but if at a distance, in the farmer's or gentleman's stable, he has not the opportunity of doing so, and can only make foot and shoe match by cutting away the wall of the hoof—a most dangerous practice.

"To those who consider the matter, it must be obvious that this tender and important organ ought not to be left to the care of an ignorant, and too often brutal, smith without supervision. His trade requires judgment and discretion; and there are no better means of ensuring careful shoeing than for the horse-proprietor to visit the forge while his horse is being shod, and observe the proceedings. More depends on the preparation of the foot than on the affixing the shoe; for the latter will hardly do much damage, unless made outrageously bad, or nailed on in a most clumsy manner; but it should be constantly kept in mind that a horse may be easily lamed from rash and ignorant paring of his hoofs.

Indeed, the great evils of shoeing are cutting the sole and frog, putting on too heavy and too small shoes, and rasping the outer surface of the wall of the hoof. Sometimes, also, the shoes are allowed to remain on the feet for too long a period. This ought to be regularly attended to, at intervals of about three or four weeks, and no misplaced ideas of economy should allow a longer period to elapse without an inspection of the feet.

PURCHASING OR ORDERING THE HARNESS.

"Knavery's plain face is never seen till used."

THE first question to consider in reference to the harness before you purchase or order is, the kind of vehicle to be used; if a heavy or light one, or whether it is to be a gig, dog cart, or four wheeler. For a gig the harness should be made up to have a light appearance, an imperial pad with straight flaps, square (or Westend) furniture and winkers, look and wear well, in both silver and brass furniture. Where practicable the horse may be used to work without winkers. If the business requires a dog cart or trap, the harness should be somewhat heavier, with an Alexandra or other saddle, at discretion. Should a four-wheeler or phaeton be decided upon, the saddle is not required to be heavy, the only weight to carry being the shafts, but a breech-band, (either a long or short one), is absolutely necessary. Many persons in setting up their first "Turn Out" decide upon having a second-hand set of harness, which system of *drawing the line at the harness*, after going to the expense of a good horse, and probably a new vehicle, requires a second consideration, and the harness, before purchasing, most minute examination. At first sight the set may be clean, and to all appearance sound; but when we consider the fact that the simple breaking of the top hame strap, or the ends of the traces, or billetts of the reins, may result in the death of a valuable steed, the total wreck of a handsome vehicle, and, perhaps, permanent injury to the driver and occupants, besides numerous risks to the public, it becomes necessary, and in fact a duty, that the harness should have as much, if not more, preliminary consideration than the remainder or most expensive part of the "Turn Out," particularly as we are aware, and now formally warned of the fact, that the welfare of the whole lot depends entirely upon the soundness of the merest strap, which is an easy matter to overlook in purchasing a second-hand, or cheap, common-made new set.

The writer's experience and interestedness in his business has prompted him to be frequently amused and surprised while reading the very tempting baits advertised in the daily papers, emanating from persons whose original trade or profession has nothing whatever to do with the article or goods they profess to laud up, and have on sale; and whose clever endeavour it is to force upon the public, or some private individual, common goods, totally disregarding the business man's pride in legitimate trading, and who's motto is "purchase and come again." Here is an advertisement, emanating from a large manufacturing midland town, which the writer read four days in succession, and ultimately followed up to the end:—"Extraordinary bargains—50 Sets of Silver Harness, Complete—all sizes—best quality—to be sold cheap. No reasonable offer refused as the lot must be cleared out immediately, the *manufacturer* wanting money."

The writer went by the first train, on reading the above, having his doubts as to the "best quality," and to prove the genuineness of the number of sets advertised, feeling convinced that the extraordinary bargain existed only in the fertile, irresponsible brain of the "puffing shark" (as these worse than Cheap Johns are called) who put forth the bait; and so it proved to be, as we shall now see. On arriving at the shop, we were surprised to find nothing in the window or premises (as far as could be seen from the street), appertaining to harness; or that the proprietor had anything to do with, or knowledge of such goods, which he professed to *deal* in so plentifully, and to sell so cheap. Certainly, the entrance and doorway was plastered up with catalogues, which seemed to have done good long service, these being much soiled and partially obliterated, their details, in wording and want of dates, appearing to be manufactured for the express purpose of standing for a considerable time. The writer entered the small front shop; then the secret business began between the principal and assistant, in certain side glances at the visitor, and undertones between themselves, which is easily detected by the visitor; their anxiety being to determine, without delay, whether they had secured by their advertisement a C. C. or O. T.—which means a "Caught Customer," or "One of the Trade," that is to say, a harness manufacturer. Had they have decided him to be an O. T., then the intruder, by virtue of their suspicions of his superior knowledge of that special article, would have been told that all was cleared out about an hour ago, or so, by a firm in town; but, thanks to the disguise assumed, the writer was ushered into—*the cellar (or underground stockroom)*, which seemed more like a lumber-hole, and the gas being turned on, to see—not fifty sets, but a hundred and fifty oddments, not altogether confined to the saddlery trade—including, broken boxes, old and rusty hames, second-hand gears, cheap pilches, and second-hand ladies' saddles, a quatity of damaged cart collars, all smothered with dirt and spider webs; and the first invitation was delivered in a light and happy tone;—Come, Buy the lot! Clear me out!!"—but on being asked for a view of the fifty sets, the expression of the man (whom, being the seller, we will call Mr. S.) was altered, and a more patronising and whining or whimpering voice was assumed, the excuse being that his assistant had made a mistake in the advertisement; the number should have been *five* instead of *fifty*, four of which he had just disposed of; at the same time opening a rough box which lay on the damp floor, and which contained the only complete set upon the premises. On our wishing or preferring to see it out of the box, we were told that if we had any knowledge of our requirements, we could tell at a glance what it was as the harness lay, and save the trouble of unpacking and repacking. The fact is, the business of the seller is not to expose the miserable make, and the light and flimsy manner in which it has been specially put or blown together for him, and his Saturday night banterings. Such leather is known by the trade as " goose hide, or tripe," instead of good solid material cut out of prime harness backs, or butts. In reply to the query as to the furniture, the answer was " Silver on German," meaning the one Buckle only—that which the seller had just placed his finger upon as it lay uppermost in the box—viz.: the Crupper Buckle, this buckle being fixed there for that special and evasive purpose. The fact is, the furniture was simply the commonest iron electro-plated, and in a very short time would have shown quite black, as soon as the thin coating of silver had been taken off by the first breeze. And it must be remembered that this man's dealings are never completed in the presence of a third party. His price commenced at nine guineas, and in about four minutes came down to five pounds, without any solicitation on the part of the writer, such being the usual " Cheap John " system of saving time. On our giving the horse's size as sixteen hands, the reply was that the harness would fit like a glove, and as true and easy as though it had been measured for, which augurs well for his judgment when he tells you the size of the collar belonging to the set is eighteen and half inches, and the fact is considered that the average length of collars for horses above fifteen hands is from twenty to twenty-two inches.

The harness is declined; then the visitor saw the "being" before him in his true colours, and was addressed in numerous insulting expressions, such as "he did not mean business when he came;—if the money is not available he could be accommodated, either with *that or anything else*,—and the sooner he was off his premises the better" (the writer considered him a perfect treat, without danger). His style of "rushing" being the way such unbusiness-like touts get their living; which treatment is the more surprising when we consider the fact that the legitimate tradesman never insults or intimidates his customers under any circumstances.

But the writer was not to be wiped out by the mean manner and contemptible language of the man so anxious to rid himself of his unprofitable visitor, and by way of retaliation, elevated a thick-knobbed black thorn, a regular double-barrelled walking stick, appearing to rub his nasal organ with the same, and addressed Mr. S. as follows :—

"Yes! Mr. 'Bad Leather Merchant,' no doubt you are quite right in all you say as to my knowledge of harness, and I may have some difficulty in finding the money for the purpose of encouraging your system of robbery, but, considering the fact that I have made a special journey here this morning, at cost and inconvenience, to see your "extraordinary bargain" with the view to purchasing, it will not be in harmony with my regular way of doing business to return satisfied with the *sight* of one set, and a job lot of rubbish, spiced with your formidable bearing and low language ; it is my purpose, ere I leave this establishment to demand an immediate apology and all expenses incurred by your inducements."

Seeing the firm stand taken by his visitor, and thinking perhaps that discretion would prove better than exposure, the half-cowed man (with his long hair and greasy collar) at once handed over to the writer the sum of one guinea, with an abundance of imitation regrets, and struggles to explain his "excitement."

But suppose, for the sake of argument, we purchase the harness, and find that we are duped by this harness seller, and bring the set home—with what result? to find, the collar in the first place, altogether a misfit. We write the same evening to the advertiser asking his explanation, and to exchange. Does he agree to it, or offer to satisfy you in any way? Certainly not! that is no part of his business; the matter is done with as far as he is concerned, the money is in his pocket, and the affair off his hands; the one prevailing idea and effort with him is, to look out for another "mark." Our only remedy then is to order a collar from a practical saddler. The collar is made and fitted satisfactorily, but alas! to find the hames far too small, in fact, they will not touch the proper sized collar, therefore your journey is again deferred with your new "Turn Out," and the result is—you order a complete set at the hands of the practical man, who is always willing to exchange any part of the harness, within a reasonable time, in case of misfit or alteration in the buyer's ideas or tastes, the practical tradesman being fully aware of the trade rule—that in adapting a set of harness, it is not only a matter of fitting the animal's back, but also of suiting the eye and taste or wishes of the purchaser. There are many kinds, qualities, and patterns of harness furniture too numerous to mention here; but the Author would refer the reader to our Illustrations, and will be pleased to send a complete list at any time on application; including the newest designs, and their particular uses, either for home or export.

And it must be remembered, that the whole and sole business of the cheap advertiser of harness is, to sell at any price, totally regardless of risk to human life, or satisfaction to the customer, the entire plot seeming to endorse the old saying—

"My son, get money, honestly if you can but—get money."

FITTING THE HARNESS.

"How poor are they that have not patience."

In fixing the harness upon the horse it is necessary that all the parts comprising the set should be a close fit, but at the same time everything must be easy, or to use an old term—" so that the hand can be placed between." The only item of the set that should be really pulled tight is the top hame strap, because the fit and form of the collar depends upon the exact manner in which the hames are attached and retained. In harnessing the horse the first part to commence with is the Saddle, and its immediate belongings. The crupper and breechband should be placed (not thrown) carefully across the back, and left loose until the crupper dock is put in position, which is done by doubling the tail under, and keeping the same held up with the left hand until the dock is fixed close under the tail, *without leaving any hairs between*, the whole of which is done by standing up near to the horse's side, with the operator's back towards its head, which will prevent the horse doing any injury, and the quicker and quieter this part of the business is performed the better, as the Americans say—"Hurry up! fix it clean, and right away."

THE CRUPPER-DOCK should always be of good substance, or thickness, and must not be made too hard; it is then considerably easier for the horse than a thin one, and will cause the tail to be carried more showily. There is some art on the part of the harness maker in properly shaping the dock; which is invariably stuffed with paper; but linseed is not only preferable, but the proper filling, and, being of an oily and softening nature, it is permanently healing. Candles have been used, hence the term—"a candle dock." When the saddle is drawn up and placed properly upon the back, attention should be directed to the pannel stuffing, the thickness of which is reduced after a few journeys in a new saddle; and it should never be allowed to come down thin enough for the tree to touch the horse, whether in new or old saddles.

Ease and Comfort

Occasional back-stuffing and examination at the hands of the manufacturer is advisable, particularly in worn saddles; and the wool should be renewed by taking out the old and knotty parts, caused by perspiration, or the pannel re-lined when necessary. The writer has supplied harness without the crupper-dock, &c., &c., but that extreme requires judgment and extra care on the part of the horse-owner and driver.

THE GIRTH should be buckled close but not tight, and the end of the girth strap run through the three loops in the girth body, and not left to swing about, which rule as regards the straps applies to all parts of the harness, and to sets of all kinds. Nothing looks more untidy than a lot of strapping ends hanging and flapping about. The ends of the traces, if too long, besides being irritating to the horse, are a great eyesore to the "Turn Out." The bellyband, which is part of the backband, should not be buckled until the vehicle is attached, and then not too tight. The saddle must never be pressed forward, because it naturally works in that direction. It is easily and nicely adjusted by loosing out or taking up the crupper-strap.

THE COLLAR should now be put upon the horse's neck, after turning his head from the manger towards the door, if in the stable. With new collars it is often necessary to open or widen them a little across the part which has to pass over the eyes, which should be done with the knee, and not by placing the collar upon a post, or hook—in fact, the writer has seen the handiest nail turned to account for that purpose,—which not only scratches and damages the collar, but too much pulling is calculated to put it out of shape, and if once broken at the throat, it will never recover its original firmness, hence the failure in open-topped collars.

Before putting the collar on, it should be formally shewn to the horse, and a little conversation introduced, including the mention of the animal's name, and a few pats upon the neck, or, to use a military term—to make "much of him," particularly if a young horse; which is done in less time than it takes to write it, and thereby does not mean much loss, but an actual saving of time. By such little attentions the help and assistance of the horse is being asked (the result of which is very noticeable in well-regulated stables), and is never refused by a horse that has been properly appealed to, and systematically trained. For putting the collar on the neck, it is first turned upside down, with the wale (or rim) towards the fitter, and when it is close to the eyes of the horse, it should never be *pushed up with* a rush or series of sudden jerks towards the ears, for under such circumstances it invariably happens that the head of the horse goes with the pressure and not against it, thus losing both power and time. The usual practice is, that a gentle twist be brought to bear with the hand each side the draught of the collar, and the housing, if any, pressed somewhat under towards the neck, and with the corresponding help from the horse, the collar is easily and quietly passed beyond the ears. It should then be immediately turned over into its proper position, housing up being reversed the way of the mane, and at once carried down to the shoulders.* The old-fashioned way of fixing the hames upon the collar while it is close to the ears at the top of the neck, and before it is reversed, is very reprehensible, being tiring and irritating both to man and horse, and also causes a larger amount of operating in front of the animal than is necessary, and likewise adds materially to the weight, encumbrance, and risk incurred in throwing the collar, hames, and traces round the animal's neck, besides causing unnecessary pain to the horse.

Before putting the hames on, it is important to know that they fit the collar exactly; in fact, the writer, as a rule, makes it a special point to have them fitted in form to the identical collar *by the hame maker*, before the collar is side pieced or finished, thus preventing any fear of their slipping off in wear by ensuring a perfect fit. That the hames should not move or spring from the position in which they are placed is a matter of serious moment—hence the importance of sound straps. The hames must not reach the top of the collar, neither must they be too short, say about 2 in. from the top. Make-shift cannot, compatible with safety, be applied to this portion of the harness under any circumstances. Any practical saddler, or harness furniture manufacturer, will safely adjust the hames to the collar, and the proper length required for that particular collar. In nicely and promptly fixing the hames it is necessary to buckle them lightly to the collar for the time, during the process of running the hands round them to see that they are properly adjusted; after which the top strap is pulled up as close or tight as possible. Hames up to 21 inches should measure 1 inch longer than the collar, and over 21 inches, $1\frac{1}{2}$ inch should be allowed extra. The hames, when fitted, should never reach the top of the collar by at least 2 inches, as before mentioned. The hames are the most important part of the whole set of harness furniture,

---

* This of course will be understood to apply only to horses that do not require an open-topped collar.

and the first consideration respecting them is the quality of the iron of which they are made. Harness hames are made of iron, body and draft, whether they be plated with silver, or brass, or covered with leather. The best brand of iron known to the trade for either hames or horse-shoes, is that manufactured by Messrs. Benjamin Bunch and Sons, Staffordshire Iron Works. The Author has several specimens of hames made of this iron on view at his establishment, both finished and unfinished, bent and twisted into every possible shape; one hame is actually tied into a knot, but neither split, crack, or flaw appears, and the draft remains intact, and as sound and tough as the best part of the hame. The most peculiar, if not wonderful, fact in connection with this hame draft is, that it is neither welded on to the body of the hame, nor is it drawn out from the solid iron. These hames are warranted to stand the roughest wear and tear for two years, and the secret of the invention and their construction is only known to the manufacturer* of the specimens above referred to. These hames are known as the "Gough" hame, being so called by the inventor out of compliment to the Author of "CENTAUR," in whom the sole right of supplying them is vested.

It is a saying that "Horses necks vary like Human faces," and it is well-known that the collar is the most important part of the whole harness, as regards comfort to the horse, whether it be used with Four-in-hand, Pair-horse, Tandem, Gig, Dog-Cart, Phaeton, Trap, Buggy, Stage, Waggon, Dray, Cart, Pit, or Plough harness; and the whole of the before-mentioned and following remarks and comments are applicable in either case. The form of the collar should be carefully studied by the saddler for each particular animal. Some horses require a very narrow collar, which must be *made so*, and not *adapted*; some are wide at the bottom and straight at the top, others the reverse. Collars have been manufactured by the Author, and are still in wear, absolutely odd-sided, and no other form would answer for that particular horse a single journey; but most collars more or less require to be full in the draught, and made perfectly true. Some horses, on account of their extreme width across the head, or eyes, require an open-topped collar, which is never advisable when it can in any way be

---

* The inventor and maker of this hame is John Warrallo, the manufacturer of the Prize hame for the London Exhibition 1862, which hame is likewise on view at the Author's establishment, exhibited by the present owner, Mr. T. Venables, Coach and Gig Harness Furniture Manufacturer, Bradford Works, Walsall, successor to the late Thomas Harvey, for whom this champion hame was originally made.

dispensed with. The constant and wide opening in putting on and taking off, causes the straw at the throat of the collar to break, and thus the firmness, so necessary in the build of the collar, is lost, and oftimes the top strap is left comparatively slack or loose by the fitter, thus making the collar 1 in. longer than the fit by causing it to drop. The writer is in favour of a light top, a light throat, good draught bodyside, and plenty of wool under the lining; and thinks such collars perfection, and the light buggy harness a real luxury to sit behind; at the same time the American light make of harness would not suit the English roads for hard wear.

In ordering a set of harness by letter, give the height and a general description of the horse. If it be heavy, or light, and its proportion; this, with the following further particulars as to the collar, will be all that is necessary.

To measure a horse for a collar, and to describe the want and form required, is a matter of no great difficulty, if an old collar is at hand, that can easily be tried on to judge by, and a piece of stick, string, or tape cut to show the length, allowing for the width of the old collar by adding $\frac{1}{2}$-in. extra to the length, although this measurement is a trouble sometimes to the non-practical. But the proper way to measure a horse's neck is with a 24-in. rule, from the near or left side, with the right finger along the end of the rule, and the left finger across the flat, to form a stop at top and bottom of the horse's neck; the left finger will shew the length required. The distance or measurement is taken from the throat or left hand end of the rule, which is pressed down close to the shoulder, exactly where the rim of the collar would rest. If a piped throated collar is necessary, one inch extra should be allowed; and if a full or spare neck, or any other peculiarity, instructions can be easily given, or the necessary items observed. Should a little alteration, or even exchange, be desirable, after a reasonable trial, the prompt and accomodating manufacturer will not hesitate to oblige, for his own credit's sake, and for the safety of the driver and the comfort of the horse. There is an old and simple method of measuring a horse for a collar, viz.—to run a tape round the neck exactly where the collar will rest, and from the length shewn deduct nine inches, and divide by two, which will give the inside depth of the collar; for example—say the neck measures 50 inches, deducting nine leaves 41 inches, dividing by two shews the length required to be $20\frac{1}{2}$ inches, which is the reliable size, thus the measure may be forwarded with confidence to the saddler or harness maker.

It is the Author's opinion that if piped collars were generally adopted, they could not, and would not, be out of place under any circumstances.

BREAST-COLLARS are never in much demand, and are not as a rule considered any improvement to the general appearance of the "Turn Out"; in fact, the writer condemns them, unless for occasional wear; for permanent wear, they are an eyesore, and dangerous to the horse.

The same argument, to some extent, applies to rush collars, but they possess the advantage of being handy, light, and non-chafing, and, if well fitted and properly leathered for the hame-draft, reindees, and top-strap, and woolled under the lining, they will wear a long time, besides being readily, and with little cost and risk, cut, altered, or eased for sore necks, as circumstances may require. Some collars are made without housings, the side pieces of which are all in one, running right round the collar, and, being as a rule manufactured of the best material, have a very neat and light appearance. These are called "broad top," or "London-topp'd" collars. The stage and van collars are frequently used now of the same form and make, but of course considerably heavier, and of plain leather; they answer the purpose equally as well as with the unsightly housing on the top. If a collar should be too large, a false collar, or shell, can be adapted, which, in case of sore neck, is very useful; they can be made either of solid leather, or double basil, stuffed with wool and quilted throughout.

THE BRIDLE is the most complicated part of the whole set, being nothing but an ingenious mechanical contrivance, or number of straps and bands put together for the purpose of carrying the bit safely and securely in the horse's mouth, and for no other purpose was it invented; therefore, in fixing the head-strap, front, throat-band, winker straps (if any), and nose-band, the *bit* must not be lost sight of. Bridles are certainly not required to be lumbering, or heavy, but all the billets must be strong. In taking up or loosing out the *cheek-billets*, the position, bearing, and action of the bit is materially altered, and the horse's temper considerably affected, as the case may be. The *throat-band* should never be buckled tight, but just as safety (in keeping the bridle in its proper position) demands. It is possible for the front to be but a quarter of an inch too short, which oversight will cause the head-strap to press against the ears, pulling them forward, and so allow the *winkers* to drop, adding considerably to the risk of the horse slipping the bridle, particularly if it be given to throwing its head about, which the pain will actually cause. Where winkers are used they should carry or hang their centre exactly opposite the eyes, and, if ornaments are worn, care should be taken that they be put on *before* the winkers are made or sewn in the cheeks. In fixing the crests, monograms, or ornaments after the bridle is made up, there is risk of the legs or wires sticking out and touching the eye from the winker lining.

THE BIT.—The name, make, and pattern of bits are legion. The best and safest bit for general purposes, and driving in particular, is the *"guard bit,"* it having no bar at the bottom, cannot catch over gates or posts; and the best guard bit is the " revolving mouth," being far preferable to the " Liverpool," or " slide mouth." The revolving mouth cannot be held in the teeth against a jerk of the reins, in the event of the horse running away; and it is very easy and humane in its action, and extra leverage can be applied the instant it is required. The term has many times been used by horseowners, in reference to the smooth revolving bar of this bit, that it will "mouth a colt;" at all events, its being perfectly loose affords plenty of occupation and amusement for restive horses while standing in the street, their whole attention appearing to be centred in playing with or manipulating the mouth-piece, which means safety, confidence, and ease of mind on the part of the occupants of the carriage or other vehicle, and the conscience of the driver is perfectly clear of the use of the brutal " high-port." In selecting the bit, the first consideration is the horse; second, the class of bridle to be worn; third, that the desired end be achieved without pain. The curb requires considerable judgment and feeling in its application. It should never be worn tight, and, where applicable, as in the case of light-mouthed horses, may be abandoned altogether. Some curbs are lined with chamois, padded, and these answer very well where curbs are required for gentle use. Of course there are numerous makes and patterns of bits, for all uses, both for riding and driving, ancient and modern (see illustrations), which the Author cannot detail here for want of space, but he will be very pleased to send his complete list at any time on application.

THE REINS are applied, or fixed, when the bridle and other parts are satisfactory, the billets being run through the near and off-side territts and hame dees, and attached to the bit. Several kinds and makes are introduced by manufacturers, viz. :—*flat reins,* **with brown hand-parts and the rest** black; *round reins*, brown leather all through, which the Author never recommends; *flat brown reins, flat lined Oxford reins,* stitched two or four rows according to the quality of the harness, all of which are adapted to any class of harness, the latter looking very neat and wearing remarkably well. For ladies driving, white buff hand parts are the usual thing.

And last, but not least, is the important item which has caused so much controversy, experienced and otherwise—

THE BEARING REIN.—Much has been said; volumes have been written; overstrained and impossible pictures and numerous dear-at-any-price pamphlets and baby poems published, in wholesale, thoughtless, and inexperienced condemnation of the bearing rein, a specimen of which literature the writer once heard condemned by a justly-celebrated London steel goods manufacturer as "mere twaddle," and who said "the contents were calculated to gain no other end or point than the one probably intended or hoped for, viz.:— "advertisement, by bringing the thoughtless and unreasonable objector before the public, and of giving him an opportunity of airing his—*barbarous*—sentiments (this being the word chiefly used by persons of this one idea only), on that subject at least." It is a strange fact, that the majority of those who write and invent wholesale against the bearing rein are totally inexperienced in its use, and in the "Turn Out" generally. Therefore, in the light of day, neither their arguments nor themselves would be accepted as authorities on the subject. The Author does not condemn the use of the bearing rein altogether, neither does he advise or advocate the regular or permanent application of it, but his motto, in reference to that particular item of the set, has always been—Discretion, and his standpoint — Humane. That there are times and circumstances which demand to the harness the application of the bearing rein for the general safety of the "Turn Out" there can be no doubt or legitimate question raised. The fact is well known that it should not be (and the Author believes it is not) as a rule attached for appearance sake only, as some arguers would have it understood, or with the desire of punishing the horse. A special case recently came under the writer's notice, where the necessity for applying the bearing rein to a valuable sixteen-hands steed presented itself, and was ultimately adopted. The animal being fresh had taken to amuse itself, after a spin of a few miles, by wandering, and throwing its head almost between its forelegs, and again in the air, whilst going at a swinging trot,—or, as some folks would term it a rattling pace,—and at times would vary the performance by the corresponding extreme—all round, constantly pulling in a tremendous and excitable manner—thus shewing the necessity for both bearing rein and martingale, whilst the driver tried by all means in his power to check it by calling the horse by name, coaxing it, shouting, and, at a risk, touching him up with the whip, thereby causing a considerable amount of swerving and danger, but all to no purpose. The risk of upsetting became more and more apparent, and would most certainly—and perhaps with fearful consequences—have come about, had the horse trodden upon a stone, or made one false step. At last the writer's suggestion of a bearing rein was adopted, and some window cord was attached, to act in that capacity, and an additional cord carried from the back of the noseband, through the bottom hame-strap to the belly-band. The result shewed itself in a few minutes, after first leading the horse, and then quietly mounting the vehicle, to the evident pleasure and comfort of the driver and all concerned; and the owner of the horse has said many times since that he has not, and never shall, go out with a spirited animal unless a bearing rein is either on the harness or ready for use in the vehicle. At the same time, in fixing the "check" up to the hook of the saddle, care and judgment are necessary. The horse should have easy liberty in standing, and in going up hill, which can be regulated by the buckle on the near side; and it should be remembered that the bearing rein acts upon the crupper-dock, and that it is not intended for compressing the animal's head to its tail. If the horse be a hard puller and very fresh, the bearing rein will save considerable arm-aching on the part of the driver, and chafing on the part of the animal. Severity or brute force is not needed in any case, and at all times the end to be accomplished should not be sought for, or brought about, too hurriedly. The check-rein should always be slackened (if worn tight for the time) in going up hill, and if the opportunity occurs for taking the extra rein off altogether, it may be done; it is little carriage, and,—the writer would add—no ornament. The less harness and strappings a well-broken horse can with safety be made to do with, the better. Now, the writer would ask, *what* the advocates of "*no* bearing rein" would use as a substitute, in the above case—the secret gag bit? The Author would cry shame!

We cannot believe that the bearing rein is, or ever has been, wilfully converted into the "instrument of torture," or made to administer one-third the amount of punishment that its hidden substitute—the "Gag Bit" (see illustration), has done. The cruel roof-working of the gag bit can be seen at a glance, and the imaginary charges and ridiculous illustrations that have been published against the bearing rein are an insult to the many owners of horses, and proprietors of large establishments, who think proper, and are perfectly justified in using their own discretion, in adopting any means they may try or decide upon for the safety of the "Turn Out," as the result of experience, blended with humane feeling for the horse, and care for the public safety; and the Author contends that his argument is conclusive when the fact becomes generally known, that *the majority of the largest and richest individual horse-owners in the kingdom adopt, and are known to use, the bearing rein*, to all animals where speed and blood are in hand, which fact is proved by the notice that appeared in the *Saddlers' and Coach-Builders' Gazette*, dated June 1st, 1877, viz.:—*That at the recent meeting of the Coaching (four-in-hand) Club, in Hyde Park, it was observed that all the Horses, save in three or four instances, wore bearing reins.**

This notice is sufficient to endorse the writer's words that the bearing rein is neither more nor less than a legitimate part of the set, and, *that no harness room is complete without it.*† One bearing rein with plain covered furniture can be used to any pattern single harness, so there is no real necessity for an extra rein to every set.

There may be some persons who, at a loss for fair argument would say, that the Author, being an harness maker, is interested in the manufacture and sale of the bearing rein. Such argument is not worth entertaining, considering the fact that the cost of a bearing rein is so very nominal, and little or no difference is made to the customer or manufacturer whether that rein is supplied or not, as far as the cost of the set or sets go. And, in conclusion, we would remark that if the amateur or prejudiced enemy of the bearing rein would hasten his non-success as a horse-breaker, he has only to

---

* It is said that the horse does not know its own strength, hence our control over it in the shafts. Therefore the writer considers the strength and presence of mind of *one man* on the box behind a team of four high-bred, well-corned, noble animals altogether inadequate, particularly in crowded thoroughfares, with vehicles before him and behind him, without the assistance of the bearing rein.

† A friend's simile in conversation, respecting the use and abuse of the bearing rein, was, that with restive and over-fresh horses, it is much the same as a drill-sergeant to the raw recruit, the natural position of the latter being known as "all over the shop."

adopt the extraordinary high-port of the "gag bit," which was expressly invented to act as a secret substitute for the bearing rein, and he will very soon find that he has established himself as an accomplished "Temper and jaw breaker," unless he be of the same class as the man who "would condemn the inventor of the barbarous bearing rein to wear one for life," and at the same moment confessed that he himself "had never *possessed a Turn Out*."

It is an easy matter to discover whether a bearing rein is necessary or not, and the sum and substance of the writer's dictum is, if the horse carries itself perfectly straight and freely with a light mouth without the extra rein, by no means apply it; but if, on the contrary, the animal is a very hard and excitable puller,* or stumbles and throws its head about as though having business on both sides of the road at one time, then the bearing rein cannot, and must not be dispensed with.

Before leaving the bearing rein, we would quote the words of JOHN PHILIPSON, Esq., of the firm of ATTKINSON AND PHILLIPSON, the celebrated coach builders, and author of a little work on "Harness," viz. :—" I have said that bearing reins have been widely condemned of late years, and this condemnation I consider deservedly merited when pointed to the 'gag,' as this method of bearing-up is both cruel and highly injurious. This remark, however, does not apply with the same force to the bearing rein in its simple form, and the most impartial summing up of all that has been said for and against them would not justify me in saying that they are always to be dispensed with, for, as a writer on coaching days says :—'bearing reins have their uses and abuses.'"

In RAWLINSON's "Ancient Monarchies," we learn that the use of the bearing rein was practised by the Egyptians of old, &c.

"NIMROD" in one of his sporting essays, writes :—

"There are many horses, sometimes whole teams (four-in-hand), that will not face anything but the cheek ; and where is the arm that could bear the weight of four horses leaning

---

* How often have we heard it said that a certain "horse shall come fresh out of the stable, and draw a vehicle and driver some miles without traces," and, again, drivers to complain that "their arms have ached enough to drop off."

upon it for an hour or more together, perhaps at full gallop? How much soever humanity towards the horse may be enjoined, *regard for our own species must prevail*, and no horse in a coach or a post chaise IS SAFE without a bearing rein, and for this reason, he is in constant danger from having his head at liberty, of loosing his bridle by rubbing his head against the pole, or against the other horse, and an accident is almost sure to happen."

Therefore, we will now leave the reader to his best discretion as regards the bearing rein, and advise him to study seriously before he resolves to use or abandon it, or to advise others either for or against it. We will now proceed with our advices and suggestions as "to fitting," and other items of the whole set.

It is not necessary to say, that for safety, the quality of the leather and furniture of the set of harness should be of the best, but *it is* necessary to intimate that no matter how good the make and quality may be, equal danger attends the "Turn Out" if the harness be not properly and judiciously fitted. The horse must never be buckled tight to its work, particularly at the traces; special care should be paid to the traces, in seeing that they are punched true, and buckled equal length each side. The piped or long loops should be well sewn in with strong threads, and creased, chequered, and bevilled by hand. If narrow loops are used throughout, they should be firm and nicely blocked; loose and flimsy loops are useless for the purpose intended after a few showers of rain, and are very unsightly. Long breechbands running up to the tugs are rather ancient and complicated, and add to the expense and weight of the harness—short breechbands answer the same purpose, and are lighter for the horse to carry. If the set be *regular best*, it should be sewn four rows throughout (by hand preferred); if it be second quality, one row round is the rule, except in the traces and backband, which should be always four rows; and if plain harness be ordered, it will be single solid leather in parts other than the traces, backband, tugs, and breechband, which are always lined, with the exception of the traces used in tramway and such work, which are made wider, and of stouter solid leather.

In running a horse without winkers for the first time, great care is necessary; and the whip should be kept in the socket. These items may seem of small moment to the practised horsemen, and manufacturers of harness; but they are of the greatest importance to the general public, for whom this work is in the main intended.

Good plain solid leather harness invariably gives satisfaction. All stitches of harness should of necessity be hand work, the threads well waxed and twisted before using, and the awl blade actually smaller than the threads, which threads should be well and evenly pulled in, or, as the trade saying is, "plump as a bird's eye." Firm sound work is then assured, and this book would be wanting in its practical sense, and would not have fulfiled the mission intended, unless it gave this real germ of the subject in hand, viz., such particulars, which may appear, from their simplicity, of minor importance; and which must have been so considered, or overlooked, by other Authors; who, have omitted them for the purpose of more minutely particularising matters not practical; and in which the average driver and horse-owner is not concerned, or at all times safe in turning to account, namely, physic, prescriptions, and trick training; which latter is the extreme of horse-breaking, and not suitable to the vocation of all horse-owners.

The writer recently made a brown leather set of harness, with square brass wire (west end) furniture, straight flapped imperial pad, square winkers, light kicking strap and tugs, flat-lined Oxford reins, London topped collar, and revolving mouthed guard bit. This model set (as the customer called it) was supplied without breast-plate, face-piece, curb, hip-pieces, bearing rein, throat-band swivels, pad-cloth, or any ornaments whatever; the only extra in the set being, that the bellyband was made to buckle both on the near and off sides, for easy access and handiness in releasing the horse from the shafts, in the event of accident.

It is a cruel mistake to run a horse in a four-wheeler *without a breechband*, which should be so adjusted as to keep the vehicle from forcing the shaft tugs from their proper position in going down hill. The foregoing applies to double harness and four-in-hand or tandem alike; other minor particulars can be advised the maker on ordering the set.

For pipe-throated collars the hames are required to be specially made in every case; the ordinary formed plain hames, being difficult to adjust, are a misfit, and altogether unsafe.

We have introduced a set of harness which we think fully endorses the name given it, viz., "The Humane," but it must only be applied to well-broken, docile horses, and in the hands of a thoroughly experienced whip, the set being without breech-band, bearing rein, crupper dock, rein billetts, cheek'd-bit, swivells, hook, collar, and rosetts, and being made very light in the leather work and furniture. The Author thinks this should meet the wishes of the most sensitive arguer against the bearing rein; but the fact remains that any part of the present existing harness can be, and often is, so adjusted as to become a greater "instrument of torture" than it is possible to make the bearing rein, *in which the neck gives way*, but not so with the cheeks of the bridle, the crupper strap, or the traces, *when buckled uneven or without play*.

The writer has invented a much needed substitute for the driving-rein "billetts," which can be applied to hackney bridles alike, and many useful points in a set of harness.

The above substitute for rein furniture, (which means economy in price, less weight for the horse, wear and tear reduced to a minimum, and, improvement in the general appearance of the "Turn Out") the Author will be very pleased to adapt to any gentleman's reins, free of charge, on the same being sent to his manufactory.

The reader shall not be troubled with wading through a long description of the different classes, qualities, and parts of harness leather, such as 'backs,' 'butts,' 'bellies,' 'shoulders,' 'hides,'—'black,' 'brown,'—&c., and the cost of production and process of manufacture; that being unnecessary in this work, and more to the interest of the harness maker, who is already experienced in every particular, and his good judgment will ensure good value. The same rule applies to the furniture, such as buckles, hames, &c., &c.

After selecting the pattern, the rest must remain with the harness maker, who will hold himself responsible for fit and satisfaction.

Specimens of modern harness furniture, price list, and drawings, the Author will forward at any time post free.

TO ATTACH THE HORSE TO THE VEHICLE.

"Slow and Sure."

IN attaching a horse or putting it between the shafts, the most deliberate way is the quickest and safest; bustling or hurrying and running round its head backwards and forwards is a very dangerous practice, particularly with a spirited animal.

A few days ago a friend of the writer's (after many remonstrations and cautions for the rushing manner in which he always put the horse in) met with a very serious accident, nearly costing him the life of his steed. To use own words—" He had just fixed the near side trace and breech-band strap, and was hastening round the back of the dog-cart to attach the off side, when the horse sheered away, at the same time catching the wheel of the vehicle against a large stone fixed in the gateway, causing it to plunge, and the owner to shout and pull at the reins; ultimately, during the brief excitement, the horse got his rump under the shafts and commenced kicking, soon cleared himself of the lot, and bolted away, fell—or was knocked—down in turning the corner, thus preventing further mischief." The moral is—Had the owner gone about his work with less bustle and in a more systematic manner the horse would not have been so likely to become nervous.

Some horses are extremely irritable and unsteady during the process of attaching to or taking from the vehicle, for which there must be a cause, and it is known to be not at all times the fault of the horse. The attendant who understands his horse, and is familiar with humane and systematic care and good treatment, has very little trouble with a well-broken animal.

It is very important that the shafts should always be elevated and drawn to the horse, and never left upon the ground for backing the horse between them.

It is a common practice to throw the cushions, rugs, and mats into the vehicle from a distance, and *vice versâ;* many serious accidents have arisen therefrom—a simple crack of the whip, and—" *Who'd have thought it !* "

The same methodical system as above suggested should be adopted in taking the horse out of the shafts as in putting him in. Some may say after a journey—"Oh! the horse is tired! —he's quiet enough now—make haste!—hurry up!—have him out as quick as possible;" but it must be remembered, that the horse has a great love for home, and is as anxious to get *into* his stable as he was *for a run* when brought out fresh. Many a shaft has been broken at the stable door, and many a set of harness partly ripped from the animal's back, through the tugs, &c., catching the latch or other impediment on or near the door in the hurry of the horse to reach his stall.

In attaching your horse, always consider the kind or class of vehicle it is about to draw, so that you may either add to or dispense with the parts of harness that may be or may not be required, or appear necessary; for instance, if the conveyance be a four-wheeler, then the breech-band should not be dispensed with, on account of the weight and forward pressure down hill, which the breech-band will assist in resisting, both as regards the horse and the brake, when the latter is used. But if a gig, light dog-cart, or any vehicle where the occupants do not exceed two in number, the kicking strap, or even the kicking strap tugs alone, will be sufficient, the last items being simply to carry the traces.

The traces should always be buckled perfectly true and alike in length on either side; to be careless or "makeshift" in this matter means torture for the horse and personal risks. When an odd trace is spliced, or a new buckle end (say sixteen inches long) is put on to the trace, as is often the case, care should be taken that both sides are attended to at the same time, and that the punch holes shall be found or made to correspond exactly; this is out of consideration for the part that bears the pressure or pain, viz., the horse's shoulder.

These matters may appear very simple to the experienced, or to the careless eye, but the Author would argue that every good huntsman knows the importance of true stirrup leathers and level irons each side, not only for his comfort and pleasure, but for the actual safety of his life; thereby the same rule more strictly applies to the most important duty in "attaching the horse to the vehicle," viz., the *draft*.

Where the hame tug is at the reverse end of the traces, the horse certainly is relieved of the weight; but apart from that consideration, it is an encumbrance, and somewhat unsightly; as is any part of the harness not actually required for immediate use.

The Author would here suggest that the finishing touch in "attaching the horse" should be, to see that its tail rests in the crupper dock perfectly free from hair, no bristles left between it and the "pad," by which title the dock really should be known, it being made large, thick, and filled with linseed;—not thin, wiry, and stuffed with paper. Hence the oily and healing nature of the *humane dock*, as invented by the Author.

Few horsemen or drivers would knowingly permit the animal in their charge to work one hour in pain, particularly if they had the remedy at hand, yet, many horses toil the whole day in actual agony; and submit to labour, under protest as it were, from sheer good temper and obedient disposition.

How frequently do we see not only marks, but scars and raw places under various parts of the harness, wounds which are frequently caused through carelessness and want of the observant eye in the attaching of the horse to the vehicle, and its afterwards working away, up hill and down, loaded or unloaded, in all weathers, without an occasional notice on the part of the driver, or re-adjustment of the different items of the set which may appear necessary. Some horses are punished into an habitual "*protest,*" such as biting and snapping with the teeth, scraping with the feet, or starting and stopping without orders, or by sudden and dangerous jerks. All these signs are weighed over by the careful horseman, and he soon discovers the cause, and in five cases out of six he will effect the cure, at very little inconvenience or expense.

To learn if "all is easy," place the hand under the saddle or pad, lift the bridle-head from pressing around the ears, wipe as it were through the underside of the top of the collar and around the throat inside, or ease the belly-band and dock, and re-adjust the curb, if one is worn, and at all times raise the weight from the horse's back when on the road, by leaning backwards or forwards, if driving, or if walking at the side, lift up the shafts, when the load is on the same; and it will be found that such small attentions as these may appear to be are most effective with the horse, and a great source of pleasure and satisfaction to the horseman, who is fully and promptly repaid by the ready appreciation of the animal under his protection, which latter may be the actual bread winner.

The horse's skin is doubly sensitive to chafing and galling during wet seasons and persistent rainy weather; therefore at these times more care and attention to cleanliness is necessary on the part of the groom.

Neglect means cruelty; and the old saying here applies, "Prevention is better than cure."

To cure occasional sores, which may be caused whilst the horse is in the shafts, let the first attention in the stable be, to clean the hair away from the wound with a pair of scissors, wash the sore, and gently rub with a lather of water and black soap, after which an application of salt and water, well dissolved, and left to dry itself, is an old and effectual remedy, and a simple preliminary "stitch in time."

Of course the above prescription will not cure defects in the formation of the shafts; which may be too narrow, and thus cause a sore; or injury may arise through misfitting harness; but these items can easily be discovered, and pointed out to the coach-builder, or saddler, as the case may be, and if these persons are only consulted in time, serious accidents may be prevented.

It is a dangerous practice to unbuckle the driving rein billetts before taking the horse out of the shafts, thereby losing control of the animal somewhat; the breech-band or kicking strap (whichever worn) should always be released first, then the belly-band and traces. The occasional mention of the horse's name, and in fact a little conversation kept up with him, during the process of attaching to and releasing from the vehicle, such as "Woa, Charlie!—Steady boy!—Stand over!" &c., saves time, tends to avoid accidents, and is calculated to cultivate patience and good temper in both horse and man.*

---

* The reader will understand that the foregoing and after suggestions and rules, apply to single and double—or pair-horse—and every description of "Turn Out" alike.

DRIVING.

"'Tis the pace that kills."

THE term "Driving" seems, as a rule, to be misunderstood by the amateur whip, and by many whose daily business it is to sit behind a steed. We often hear it said that "a good horse requires no driving," and so it is. The holder of the ribbons should take his position, with a view to steer or guide the horse, and not for the express purpose of "driving" it, which term may be, and is, often misconstrued into frequent floggings, constant shoutings, pulling or jerking at the reins, and other demonstrations, which frequently call to mind the poetical lines—

"To see ourselves as others see us."

Before taking charge of your "Turn Out," the first business is,—to learn how to pick up the reins; mount the vehicle; and keep your own side, for, as before quoted—

"The rule of the road is a paradox quite,
    As the drivers jog it along;
If you keep to the left you are sure to go right,
But if you keep to the right you go wrong."*

The reins should be taken in hand before the vehicle is mounted, therefore the responsibilities commence at that moment. If there are any other occupants, the driver takes his place last, (unless an attendant is at the horse's head), and that without the least hurry or excitement, by stepping lightly and firmly to his seat, the reins being already in hand the proper length, and the *whip in the socket*. The horse should be allowed to start itself by a gentle movement of the reins between the fingers, without the slightest flourish or noise on the part of the driver, he at the same moment moving his weight a little to the front. The horse may be quietly spoken to, or made to respond to his name being mentioned by starting immediately and freely.

---

* Where repetition of the same lines or suggestions occur, the Author wishes it to be distinctly understood that it is done for a deliberate purpose, viz.:—that of "*driving*" THE ARGUMENTS home; where the reader may miss the first, the second may catch him.

The position of the driver is to lean a little forward, after taking a firm seat and keeping the legs well out towards the dash, and never to hang backward, excepting for the purpose of balancing the vehicle in going down hill, the feet being kept to the front at all times. In driving, the reins are taken up the reverse way to riding, viz.:—from the bottom, or underside, and kept with a steady pressure constantly feeling the animal's mouth.*

Should the driver at any time become nervous or irritable, the same is communicated to the horse through the reins, which communication is calculated to give the horse increased license and want of confidence, and the driver considerable anxiety. At all times the driver should sit square and perfectly easy, without the slightest appearance of stiffness or carelessness, and must keep a good foothold in turning corners.

In our travels we see numerous styles of holding the reins, but there is only one proper and safe way, viz.:—in the left hand; the right, or whip hand, being kept ready for emergencies. The driving hand, with the reins, should be held to the front, a little way from the body and on a level with the elbow; the finger nails are slightly uppermost in driving, and the reverse in riding. The *near* side or left rein passes between the thumb and first finger; the *off* or right side rein between the second and third fingers, which are kept close together, thus securing the purchase or grip.

To hold a rein in each hand† is a most awkward and helpless plan, and seems to be the system adopted in America, where the writer has witnessed many accidents arising from that cause alone, both on the road and upon the trotting track; in one case the driver was thrown backwards out of his buggy on to the ground, through hanging on, which ended in the breaking of the reins; in fact, it had been his constant boast that the horse did not require traces, but could pull the vehicle by the reins alone.

Some persons hold the reins close to the body; others up to the chin, with only the first finger between them; this is very unsafe in the event of the horse stumbling, particularly if drivers themselves indulge in the habit of keeping their

---

* The reins should never be allowed to fall or lay upon the horse's back.

† The witty carman says he holds a rein in each hand, and the whip in the other.

legs under the seat, which is altogether a very helpless and nervous position, and is calculated to land the driver into the gutter on turning the first corner.

The occupier of the box should be particular in pulling up gradually before arriving at his destination; and in turning corners, by giving a full sweep; going wide where there is room and all clear; and the fact should be kept constantly to the front, that the driver's position behind the horse is exactly the same as the man at the wheel of a vessel.

The frequent use of the horse's name is a very important item in travelling long journeys, it being not only cheering to the animal, but company for him; and the same practice is of very great service when the horse is standing still in the street.

In driving along, should anything occur ahead to necessitate your stopping or pulling up suddenly in crowded thoroughfares, the whip or hand should be elevated as a signal to those who may be in the rear.

The following is an illustration of flourishing starts on the part of drivers:—

A doctor acquaintance of the writer's was in constant danger of his life, and could not account for it. After each call throughout the day, the moment on opening the carriage door, the horses would bounce off at express speed, sometimes rearing or swerving round, and invariably landing the doctor's hat against the top of the door-way. The cause of this very restive starting on the part of the horses was not discovered until a change of coachmen came about, and it was then found out that the horses had been regularly cut with the whip at the sound of the handle of the door turning. And it took considerable time and patience on the part of the new Jehu, to persuade the horses to start steadily, without bounding or plunging.

Special care should be taken in driving down hill. An Hibernian friend of the writer's used to say that—"*He* walked the horse down hill, and the *horse* walked himself up," which indicates plenty of consideration for the animal.

Many serious accidents would be avoided if drivers generally would adhere strictly to the rule of keeping their own side, viz. :—to the left, at all times, except when overtaking a vehicle.*

This is the simple rule of the road in England:—You start out to the left and you come home to the left.

The whip should never mount the box without previously taking a careful survey of the "Turn Out,"—to see that all the strappings are properly attached, the traces not twisted, or buckled up too tight. One of the greatest evils attending the attachment of the horse to the vehicle is buckling him too tight to his work; either in the kicking-strap, breech-band, bearing-rein, belly-band, traces, or any of the bridle parts. The writer has known even the simple hip cloth, through its not being properly adjusted, to cause the horse to bolt away at a furious speed for some miles (and unfortunately the occupier of the box was a lady†), happily without accident other than a severe shock to the nerves of the occupants of the vehicle.‡

Another case of oversight on the part of the owner of the "Turn Out" only recently came to the writer's ears.

A gentleman started rather late in the evening from an hotel yard, accompanied by his son, whom he was bringing from school for his holidays, and on stepping into the gig (without taking his customary survey of the harness) the animal, a very fast mare, bounded away. The driver, losing all control of his steed, tried and tried again to check her headlong anxiety to reach her stable, by jerking the reins, coaxing and shouting; all of which was of no avail; and to add to the agony of the father, the boy began to scream and cry; but not a solitary human being could be seen on the road, and fortunately no vehicle was passed the whole distance, eight and a half miles, and the mare being used to that road, and usually a good tempered animal, deliberately pulled up of her own accord, and trotted them gently and safely to their own door. The cause of her wild behaviour was discovered to be, that the bit had not been put into the animal's mouth before starting, and the driver had been constantly pulling away at, and hanging on to, the nose-

---

* Or meeting ladies on horseback; or a drove of horses or sheep.

† The Author's wife, accompanied by her little son, 6 years old.

‡ Similar accidents have been known to arise from strangers fixing the rein billetts upon the single ring of a Wilson snaffle, the horse having been used to the double rings being billetted together.

band and cheeks of the bridle all the distance, which novel proceeding was more calculated to excite the mare than to stop her.

Therefore, the moral is, that no matter who may have the care or charge of the steed, in the temporary absence of the owner or driver, all persons or attendants are liable at some time or other to have their attention called away during the process of fixing the harness upon the horse, and attaching the horse to the vehicle; so the driver should never mount the box without having first felt and examined the easy bearings and proper adjustment of the whole set.

Great want of consideration for the horse is at times noticeable in the loading of vehicles, especially waggonettes and brakes for pic-nic parties; and, it is a standing disgrace that market carriers generally, and pleasure seekers also, seem to think more of the capabilities of the conveyance than the horse, and the writer has many times put the gentle reminder to those in charge :—" In considering (or risking) what the *cart will hold*, think how much the *horse can draw*."

In the summer time, and at holiday times, it is the usual practice to pack human beings behind a horse as close as a tin of sardines, and often with the tugs too low, the shafts swinging about, and the cart body bumping upon the axletree, caused by the springs being over-weighted. This kind of thing together with "We won't go home till morning" and other lively melodies in harmony with the time of evening and the quantity of stimulant deposited, are all apparently necessary to complete the day's enjoyment. But how little can the occupants be thinking of the enormous risk they are running whilst rocking backwards and forwards, as though they would roll in one mass out of the vehicle, and their whole attention seeming to be centered in getting to the top of their voices on the return journey; flogging, and racing up hill and down, frequently, at least as a rule, more excited or helpless than when starting out, and their last thoughts being—the Horse.

Gardener's carts, although to all appearance a big load, are, as a rule, packed with more judgment, the gardener generally putting the finishing touch to the balance by stowing himself away either on the front or extreme back of his strong and well-built cart, as the case requires; and, generally speaking, his horse is well-cared for, and never to be seen distressed or neglected. There is sometimes a risk in allowing the faithful animal to hurry home in the evening, almost on its own responsibility, the driver being in a kind of semi-sleep, after his very long and laborious day's work, which generally commences with the daylight in the summer time and long before the dawn in the winter time.

The writer has known several cases of complete smash-up, which in one or two instances could have been easily avoided, had not obstinacy on the one part and vacancy on the other prevailed.

Those in charge of gigs, traps, dog carts, carriages, or other vehicles, should always be prepared *to take either side* (although there is only one proper side), or go *clean off the road altogether* (where practicable) in cases of emergency, taking care to be in constant readiness and on the look out for runaways, or heavily laden waggons that may be slowly trudging along on the wrong side, and the attendant some distance in the rear; likewise for "sleepy" drivers, "ignorant" drivers, and "indifferent and amateur" drivers, all of which are frequently to be met with on the road.

The writer thinks the Shakesperian lines (which he once saw nailed up in a certain nobleman's harness-room) peculiarly applicable to the foregoing remarks, namely, that " 'Tis a cruelty to load a falling man," and " Good words are better than bad strokes."

The art of driving can be summed up and condensed into a few simple rules, viz. :—

1st. Always mind your own (*near* or left) side, except when passing a vehicle, which takes you by the right or *off* side.

2nd. Never turn round a corner at full speed, but always pull gently in beforehand, and take a full sweep, to give clear space to any vehicle that may be coming.

3rd. When you pull up or turn round in crowded thoroughfares, always intimate your intention to probable drivers behind, by holding up your right hand or whip, as a danger signal.

4th. In driving down hill, hold the horse well in hand, by keeping the grip somewhat short, and the reins comparatively high, which will tend to support the horse, and promote confidence in man and horse alike. In going up-hill, slacken and ease the back if necessary; prepare to check in case of stumbling.

5th. Do not use the whip at any time without a thought as to the necessity for it, and by no means irritate or tease the horse by tugging at the reins. This habit renders the horse callous and indifferent.

6th. If the journey be a good distance, to be covered in a given time, drive at a moderate pace throughout, and by no means play at galloping and walking, which means actual torture and loss of time.

7th. If the horse is known to be nervous and to shy at times, the driver must be beforehand with him, by preparing the horse with a word, and giving the object likely to be shied at a wide berth. To practise horse-breaking by taking him up to the object again and again is not always convenient or advisable.

8th. If a shoe becomes loose, do not postpone the fixing of it until you get home. If you can anywhere have it properly secured, this will prevent accident and probable lameness.

9th. If the horse bolts or runs away, try, by all means in your power, to keep your presence of mind,[*] by which you will not abandon all control over him. Continue to guide him, and speak to him; he may yield mechanically to the rein, and the danger may be, and often is, averted by so doing.

10th. It is as well to remember that the horse is, at all times, grateful for any gentleness or kind act shown towards him.

As proving the value of a cautious driver, the following will show the kind of man preferred by most gentlemen. A gentleman advertised for a coachman; three persons applied, and were admitted into the parlour. The road leading to the hall went near a dangerous precipice.

---

[*] A friend of the Author's once argued that he knew something better than "presence of mind" in a railway accident, viz.—"absence of body,"—which the writer thinks equally applies to carriage accidents.

"How near the edge of this precipice can you drive me without the danger of an upset?" inquired the gentleman of the first applicant. "Within a hair's breadth!" answered the man. "And how near could you drive me?" said the gentleman to the second. "Within a hand's breadth," was the reply. The third man had taken up his hat and was leaving the room, supposing he had no chance of competing with either of these two. "Stop, stop!" said the gentleman; "let us here what you have to say!" "Why, sir, I cannot compete with either of these. If I were to drive you, I would keep as far off as I possibly could." "You are the man for me!" said the gentleman, and engaged him right away.

MEMOS. NOT TO BE FORGOTTEN IN CONNECTION WITH THE HARNESS.

The most important items to be observed in reference to the *comfort of the horse* are :—

>THE BIT,
>>THE COLLAR,
>>>THE SADDLE,
>>>>and CRUPPER-DOCK.

The most important items to be observed in reference to the *safety of the driver*, are :—

>THE REINS,
>>THE BACKBAND and TUGS,
>>>THE TRACES,
>>>>and TOP HAME STRAP.

These should be systematically examined before mounting the vehicle.

UNHARNESSING AND CLEANING.

"I rather tell thee what is to be fear'd."

NO doubt there may be a few rough and ready readers of the above title who would ask the question—"What art can there be in taking a set of harness off a horse?" or say—"I can soon rip it off, and without any ceremony." The writer would answer—If there is no art in the business of releasing or unburdening a horse with the easiest and quietest despatch, after its hard day's work, or perhaps after a long and tedious journey under the broiling sun or drenching rain, there is at least a certain amount of judgment and consideration necessary; and it is, therefore, the successful horse-keeper's rule that a certain system shall be laid down and regularly adhered to.

It is the general practice, in fact it may be said to be the universal custom, when undressing or taking a set of harness off a horse, to *commence* at the driving rein billets, by unbuckling the same from the bit and bringing them back to the hind part or territt of the saddle.

The writer's opinion is that *time is lost* and unnecessary *punishment* is inflicted upon the horse by so doing.

If the *girth be first unbuckled*, it has the immediate effect of releasing the pressure of the saddle from the horse's back, and allowing a gentle current of air to pass under the same without fear of chill or other consequences; and it also has the effect of easing the dock of the crupper from the root of the tail, particularly if the saddle be slightly moved backward, say a few inches (as it should be in all cases and under all circumstances, whether after riding, driving, or carting), a little while at least before taking the saddle and crupper finally from the horse's back. The heated parts are thus gradually cooled and relieved without the risk which attends the instantaneous removal of the saddle. Prompt removal of the saddle invariably follows the system of unbuckling first of the set, the billets at the bit, which bad method, or want of thought, is alone responsible for the many sore and scaly tails we see about the region of the dock; so much so that some tails that have been thus neglected, have the appearance of a number of permanent sores and running wounds underneath, which is caused by the horse pressing and keeping down the tail when the saddle is unbuckled and dragged off, with all its surroundings, at a moment's notice; and very often the behind part of the steed is pulled half across the stall. Before the saddle is taken off altogether, after loosening the girth, the reins should be cleared of the harness and hung up, not doubled or twisted in any way, but suspended as nearly straight as possible.

THE HAMES follow in due course, being unbuckled whilst upon the horse's neck and then removed. They should never remain upon the collar, to be taken off at the same time, and left upon it; this method is a strong illustration of want of feeling for the horse. It may be considered a saving of time and easy enough to take old and wide collars off the neck with the hames attached, but the quickness of the business, if done quickly at all, is chiefly owing to the extreme anxiety of the horse to wriggle through the infliction, and get it over. It is usual on taking the hames off to examine the top and bottom straps, as they are an important item in the set, and it is necessary to see that the punch holes are all sound. The advantage of taking the hames off before the bridle is that the collar can be moved a few inches up the neck, relieving the same of the weight, which is to the horse, during the brief moment of removing the bridle, as great a luxury and equally refreshing as the easing of the saddle and dock before taking off altogether. Good fitting hames should not reach the top of the harness collar.

THE BRIDLE should first be unbuckled at the throat-band, and even then it should not be *pulled* down, but *lifted* off with the two hands, the fingers being placed under the head-strap of the bridle behind the horse's ears; the top part being brought to the front allows the bit to *fall* from the mouth without danger to the teeth. The bridle should never under any circumstances be taken off, or the bit be taken out of the mouth while the animal is in the shafts; many serious accidents have been known to come about owing entirely to this practice. An instance recently came under the writer's notice where a pony and trap had been left at a public house door with the bridle hanging upon the points of the shafts, and a feed of corn in a bucket upon a trestle before it. The pony was startled by a boy coming round the corner playing with a whip top. The bucket of corn and trestle were upset, and away went the animal with the bridle dangling between its legs, and there being no possible chance of controlling the bare-headed runaway, a general smash up was the consequence, and in less than thirty minutes from the time of stopping to feed, the pony was killed (put out of its misery), having staked itself by trying in its mad career to leap some iron palings with the trap behind it. The wonder was that several persons were not killed in their efforts to check the animal.

In removing the SADDLE or PAD the left hand is put under the front, and the right hand to the dock, after first throwing the breech-band (if worn) over the back, across the top of the crupper, and the lot is instantly and easily taken off without any opposition on the part of the horse, such as tucking the tail under, or as some say, biting the dock. By adapting the above simple system a great deal of time and trouble (besides pain to the horse) is saved, and the ready assistance of that noble animal is secured, particularly when he becomes thoroughly acquainted with the new, easier, and more humane regulation.

To take the COLLAR from the horse's neck it has been before mentioned that the (hard iron) hames must not pass over the eyes of the horse at the same time (that is, the hames should be seperated from the collar) in any class of harness, whether gig, cab, or cart; and whatever is done through carelessness or clumsiness to irritate the horse, is sure to be communicated to the attendant, and thus both become chafed, which invariably leads to constant shoutings on the part of the man, and persistent dancing about on the part of the horse; probably the fork is introduced, which frequently ends in the animal being pricked and spoilt.

In taking the collar off it is usual to drag or lug at it from the front of the horse with both hands, and if it be at all a tight fit, one tremendous pull is given, after a series of jerks, in which the whole weight of man and horse is brought to bear, which invariably results in at least three, and sometimes four, ungraceful, if not brutish events occuring, viz. :—The moment the collar is past the eyes, after being pulled in the above helpless way, the inside of the throat cannot possibly miss striking the animal's nose, which blow is always a violent one; and if the stable has a low roof or is a temporary structure, the top of the horse's head comes in contact with the timber above the moment its nose is struck, causing the horse to rebound or reel to the full extent, which accounts for the rough and bristle like tops of the tail frequently to be seen, and is the effect of collision with the rear of the stall. All the brushing and combing that can be done will not make these broken bristles lie down or wear any other appearance than that of having been gnawed by rats. When the collar is thus pulled forcibly from the head, another event frequently occurs in the heat of temper, or (to use a milder term) under the impulse of the moment—that the collar is either thrown upon the floor, or, in no gentle mood, landed in the manger (which, of course, means wear and tear) during the process of fixing the head stall or halter.

That the above illustrations of the results of rough and ready treatment are facts, and occur every day, is well known, and the writer (from many opportunities in connection with his business and sundry other surroundings) can vouch for and verify any illustrations a personal interview may suggest, and he, at the same time, places before his readers his own system of taking the collar off, which puts any and all of the items or results before mentioned out of the question, and renders the possibility of a horse slipping backward upon its haunches unlikely. As before intimated the collar is the most important part of the whole set, both to fit and in wear, and the putting on and taking off, if not done carefully, is seriously calculated to affect the temper of the horse.

It is not necessary to stand directly in front of the horse for drawing the collar off; the quickest, quietest, and safest method is to stand a little to the near side, bringing the collar close up to the ears with the right hand only (after it has been reversed or turned over the way of the mane); the left hand is placed up the face with a quiet rub, which humours the temperament of the horse, then, by leaning stiffly to the steed and pressing the collar towards the operator, he becomes, as it were, for the moment, a part of the horse, and with this assistance, a little twist of the head is given, and the collar glides or falls quietly upon the left arm, without having caused the least confusion, and this is done much easier and in shorter time than the bungling and helpless way of hanging at the horse's head with both hands to the collar. The improved system is looked upon by the horse, in the course of an experiment or two, as a luxury and pleasurable relief. Indeed, he will quietly reciprocate any good feeling shown towards him, particularly when his help is asked.

Rubbing the ears with the hands for a few moments is always appreciated by the horse, after taking the harness off, and is calculated to promote early and permanent friendship.

After the steed is cleared of its harness, the necessary cleaning, such as washing, whisping, feeding, watering, &c., follows, which should be done with as little fuss and blowing on the part of the groom as possible. The hissing of some men during their stable business can only be compared to a small steam engine, and the inhaling the dust on the part of the man (it is at times tolerably plentiful) cannot be looked upon as in any degree a healthy habit.

After the horse is made comfortable, the harness should be cleaned and put in its place; the lining of the collar and the crupper dock should be immediately sponged over with clean water; and the pannel of the saddle brushed; the reins wiped straight down with a clean dry cloth, after damping; the bit and curb taken from the bridle, washed, dried, and then thrown into a box of slacked lime, which should be kept for the purpose; the traces, back-band, breech-band, &c., straightened out and shined up with the compo brush; the furniture rubbed over, and the flaps of the saddle, side pieces of the collar, housing, and other patent leather parts, wiped lightly over with an oil rag, and polished off afterwards.

A clean and respectable "Turn Out" always conveys the impression at sight that it is in good hands, and in the care of what is known as a "Thorough Groom," whose study is not altogether to cultivate the outward show and that which is most attractive to the eye, but to look after the inward corners as well, such as the coach-house and harness room, which have their regular share of attention. All these facts are indicated in the permanently smart "Turn Out." Regular attention to the surroundings of the stable, harness room, coach-house, and yard, actually reduces labour and makes the daily routine a pleasure.

The harness in regular use should have systematic attention, and, if possible, it should be taken to pieces and hung up in parts; hence the saying, "that good harness actually improves in wear," which remark is frequently suggested by the mellow and clean appearance of some old sets.

The most important matter in assisting the groom is that he be supplied with the best materials and tools (as he calls them), especially that item which it is intended shall preserve as well as clean the leather, and so produce a substantial and quick return for labour; hence the prominence given to the composition known as compo.

It is not our duty to give the various modes and processes of the manufacture of this or other trade specialities for harness, or harness room requisites, and the different ingredients comprised, although professed receipts of "A 1 stuff," are common enough.

The Author supplies many (or most) of the kinds known in the trade, but the compo he finds to give the widest satisfaction, and which he has used and is using almost daily in his harness manufactory, is that made by Messrs. Jamieson & Co., of Aberdeen.* The Author thinks there are others in the trade of the same name, but the above is the actual title of the firm he refers to. Of course there are other *good* compos in the market; but *the* care should be, to avoid the *bad*, of which there is a very large proportion which give no return for labour, but make work for the groom, and actually burn and destroy the substance and beauty of the harness by killing the leather and spoiling good workmanship.

The same rule applies to the polishing pastes for cleaning the furniture, many of which not only injure the silver, or whatever the metal may be, but are dirty in use. Harris's is a good old-standing name for that and many other specialities of its class. The Author will gladly forward any gentleman a list of the makers of note of all items in that line, from boot-top powder to silver sand.

The above items may not seem of vast importance to the careless eye, but they are of recognised value to the systematic horseman, who exercises the greatest discretion in all his selections, and in his prejudices is equally firm.

In giving his recommendations to probable enquirers, the Author would here say that it will be with the same feeling

---

* See Advertisement.

which prompts the writing of this book, viz.: to save the horse-owners and horse alike, to obviate risk, and to economise time and money.

The one requisite of the "Turn Out" which often suffers most in small stables is the whip. When done with for the moment, it is allowed to stop where it falls, and to lie about until it may be required again, at which time it cannot be found, an outsider having borrowed it to flog the fowls or the dog. This means a new thong and probably a new handle and caps, which altogether unbuilds and for ever ruins a whip of value; some coachmen prize their hollystick, and in such hands it will last for years. The rule is that the whip should never be thrown or placed in the corner, but hung up by the thick part of the thong upon a wooden block or spring fixed in the harness room; after which the vehicle must be looked to and put under cover.

During a conversation respecting the harnessing and unharnessing of horses, a friend of the Author's once complained to him of the extreme restiveness of his animal in the stable, when fitting for the road, after a journey, and in grooming; so much so, to use his own words, that it became positively unsafe and dangerous to approach the animal in the stable with any part of the harness or tools, the horse seeming to get every day "worse and worse." The writer, on visiting the stable, perceived that the moment the owner approached his horse to take the head collar off it began to tremble from head to croup, and literally danced about the stable at the merest touch, ultimately becoming actually savage, biting and kicking at the same time. The Author watched the business quietly through, and decided in his own mind that the blame rested entirely with the man, and not with the horse, the fact being that the owner commenced with, and kept up, one continued system of shoutings at the terrified and nervous-tempered animal—(which incessant and excitable bawlings were mixed with anything but poetic language)—together with numerous gestures, as though it were his (the owner's) momentary intention to suit the action to the word with the aid of the nearest stable implement, causing the poor animal to fly from side to side of the stable in a most frantic manner. The time consumed in this most disgraceful and ridiculous performance was over thirty minutes ere the horse was between the shafts and ready for the road.

In answer to the owner's query—"What's my remedy?" "I've made up my mind to sell the brute," and several other signs of thorough upset, the Author's answer was "Lend me your horse for a week," which was agreed to, the writer sending it to his own stable; and that day week the owner, to his very great astonishment and delight, witnessed the fact of his once savage brute being harnessed, attached to the vehicle, taken down the lane a hundred yards, unharnessed, put into the stable, and everything in its place, unaided, in about fifteen minutes, and all without the slightest noise or commotion, the only movement in the stable on the part of the horse being when it came round of its own free will to put its nose into the collar. In reply to to the owner's second query—"How have you done it?" the Author's answer was, "System, sir, made up of kindness and patience, in equal proportions;"—

"Cela saute aux yeux."

THE VEHICLE.

"Who dares not drive by day, must walk by night."

AS the Egyptians were the first to capture and train the horse, so they were the first to use chariots, and the first mention we have of a chariot is in the 43rd verse of the 41st chapter of Genesis, where it is written—"That Pharaoh made Joseph ride in the second chariot which he had." These chariots, although no doubt very elaborately decorated, were very different vehicles to the modern chariot, as may easily be ascertained by examining any of the pictures of the Egyptian, or even the more modern Greek and Roman chariots. We are told in the 3rd chapter of the Songs of Solomon, that "King Solomon made himself a chariot of the wood of Lebanon." But in those early ages chariots were only used in battle, or to swell the processions and increase the pomp of monarchs, and were never used by private individuals, who rode on horses, asses, mules, or camels.

At what time carriages were first used by private individuals is somewhat doubtful. According to a writer in the "Encyclopædia Britannica," carriages for the conveyance of private individuals were established first by the Romans, who, it is asserted, had a great variety of these vehicles; which at first—owing to the narrow streets and roads, which were mere bridle paths—were very small. The use of the carriages becoming more general led to the formation of those excellent roads—such as the Appian Way, which was made 331 years before Christ—for the construction of which the Romans were justly celebrated. The carriage which figured in public ceremonials was the *Carpentum*. It was of slight construction, mounted upon two wheels, and was sometimes covered. The Gauls had a kind of carriage called the "Benna" or "Sirpea," constructed of wicker-work. The "Essedum" of the Romans was a two-wheeled carriage, copied by them from the war cars of the "Belgæ." These various vehicles were splendidly gilded with gold, and ornamented with precious stones.

Pleasure and Action.

When the feudal system, which was founded upon military service, was introduced, the use of carriages was for a time prohibited, as it was considered to have an effeminating tendency, which rendered the people who used them less fit for military purposes. So early as the beginning of the sixteenth century there were covered carriages; but their use was restricted to ladies in the highest ranks of society only—it being considered effeminate for gentlemen to ride in them. In 1474, however, the Emperor Frederick III. visited Frankfort in a close carriage; and in the following year he returned in a still more magnificent covered carriage. At a tournament held at Ruppin in the year 1509, the Electress of Brandinburg appeared in a carriage gilded all over, while that in which the Duchess of Mecklenburg rode was hung with red satin. When Cardinal Dietrichsten entered Vienna, no fewer than 40 carriages went forth to meet him. That same year the Consort of the Emperor Matthias made her entry in a state carriage covered with perfumed leather. The carriage of the first wife of the Emperor Leopold was said to have cost 38,000 florins. The panels of the Emperor's coach were of glass. Pepys, in his diary, relates a curious accident that occurred to Lady Peterborough through her ladyship using a carriage with glass windows. He says—"Lady Peterborough being in her glass coach with the glass up, and seeing a lady pass by in a coach whom she would salute, the glass was so clear she thought it was open, and so ran her head through the glass." We are not informed that any such accident occurred to the Emperor Leopold in his glass coach. At the magnificent Court of the Duke Ernest Augustus at Hanover, in 1681, there were 50 gilt coaches with 6 horses each; and shortly after that grand display, carriages, despite the feudal laws, became common all over Germany.

Carriages were used in France at a very early age. So far back as the year 1294, an ordinance of Philip the Fair forbade citizens' wives from using them. If one might judge from Chaucer's poem, entitled "The Squyre of Low Degree," it would appear they were used in England in his day (1328-1400), for he says:—

> "To-morrow ye shall ride on hunting fare,
> And ride my daughter in a chare;
> It shall be covered with velvet red,
> And cloth of gold all about your head,
> With damask white and azure blue,
> Well dispers'd with lillies new."

When Richard II. fled from his rebellious subjects, his mother was conveyed in a carriage. It was not, however, till the time of Queen Elizabeth that coaches became common in England. Probably those famous state journeys called "Royal Progresses"—like the one to Kenilworth—of which Her Majesty was rather fond, created a demand for carriages, and gave an impetus to coach building, which, during her reign, became a very important branch of industry, and continued to flourish so rapidly that at the commencement of the seventeenth century it was calculated that in London alone there were upwards of 6,000 carriages.

Hackney carriages were first introduced into France in the beginning of the reign of Louis XIV. by one Nicholas Sauvage. In 1650 Charles Vilmere secured the exclusive right to hire out carriages in Paris, and for this privilege he paid 5,000 livres. The first vehicle similar to our modern omnibus commenced running in Paris on the 18th of March, 1662. The fare was five sous. Hackney carriages were first established in London in 1625, twenty-five years before their introduction into France. In 1634 there were about 20 such vehicles plying for hire from the "May-Pole"; in 1637 there were 50; in 1652 they had increased to 200; and in 1654 to 300. In 1694 they were limited to 700, but in 1715 the limit was extended to 800. The hackney carriage maintained its place till superseded by the more modern vehicle, the *Cabriolet de place*, better known by the shorter title of "cab." In 1834, Mr. Hansom introduced the vehicle which bears his name, and upon which several improvements have been made. The oldest coach in the kingdom is the Lord Mayor's coach, which was built in 1757 for Sir Charles Asgil, the Lord Mayor elect that year. The next oldest is Her Majesty's state carriage, which was built in 1761, from designs by Sir William Chambers. From the official description of this carriage, which is said to be the most superb ever built, it appears the body of the carriage is richly ornamented with laurel and carved work, and beautifully gilt

Such, then, is a brief history of carriages from the earliest ages to the present time; but to give a detailed account of all the various descriptions of vehicles would be impossible in a work like the present. Indeed, to enumerate all the improvements that have been made in coach building would occupy our whole space. There are, however, two very important improvements which cannot be passed over. One of the most useful improvements in connection with coach building is the Collinge Axle, invented in 1792, and by means of which wheels only require to be oiled once in several months. The other great improvement is the Eliptic Spring, patented in 1804 by Obadiah Elliot, and by means of which carriage travelling is made more comfortable, and the labour of the horses much lighter. The Collinge Axle, although it obviates the necessity for frequent lubrication, does not dispense with it entirely. The axle of all vehicles, whether those of carriages or carts, should be regularly oiled or lubricated, as it not only renders the labour of the horse much less, but preserves the axle and wheel from wearing so rapidly. It not infrequently happens that through the axle not being regularly lubricated it becomes uneven, and both it and the hub of the wheel wear out much sooner than they would do if carefully and regularly attended to.

Care should be taken on the return from a journey to see the vehicle is properly washed, and that all soil, sand, or grit is removed from the axle, as it is very apt to get into the hub and grind either it or the axle into grooves or ruts, which if not noticed in time may lead to serious accident. In order to prevent break-downs, or spills, the vehicle should be regularly inspected and kept in good repair. It is a bad plan to leave vehicles exposed to the weather; they should, therefore, be kept under cover when not in use, as the sun not only spoils the paint and varnish, but shrinks the wood to such an extent as to render travelling in a carriage long exposed dangerous, as very frequently after long exposure to the sun's rays the tires become loose. For this reason it is not always safe to purchase a second-hand carriage, as such are often exposed in open yards and places without any cover from the sun and elements, and before it can be made sound and comfortable or safe, a greater expense has to be incurred than would have purchased a substantial new carriage. It is no uncommon thing for old ramshackle traps to be painted up and sold—"a bargain!" but the unfortunate purchaser finds, after spending pounds upon it without being able to make it comfortable and secure, that the bargain is anything but a bargain to him, and he is very glad to sell it for very much less than he gave for it.

Our suggestions are endorsed by Mr. Phillipson, who is not only an authority upon the subject by virtue of his publications, but from the fact that he is a very extensive carriage builder.*

---

* Attkinson & Phillipson, Newcastle-on-Tyne. See Advertisement.

The following brief rules respecting the conveyance should be particularly noted.

Vehicles should be kept in a dry, well ventilated coach-house, and, not in total darkness, or the colour will be destroyed, and the coach-house must not communicate with the stables or manure deposit. Ammonia fumes cracks the varnish, and fades the painting and linings of the carriage. A thin cover should be kept over it, which cover must not be damp.

Newly painted carriages should have a few weeks to set before using.

A vehicle should never be put away dirty, or with the slightest speck of mud upon it, or a stain is sure to remain.

Do not wash your carriage in the sun.

Levers or jacks should be covered with leather where they come into contact with the vehicle.

Use plenty of water, and be careful to keep it from splashing the linings.

Best tools, such as sponges, chamois leathers, &c., should be used; and all of a good size, and free from cuts and grit.

Never leave a carriage to dry of itself, or stains will show.

Be careful in using the spoke brush, particularly if a new one; the best quality are the cheapest, and are not so likely to scratch.

Carriage heads and aprons should be washed with soap and water, and then rubbed lightly off with linseed oil.

Turpentine and camphor will prevent and destroy moth in woollen linings; placing the mixture in a small dish at the bottom of the closed carriage is a certain cure.

The bearings of the fore-carriage should be greased to turn freely, and thus prevent locking and ultimate overturning.

Axles should be kept well oiled, and the washers in good order. Castor oil is best for oiling them. Sperm oil answers the purpose, sweet oil never; it congeals or "gums up."

Touch the steps occasionally where worn with the feet, &c., with thin quick drying japan.

All vehicles should be pushed into the coach-house by hand, and never drawn out by the horse, and—

The carriage owner should impress upon his coachman the importance of the legend—

"Nul bein sans peine.

JIBBING.

"Good words are better than bad strokes."

SHAKESPEARE says—"We cannot all be masters;"—therefore if it should happen, as it sometimes does, particularly with strange horses, that the animal be undoubtedly master of the position for the time, and will not go forward, brute force should never be resorted to by the driver; it not only being, as a rule, labour in vain, but serious risks are involved, particularly in streets and crowded thoroughfares, as the horse is very apt to rear and plunge, and sometimes to suddenly bolt, after backing through shop fronts and overturning the occupants of the vehicle. On a horse becoming stupid in the shafts, the holder of the ribands, if an amateur, should first ask himself the question—Is it my bad driving? A new purchase that had previously been handled with a light hand, kindly spoken to, and considerately driven, is particularly sensitive to the jerking and bustling of an inexperienced whip—

> "Bold Erechonius was the first who joined
> Four horses for the rapid race design'd,
> And o'er the dusty wheels presiding sat.
> The Lapithæ to chariots add the state
> Of bits and bridles; taught the steeds to bound,
> To run the ring, and trace the airy ground,
> To stop, to fly, the rules of war to know,
> T' obey the rider, and to dare the foe."

On being satisfied that the sudden obstinacy of the horse is from no fault of the driver, the harness should be carefully examined, it very frequently being the case that the collar will prove too short, or the traces twisted, and, like the curb, too tight, or a breechband is required, or may be dispensed with altogether, according to the vehicle in use; the whole bearing of the harness and load should be carefully noted, and if found satisfactory, the horse is either a jibber, or is not as yet familiar with the strange handling above referred to. The first business, after the horse has given repeated illustrations of his capabilities by dwelling on the road, is to descend quietly from the vehicle, and go to his head, having previously handed the reins to your friend (if accompanied) to be held slack or loose—at the same time patting and speaking to the horse, and using his name. Wiping him over with the hand; rubbing his ears and mouth, and moving parts of the harness has been known to turn the attention of the accidental jibber, and a steady day's work has been the result. After this little attention to the horse, the box should be mounted quietly, and not with a rush; the horse should be led, if anyone is at hand, and afterwards allowed to proceed of his own will, and, for a time, must be repeatedly spoken to. The application of force—such as turning the wheels round, and pushing behind, should be avoided, as it is calculated to make the horse more obstinate, and, although it may succeed at first, is rarely effectual in the end. The following experiment the Author has many times found to be successful in making the steed glad to go forward, namely, standing immediately in front of the horse with a rein billett in each hand, at the same time putting the steady weight of the whole body against the horse, taking care to keep him in the middle of the road; and it must be remembered that sawing the mouth must not be resorted to, but firm and steady pressure, backing as quickly as possible until the horse expresses an anxiety to proceed onward by pushing against you, when it will be invariably found that the animal is anxious to start right away, but must be made to stand quite still until the driver is in his place again on the box, which must be mounted without the least flourish or noise. Care must be taken not to thrash the horse when he does go, and should he during the journey forget the foregoing lesson, it should be repeated, and the dose slightly increased, conversation being kept up with him the whole time. Should this fail, the animal is a confirmed jibber, more or less, and the owner should take the earliest opportunity of devoting a few special drives in the country, where there is plenty of space before and behind, and when time is no particular object.

Some drivers have a very good system of operating upon one foot only, viz., by taking up the near forefoot in the right hand, and pressing it upward and inward towards the belly, as high as possible, thus making the horse stand upon three legs until he begins to rock and show other signs of impatience to go on. In loosing the foot it must not be thrown down or dropped, but put quietly to the ground, at the same time observing the same rule in mounting the vehicle as in the previous operation, which when done promptly and quietly is, as a rule, effective after a few lessons. Some horses have been used to travel on the wrong side of the road, and exhibit a strong objection to keep their own proper side. Such is the result of bad or careless driving, and is very dangerous, particularly in return journeys on dark or foggy evenings. The cure is soon brought about by a watchful driver, in keeping a steady pressure upon the near-side rein; and occasionally stroking or touching up the off side of the horse with the whip invariably learns the horse his own side, after a few journeys. An irritable driver is greatly calculated to make matters worse in case of jibbing, so it is strictly necessary to keep cool and steady, and not to display the slightest temper or impatience. The frequent use of the horse's name will accustom the horse to the voice of the driver, and promote confidence and obedience. If the owner be altogether inexperienced, the assistance of a practical coachman should be solicited, and in the event of no speedy improvement, the horse should be put in the shafts of a heavy cart, with one or two horses in the front of him. Each start should be done without the whip, and for short distances only. It has been found that the most obstinate jibber has been glad to go freely in the shafts of a light vehicle, after a few lessons in a loaded cart with two good steeds in front of him. If a horsebreaker be engaged, particular attention should be paid to his system of treatment, and strict observance of his instructions, both in the stable and out of doors. It has been said of many horses that they were "not able to pull the cap off a man's head," but after a few patient lessons and kind treatment they have been termed willing to "pull at a standing tree."

> "The gen'rous horse,
> Restrained and awed by man's inferior force,
> Does, to the rider's will, his rage submit,
> And answers to the spur, and owns the bit."

RIDING.

'Hold fast, sit sure."

IDING is said to be the poetry of motion; anyway, it is the most invigorating and healthful of exercises. We are taught that horsemanship emanates from Egypt, and that Egypt was the great and original breeding place for horses; we are likewise told that Soloman obtained all his horses from Egypt, the price averaging 160 Shekels, or about £18 English money, for each animal. According to the Greek writers, Sesostris was the first who taught men to tame and ride horses. Six hundred years after Solomon, Xenophon says that Persia possessed no horses before the age of Cyrus, but afterwards produced the finest in the world, that all Persians were horsemen, in fact the very name of Persia became associated with horsemanship, and the present of a Persian horse was a gift indeed. The Greeks became famous for their horsemanship about the time of, or just before, the Trojan war (1192 B.C.), hence the Grecian fables of the *Centaurs,* or as Ovid calls them semi-human horses, and semi-equine men.

The *Half Breeds of North America*[*] are considered the most extraordinary and wonderful horsemen in the world. In their hunting with the lasso and trapping, and other expeditions on horseback, the saddle and bridle were not thought of; sometimes a piece of fish skin or strip of animal's hide to guide with, and a similar strip-noose for the toe, was sufficient to act as a stirrup, or a plain cord of the same material for a bridle and bit, and a piece of cloth or hide underneath the seat. In fact, they have been known to mount the wildest steed, and give him full

---

[*] See Illustration. The Author's "Centaur."

play over hill and vale, mountain and torrent, through river and marsh, and ultimately bring him home (guided by the hand alone) as docile and tame as a lap-dog.

The Arabs are good riders without the bridle and saddle, and are frequently to be seen with a common halter and piece of linen for the horse's back. The Arabian horses are considered by some more active and pleasant to ride than the English thoroughbred; but such is not the general opinion. The Arabs are known to be particularly fond of the horse, and would rather lose their lives than part with their steeds. It is said the horse reciprocates the good feeling, fully appreciating the constant care and attention shown towards him by his master—whom it is no strange sight to see fondling and embracing, and sometimes even kissing his horse.

The Turkish horse is descended from the Arab, and is a splendid creature. The Turks* are good riders and very kind to their horses, and the steeds are always very gentle and obedient. The men are never known to thrash or abuse their horses, and a vicious animal is rarely to be found among them. It is a common thing to see a Turkish horse kneel down to receive its rider; such is the result of good training. In Turkey riding is the rule and driving the exception, coach building being somewhat in its infancy, at least compared with our own country. For riding, the Turks prefer horses; the Arabs are more in favour of mares. The Ganchos are supposed to be the cleverest horsemen at lassoing wild horses, which are to be seen in their native state on the prairies of North and South America, in Tartary, the centre of Africa, and the deserts of Arabia.

Among the wild horses of South America the mares are seldom tamed, but allowed to roam about with their offspring at pleasure. It is the great ambition of the young Indian to possess a good horse for buffalo hunting, and if he cannot get it by fair means he will steal one. In the art of riding they are entirely self-taught, having no knowledge of the "hunting seat," which is so much preferred and generally adopted in England. The Indian stands astride, as it were, in performing his wonderful evolutions; his grip to the horse is (as we should term it) the "fork" or military seat. The position of the Indian upon the horse's back, and that of the jockey of the present day are great extremes.

---

* Turks, as soldiers, are unsurpassed in the World; hence the saying, "Fight like a Turk."

It is said that races were first instituted in England in the reign of Charles I.; and it is also asserted that Cromwell kept fleet horses, no doubt for the purpose of carrying the mails and other despatches.

Horsemen should be careful not to ride long stages without feeding their steeds; some have been known to ride thirty and forty miles, which is a great act of cruelty; occasional small feeds, and a good meal at the end of the journey are most beneficial to the horse. In riding a journey the horseman should start at a moderate pace, and finish in the same way, thus graduating the horse to his work and coming home cool. If quick travelling is necessary, the saddle should be eased occasionally in going up hill. The tired hack should have his feet washed, and legs bathed with warm water at his journey's end, and the hands should be carefully rubbed down the horse's legs for thorns, &c. If the steed should go off (or appear to despise) his food, it is a sure sign that rest is required.

It is an important item that the hackney saddle should be a close fit, but must not hurt the horse's back. The larger the saddle the better for the horse, the weight of the rider being spread over a larger surface; and the same rule applies to the comfort of the rider. The girths should not be buckled tight, particularly when a breast-plate is worn. The life of the rider should never be trusted to a single girth, and when two single girths are used, they must be crossed. The best and safest girth is the "Fitzwilliam," which is not only the most secure, but most comfortable for the animal; as it consists of one broad web band as the main or body girth, and a narrow one passing through loops on the top of the broader one as the safety girth, each one being buckled independently, with three buckles in all at each end.

The saddle pannel should be carefully and constantly attended to, both as to stuffing and cleanliness. The back-stuffing (as it is termed by the trade) of a saddle is a very important item in connection with the welfare of the horse and the safety of the rider—none but the very best and cleanest wool should be used; where common wool or flock is used, a hard or long ride will cause the perspiration to clog the wool, and form it into knots, hence the term "cut like a knife," thus causing wounds and sores.

The crupper and breast-plate should not be worn for wearing sake, neither should double reins or bits be used for ordinary exercise or short journeys. After a day's hunting, or few hours' ride, the saddle should by no means be taken immediately from the horse's back on reaching the stable, but the girths should be unloosed and the saddle moved a few inches towards the croup, for the purpose of allowing the horse's back to gradually cool during the process of swilling the legs, &c. (*see* "Unharnessing"). Hackney cruppers are considered unsightly, and have been frequently the cause of sore places about the region of the dock. The necessity for the crupper is invariably more the fault of the rider than the horse; a good rider never shows his stockings, but it is frequently the case that many whose daily business it is to sit upon a horse are frequently to be seen with their trousers up to their knees; such are the rollocking horsemen that require cruppers, trouser straps, and frequently tying or holding on. In riding, or attempting to ride, the old rule is "To look before you leap," and the real horseman says "Keep close to the pigskin," hence the term "daylight" between saddle and man. It is, therefore, equally important that the saddle should fit the horseman as well as the horse.

The first business of the amateur is to learn to exercise patience ere he can excel as an equestrian; next, never to start until he is ready (which rule applies to everything through life); and to avoid flourishing, or irritating the horse. The saying, "Put a beggar on horseback, &c," is an old one, but is a very true and trite one.

The writer thinks that nothing looks so thoroughly ridiculous as the back view of a full-grown green amateur, who appears mounted for the first time, trotting through the public streets at holiday times, specially got up with frock coat and button-hole, patent leather shoes, and stirrups too short, a "bran-new" saddle and bridle, and himself hanging on by the spurs, his elbows elevated, and shoulders up, as though endeavouring to overtake the horse or imitate the monkey.

Such is the picture (often to be seen on Easter Monday, and other times) of the ambitious green-horn, who, even at an advanced age, and without any preparatory lessons or practice, vaults into the saddle. It is not the *forte* of all men to excel in horsemanship, and the Author knows several horse owners who have not yet, and in all probability never will, get beyond the perfection of a walk; their sensible motto is discretion, and if a trot is ventured upon, it is not taken advantage of in towns, but out in the country where there is no fear of making an exhibition of themselves. This is sensible discretion; but, the poor horse suffers from being jolted and jerked, pulled and spurred by the clumsy, awkward, and weighty rider.

The amateur horseman, after he has got proficient in mounting and dismounting, should learn to walk the horse.

In riding, the reins are taken the reverse way to driving, viz.: from the top, and the fingers held down and kept towards the centre of the body, neither up nor down, and a little way from the body, in much the same position as in driving. The mouth of the horse should be felt lightly and regularly with the reins, and at all times be kept well in hand; the rider's elbows and toes should be kept somewhat in, and heels down; the head erect and the back hollowed, but he is by no means to lean backward; a good grip of the saddle should be cultivated, and the feeling to be cultivated and persisted in is one of firmness, ease, freedom, and independence.

In trotting, the horse must be allowed to start before the rider, which should be done without using the spurs, flourish of the whip, or noise of any kind; a gentle touch or raising of the reins and pressure of the knees, together with a slight leaning forward, will put the educated horse upon the steady and straight track immediately, the rider keeping to the saddle a few seconds and then lightly falling in with the step of the horse; then, and only then, can the luxury of a steady or fair swinging trot (such as Lord Palmerston and the noble Duke of Wellington were wont to enjoy on the Row) be appreciated. Care should be taken in pulling up or stopping the horse. It should not (as is often the case) be done on the sliding scale, but the horse should be consulted, and the walk will be brought about without the least jerk, strain, or effort. The same rule applies to the canter, which is beautifully illustrated by the hand gallop of a lady's hack with the musical accompaniment (especially on a clear frosty morning) of the firm trot of the companion at her side.

The hunting rule is to ride "slow at timber," and "fast at water."

As regards the bridle, the least complicated and easiest for the horse in business or pleasure is the "Snaffle," which simple bit can be made more effective in the hands of an experienced horseman than the most expensive "Weymouth" when used by a heavy-handed amateur. The "Snaffle" consists of a single head, single rein, and single bit, which is invariably used for racing over turf, allowing as it does, the full stretch of the horse's neck. For general business the "Pelham" is used, consisting of single head, single bit, and double rein. For hunting and military purposes the "Weymouth" bridle is adopted, which embraces double head, double reins, double bits and curb, in the use of which great judgment and feeling are required, on account of the excessive leverage on the curb bit. The Author does not agree with twisted, jointed, port-mouthed, or complicated bits, unless applied under the advice of a practical man, and in any case objects to the high-port* or gag bit. The bridle should be adjusted so as to fit easily, and the cheeks should be regulated according to the carriage of the bit in the mouth. The throat-band should have fair or easy play, just being sufficiently tight to keep the bridle in position without danger of being thrown off by the horse jerking his head up or down. All extra trappings or superfluities should be adjusted with equal judgment, so as not to chafe the horse, or risk the rider's life.

Shakespeare says—"What wound did ever heal but by degrees," which well applies to the use and abuse of spurs. Many indifferent horsemen seem to think that spurs were invented for the special purpose of holding on by, and have come to grief accordingly; but not until the horse has been unnecessarily punished by having its sides gored and gashed several inches, very often causing blood to trickle freely down.

The cruel spurs and gag-bit were not known in early days, as we learn by the fresco representations of the Parthenon at Athens; the horse being guided by a word or movement of the hand of the rider, the same, in many respects, as are our cart-horses of the present day. The amateur horseman should by no means wear spurs until he can sit a horse properly, and has become perfectly familiar with the real use of them. The military horseman rarely touches the skin with the spurs, yet he can guide (or ease)

---

* See Illustration.

the horse to the right or left, and forward or backward by a slight pressure of the knee, and sometimes is understood by a slight shake of the foot or leg. Spurs, used without discretion, not only wound the horse but affect his temper, and endanger the life of the rider.

The writer would here remark that the unnecessary application of the whip, either when riding or driving is both brutal and dangerous, and it must be remembered that a "long journey and swift" is bad form, and that it is good policy to frequently pat, or "*make much of*," your steed, at the same time calling him by name. The horse should never be flogged for shying, but the object shied at should be steadily and carefully approached, or rode up to, if time permits; this will satisfy the horse, and tend to give him confidence in the future. The same rules should be observed in riding as driving. The horseman, before starting or mounting, should "cast his eyes round," and see that every part of the equipment is as it should be, sound and properly fitted, the girths not slack, nor too tight, the bridle and bit or bits a comfortable and safe fit, and the foretop hair placed under the front of the bridle, and the reins untwisted; the saddle centrally fixed, a nice large easy fit, which means comfort for the horse and horseman alike, and the motion of the animal's shoulders not impeded. Systematic inspection detects the careless groom, and certainly provides against accidents.

The position or seat of the rider being upright, smart but not stiff; he depends in a great measure upon the stirrup leathers, which should therefore not be too short or too long. If the irons are high, the rider is shot as it were into the air, and he cannot possibly "sit close to the pigskin;" if they be too long, the grip of the saddle is missed to a great extent, and the rider is known as a straight-kneed jockey, which position not only detracts from the appearance, but is actually dangerous, sometimes causing rupture. In either case the rider has less power or control over the horse.

On starting out, say for an exercise or pleasure ride, the horse should be kept to a walk for a short time, then jog-trot, and gradually into a fair swinging trot. If in the country a "hand-gallop," or on grass a "stiff-gallop," is enjoyable both to man and horse.

A full, firm shoulder is the principal choice in either hackney or hunter; it means strength and power.

Great knee action or "high-stepping" jars the rider, and batters the horse's feet.

"Daisy cutting" is very pleasant on turf, but as a rule suggests insuring the neck of the rider.

Putting the foot down is more important than taking or lifting it up, a big foot put down full being far safer than tripping the toe, as it were, on the "sliding-scale."

For pleasant riding the hackney should not carry his legs too high.

All horses are liable to come down or fall; therefore the rider should "feel the mouth" lightly, yet firmly as a rule; but by no means hang on, or pull or saw the mouth.

Rough usage with the reins spoils the horse's mouth, and produces ill-temper.

The average speed should be eight or ten miles an hour, or on a long journey six or seven.

Fast trotters are rarely easy in their paces, and are ofttimes disabled and worthless when they should be only in their prime.

The faithfulness, memory, and sagacity of horses is indeed remarkable, and has commanded the wonder and admiration of all countries and climes, from the earliest ages to the present day. The horse enters into the full spirit of his duties, whether they be pleasure or business, in peace or war, and many are the affectionate recollections and adventures that could be recorded by the writer, and doubtless by the reader. The horse will often show greater or safer judgment at times of doubt or difficulty than the most expert rider. Many is the sportsman who has to thank his horse for landing him safely between the sheets after dining freely, or accepting too deeply of the parting cup, "just to keep the cold out." A horse has been taken over new ground, and the return journey has been in pitch darkness, in a drenching rain and driving wind, and though left to himself, he has brought his driver and party safely home.

The writer once started out late (with a favourite mare) one November evening in '72, to see a sick friend some eight miles away, and had to cross a wild region (The Chase), which has lost many a horseman in broad day-light. Soon after starting for the return journey a fog collected and thickened till it became an absolute black, wall-like mass; nothing could be seen or heard besides the breathing and feet of the horse and the creaking of the saddle. Many are the riders who can follow this experience. It was a regular out-and-out "Tam o'Shanter" night, and only wanted the witches to complete the solitary surroundings. It was, indeed, "darkness that might be felt," and fog that "could be cut with a knife." To proceed seemed impossible, and to turn back was out of the question; the state of the road was simply no road at all, being wild, rugged, and as it were self made, the luxury of a lane being remote until nearing the town. The horse slipped and snorted, and the rider cheered the faithful animal on, at the same time wanting a cheer much himself. On coming to a canal bridge he determined his programme, namely, to raise up his great coat collar still higher, if possible, pull his gloves up his wrists, pull down his broad brimmed soft hat, slacken his grip of the saddle, and leave the steering home to the horse. Never did faithful creature come straighter or safer; therefore, the writer would advise all horsemen, under similar circumstances, to "keep awake and leave the rest to the horse," and by no means to communicate the least sign of nervousness through the reins, which can be easily done, as before said, whether in riding or driving.

We will now take a few of the most conspicuous or frequent of the shortcomings and failings peculiar to the horse, known as "The Vices," and, in as brief a manner as possible, for easy perusal and reference, consider how best to treat them.

A LIST OF VICES.

Defects in the tempers of horses often arise from their being in their early days either in ignorant or brutal hands.

The defects naturally are few, the excellent qualities many.

Restiveness, arises either from bad temper or worse education, and shows itself in various ways—by kicking, rearing, plunging, or bolting, and which, if established or confirmed, rarely admit of cure. An accomplished, daring and determined rider can work wonders, or the horse may have his favourite; but let him depart from the hands who (by, as it were, a fluke) control him, and he will, even years after, return to his old tricks. Some horses have a habit of turning the head round, and (after all other efforts have failed to dislodge him from his seat) worrying or biting the rider's legs, the only safe remedy for which is attaching a piece of strong flat wood (known as a sword) to the bridle cheek and to the girth.

Backing and Gibbing, are much the same; at first they may be the result of playfulness or pain, which the rider must determine. In any case, horsebreaking, either professional or amateur, should be practised in smooth, even temper. Hasty or passionate fits cause loss of control of oneself and the object to be attained. Some horses have vices, and, to all appearances, savage dispositions, which, in reality, is mere playfulness, caused by being played with, which frequently ends in teasing, and thus brings about habitual ferocity.

To cure biting the billetts, fix a large solid leather pad on each side of the bit, or ride and drive with none but the Author's recently invented " *Vice versâ* Billettless Reins,"[*] which are a sure cure, absolutely safe, and wear much longer than the ordinary billetted reins.

Kicking, is considered incurable, either in saddle or stable. In harness, kicking has been frequently stimulated by allowing the reins to get under the tail, and glorious results have ensued, from the fact that when the reins are once there the horse holds them there by pressing the tail down upon them. Such horses are, at least, unreliable.

Rearing, is frequently caused by bad horsemanship. Leaving the spurs at home, or a change of bit, and dropping the curb may cure. Brutal means are, as a rule, useless, and are neither modern nor worthy of any man.

A runaway horse is best controlled by presence of mind and a good firm hand. If there is plenty of "sea room," give the bolter all he asks and a little bit more, "just for

---

[*] See full description in the Chapter "Saddlers' Guide," page 163.

your own pleasure," assisted by a moderate touch of the whip, and if he repeats the performance, sell him to those who will give him heavier and slower work, between other horses, say on a farm.

Some horses who are vicious to clean may be cured by a change of tools, and in some cases by a change of groom. Old and worn out tools, or rough common new ones in careless hands, are absolutely painful when thoughtlessly applied to the tender and more sensitive parts of the horse.

Vicious to shoe, must be left to the inventive powers of the smith. If it can be avoided, never have the horse shod at his own stable, for many reasons; the blacksmith has all the appliances at hand that are necessary, and has certainly more confidence and tact in his own shop. The horse should always be taken by the same man, and have his regular groom, and be shod by a smith who can coax and persuade. If possible, a quiet horse should be shod first, under the nose of the restive one. Blows and twitches are best left out.

Swallowing the corn whole, is often the result of feeding two horses in the same manger and at the same time, which promotes greediness. Some horses are naturally greedy and carry very little flesh, hence are not as a rule strong workers. Such horses must not be allowed to fast long or go far without the nosebag; mix good chaff with the corn, and plenty of it.

Crib-biting and Wind-sucking, are serious vices; the horse chiefly operates upon the manger, biting and sawing it with his teeth, to the neglect of all his other comforts. Whether the "sucking" is actually drawing air or expelling it is not thoroughly arrived at. A strap round the neck with a square pad of leather enclosing a small iron plate to press close up will prevent and ultimately cure, if worn regularly; but care must be taken not to bring about another evil by causing irritation of the windpipe, which will produce roaring. Medicine is of no service for crib-biting or wind-sucking; a muzzle should be worn at all possible times, and constructed so that the horse can be feed with it on.

Crib-biting, is sometimes caused by the horse being groomed in the stable; partial starvation and bad food has brought it about; and even being over fed will cause it, from the horse's love of mischief.

Wind-sucking, is closely associated with crib-biting, hence my coupling them, and it arises from the same causes. Either tie the animal's head up, or muzzle him, or let the saddler fit him with a spiked collar; in the fixing of which great care is necessary.

Cutting, can be remedied either wholly or partially by an arrangement of the shoe and somewhat shaping the foot by the smith. A thin, firm, nicely hollowed cutting boot should be fitted by the saddler and worn for a time.

Pawing in the stable, some horses will get to a violent pitch; shackles are the only remedy.

Over-reach and clicking, can be cured in a young horse, but are very difficult to deal with in an aged one; the toe of the hind foot should be kept as short as is compatible with safety.

Quidding, is not unfrequently connected with sore throat, or from irregular teeth, which the veterinary surgeon will soon cure.

Rolling in the stable, is dangerous, and particularly expensive if the horse happens to be in harness. When naked in the field it is equally pleasant for the audience as for the performer, but in the stable shorten the head collar rein, to keep the horse's head from the floor, and then he cannot roll. It may be a most inconvenient cure for the horse, but better that than the greater evils which result to the habitual roller.

Shying, is from either nervousness or playfulness; sometimes it arises from defective sight. The rider or driver should be always ready, and in correcting, should blend the seeming severity with coaxing—that is, be firm and gentle, for the cure of the horse, and, at times, for the sake of your own neck. A horse which shies on coming out of the stable is simply incurable; it has either been caused by a bump at the top of the door-frame, or the horse has been caught by the stirrup-leather or reins at the door-latch. Hence care must be taken in bringing the animal out of the stable when dressed.

Stumbling; an habitual stumbler is not fit for riding or harness, being simply dangerous and unreliable. The horse should be put to slow work, if shortening and rounding the toe and shoe does not remedy the evil.

THE STABLE

AND

STABLE FITTINGS.

CLIPPING, CLOTHING, SHOEING, FEEDING, CLEANING, AND
GENERAL STABLE MANAGEMENT.

"Allow not nature more than nature needs."

HE old proverb says—"It is usual to lock the stable door after the horse is gone," which figurative expression plainly indicates to all horse owners, and particularly to those *about to set up* a "Turn Out," the real necessity, not only for a good system in reference to the steed at the outset, but a watchful eye upon all its immediate surroundings. The first object should be to secure, if possible, a roomy home or domicile for the horse, which must not be too dark or too light. The next considerations are good ventilation and perfect drainage; general cleanliness must be observed; pure corn and prompt attention are absolutely necessary.

Loose boxes possess great advantages over the stall in many ways, particularly as regards the exercise given the horse by having his liberty. The floor should be laid with best hard bricks, which are easily kept clean and sweet. Sloping floors are very objectionable, and are injurious to the horse, particularly when he is tied up in the stall, hence his invariable resting position being either across the stall or with his tail in the manger; oft-times the horse is found at the full length of the halter rein. Gratings in the centre of the stall are very unwholesome, somewhat draughty, accumulate deposits, and unhealthy fumes arise from the sewer gases. All urine should be conducted outside the stable by a gutter from behind the horse, and no dirt should be permitted to remain in the corners of the stable.

The arrangements for ventilation should be complete, and be fixed above and below, but not immediately behind or before the steed. The stable should not be kept too cool or too hot; the proper temperature can be easily regulated by the thermometer, without which no stable is complete. The average should be 50° in winter and 70° in summer.

The walls of the stable should not be perfectly white, but somewhat of a drab or grey colour, and paint preferred, which can be washed over as often as desirable— say once a month. The stable should be boarded round a few feet up the walls from the ground; no rails, or other impediment or obstruction should be within reach. Dark stables are never clean, and unclean stables are extremely unhealthy and dangerous for the animal's eyes. Too much light is not advisable; therefore, this particular department rests more or less with the judgment and humane feeling of the horse owners. The windows should be as high up from the ground as possible—say about 8-ft. to the bottom pane—and if the window frame is made to revolve it will greatly facilitate the ventilation. The glass should not by any means be low down, on account of its liability to be broken.

The manger should be a good depth, and about 2-ft. long, and so constructed as to prevent the possibility of the corn being wasted. The hay rack should be on a level with the manger, and on the near (or left) side of the horse. The hay rack should never be above the manger, for many reasons, such as the great and constant strain caused to the animal's neck, the falling of dust into the corn and into the horse's eyes, and the great waste which invariably results from such an arrangement. Hay lofts immediately over the stable are very objectionable, yet cannot always be avoided, but the hay hole over the horse's head should by all means be dispensed with, as it is dangerous for restive horses, frequently spoils the corn and water, and causes the dust to affect the steed; and, in addition, foul fumes ascend, which poison the fodder stored above. The water is best kept in a small cistern by the side of the manger, so that the horse can help himself. If two horses stand in the same stall, as is frequently the case with cart horses, the rack should be fixed in the centre and a manger at each end, on a level, and constructed strictly with the view to promoting facility of movement, comfort, and economy.

The head collar rein may be leather, and so made to buckle with a billett, or a rope may be substituted; chains are not so good, being noisy, heavy, and sometimes dangerous. The log must not be heavy, and should be encased so as to slide up and down a wooden tube to and from the ring.

A good groom will not permit the slightest particle of dirt to accumulate in the manger, or dust in the stable or its precincts. Rising early every morning he will commence his duties, with a cheerful good will, at one systematic time, say 5:30 in the summer, and 6:30 in the winter, and will apply the same rule to the punctual (where applicable) and steady "supping up," or making the animals comfortable for the night.

Cats, dogs, goats, or pigs should not be allowed in the stable at any time, the horse being particularly sensitive to hay or other food which has been lain upon or otherwise damaged, and this means waste, and is the general result of encouraging such pets to locate themselves in the stable or hay loft.

That the groom should be even tempered and sober is strictly necessary, if the steed is to thrive and do well whilst in his hands.

In grooming, a certain time should be laid down as a rule, and devoted to the horse systematically, supported by a good share of elbow grease. The business of grooming must not be skipped over at any time, but the horse should be thoroughly cleaned from head to croup—not merely polishing the most conspicuous parts, and slipping over what may pass muster with the inexperienced or careless owner, for it must be borne in mind that the genuine horseman cannot be deceived.

The groom commences first by using the curry-comb, with great caution. If the horse is long-coated the curry-comb may be applied pretty freely, but if the steed be clean-coated, thin skinned, and of nervous temperament, very delicate manipulation is essentially necessary, and in fact the comb may be dispensed with altogether. Some grooms merely use the curry-comb for the purpose of cleaning and dusting the brush.

The entire art of grooming a horse consists in cleaning the dirt from its hide, whisping, brushing, wiping down with a cloth, combing the mane and tail, sponging the croup, eyes, and mouth; examining, picking, and (if necessary), washing the feet; rubbing the legs and ears, adjusting the head-collar, clothing, and body roller; all of which should be promptly and quietly done, and without the hissing on the part of the groom so frequently to be heard in stables; which hissing, it should be remembered, is neither musical to the horse, nor healthy to the operator.

The stable requisites are,—pitch-fork, shovel, broom, manure basket, body brush, water brush, weed or whalebone brush, scraper, mane comb, curry-comb, hoof-picker, chamois leathers, compo-brushes, sponges, bucket, corn measure, sieve and server, poultice boot, sponge boot, dusters, bandages, linen and woollen ("Newmarket" or "stocking"), drenching horn, stopping, spoke brush, jack, compo. and harness pastes, whiting, button stick and brush, manger log, rock salt, hay wisp, black oils, hoof ointment and embrocation, singeing lamps (with large and small heads), tubing, hose-piping, trimming comb and scissors, clipping machines (large and small for body and head), twitch, and a supply of tow and tar, the great usefulness of which any Vet. will advise, for checking the common disease known as thrush.

The following good advice, as circulated by Mr. Gregory, M.R.C.V.S., Bristol, we think can be profitably noted by our readers:—

"A sick horse should not be fastened to the manger, but have freedom in a loose box, and be treated with kindliness and gentleness.

"He should have just sufficient clothing to keep the skin comfortably warm, and if perspiring should have a little hay or straw between the skin and clothing.

"A sick horse should have a constant supply of clean water at stable temperature; also, in small quantities, bran, linseed or oil cake, oats and hay of the best quality.

"He should not be taken out to exercise unless the weather be dry and genial, and then quietly until he has recovered.

"He should be groomed with a brush and dry cloth quietly and quickly, and if the legs be cold, put on dry bandages lightly.

"The stable should have sufficient ventilation without draught; if any foulness arise from the floor, a little fresh lime mixed with ashes or sawdust, or other disinfectant, should be sprinkled over the floor, and a clean bed kept."

It should be borne in mind that the horse cannot work upon a full belly, hence the necessity for its first feed being given early in the day, and with punctuality,—as much earlier, and certainly not later, than the times set down above.

For the Hackney Horse, the quantity of food should be regulated by the judgment of the groom, but the quality should be none other than the best. The horse that is worked hard requires more food than the one that has little work, and the number of feeds and quantities given should be in accordance with the work, size, build, and stamina of the horse One peck of good, clean, sound oats, a few handfuls of beans, and about ten pounds of sweet hay divided into three or four meals per day is the usual quantity for the average hack. A little cut hay or chaff will cause the horse to masticate his food, and take more time over it; and this is very desirable, it being a well known fact that corn greedily bolted loses half its nutrition. A handful of bran gives the feed a wholesome fragrance, and a little water* flavoured with salt and sprinkled over the hay and chaff makes it exceedingly palatable. A lump of rock salt in the manger is decidedly wholesome, and is calculated to find good occupation for the horse, and will at the same time tend greatly to prevent crib-biting.

For the Cart Horse, 8 lbs. of oats and 2 lbs. beans to 20 lbs. chaff, or average 34 to 36 lbs. of the mixture for each horse

---

* One extensive firm of horse owners (Messrs. Walter Showell & Son, Crosswell's Brewery, Oldbury, near Birmingham) have adopted an original system of substituting porter, with success, which treatment carries one back to the good old days "when George III. was king;" and, to the indulgences shown to "Bonny Black Bess."

G

per day, with regular work. Dray horse, 40 lbs. Damp the provender at time of feeding, and not before. Damaged hay must not be totally set apart for chaff; it is injurious.

Some farmers bruise their oats. Half bushel sliced carrots per day, mixed with chaff, and the 2 lbs. beans, and *6 lbs.* oats may be withdrawn. The healthy horse is very fond of this provender, and the virtues of the carrot are not sufficiently known.

As a vegetable food carrots are greatly relished by the horse, and are considered more than wholesome, but must be particularly cleaned, and are usually sliced.

The general quantity of water, if the permanent cistern be not adopted, is half a bucket three times per day. The horse should be exercised on idle days for at least two hours, during which time the stable should be washed out and thoroughly cleaned, the wet straw taken away—but by no means should it be pushed under the manger—and a little dry litter left and spread under the horse for it to stand upon.

The test for oats is that they should be old, heavy, sweet, perfectly dry, plump, and a bright colour. If beans are given they are best bruised. It is usual to water the horse after dressing it. New hay is not calculated to improve the working condition of the horse.

The following is a safe cooling lotion for over-heated backs on reaching the stable after a journey:—4 drachms sugar of lead to a wine bottle full of spring water.

The groom should never be allowed to physic or bleed the animal under his care; if anything of the sort is thought necessary, the services of the veterinary surgeon should be immediately obtained.

Great care is necessary in working horses that have been brought up fresh from grass, and special attention should be paid to grooming them. It should be remembered that a well-groomed horse is always more buoyant and healthy than those that are comparatively neglected or never thoroughly cleaned. Good grooming is half corn, and waste or over generosity should be discouraged. The cratch should never be crammed with hay, or the oats unmeasured and thrown recklessly into the manger. The quantity of food should be calculated and measured out, in strict accordance with the clean manner in which it is eaten up.

Beware of amateur horse doctors and the groom or stable man, with his head crammed full of useless and dangerous receipts and experiments, or, as he would term them "fakements," in addition to his wonderful ball prescriptions, which are "a family secret."

The waggon horse, carrier's horse, cab horse, or boat horse, should never be sent out without the nose-bag or nose-tin, and spare cloths or waterproof sheets that will cover the whole body and strap on against the wind while standing still.

Whole corn, coarse hay, irregular feeding, and careless treatment, are frequently the cause of indigestion in the horse, or chronic colic, as it is called.

The corn should be kept under lock and key near the stable, and proper shelves and drawers should be fitted for brushes and general tools, and be kept clean and handy for use; the fork, shovel, and bucket, should be kept outside the stable.

Some judgment should be brought to bear in feeding working horses at holiday times; the measure of bran should prevail.

Singeing and clipping should be performed with great caution, and by no means hurriedly, and none but the very best machines* be used, by steady, sober men only.

The clothing of the horse demands immediate attention after clipping and singeing. It is a well-known fact—and illustrations may often be seen—that the horse is literally smothered with sheet after sheet of clothing and rugs for the first exercise after clipping, and the horse remains so smothered up for days in the stable. After a time the animal is left in the open air in snow or rain, or perhaps a biting frost, altogether unprotected from the elements, which contrasts strongly with the driver, who appears muffled, coated and gloved up, his last innocent

---

* "The Newmarket, and Toilet Clippers," manufactured by Mr. W. Bown, 308, Summer Lane, Birmingham, are well known all over the World as thoroughly reliable, and excellent value.

thoughts being the poor horse. A sharp trot is expected to warm the animal, which has to be pulled up again for another starving spell during the transaction of the owner's business. It cannot be said that any man would, or could, wilfully neglect his faithful companion as above shown, but it is the result of sheer want of thought, or carelessness, which is equally blameable; the same man will be most particular in stopping every crevice and hole in the stable on returning home, to (as he thinks) prevent draughts, whereas he is excluding the air that is necessary to the preservation of the health and life of the horse.

The clothing sheet proper (say the "Newmarket") should reach within 9 or 10 inches of the croup, and be made to fit easily and nicely round the neck, and should be duly strengthened at the chine and double at the wearing parts. If a horse be overloaded with clothing in the stable, he is much more susceptible to cold outside; in fact, everything connected with the "Turn Out" depends more or less upon the discretion and judgment of the owner. Most good stables have different systems, and in many cases they will be found admirably adapted to their individual surroundings.

The body roller and surcingle are an important part of the clothing suit, and, like the head-collar, should never be buckled tight. Knee-caps are useful for exercising valuable horses, but are not considered any improvement to the appearance of the "Turn Out."

The shoes demand the regular attention of the groom, and the feet should be carefully examined every morning, and listened to occasionally during the drives. The horse's shoes require changing on the average once a month, but much depends upon the nature or kind of work the horse is engaged upon. The heavy waggon horse does not wear out his shoes so fast as the hackney. Speed grinds shoes down much quicker than steady draught. Many a horse has been lamed and crippled by careless or indiscriminate shoeing, but where the farrier is an acknowledged practical man, and known to make a study of his business, his judgment should not be subjected to dictation, but appealed to in any particular case; it will then secure his most careful attention. Heavy shoes are not considered any advantage, as they tire the horse. It is always very necessary to exercise great care in paring and rasping the feet, and the less nails used (compatible with wear and tear) the better. Roughing and sharpening should never be deferred in frosty and slippery weather. Rather keep the horse at home than send him out imperfectly protected, or, as it were, in a helpless condition. A good farrier makes the anatomy and physiology of the horse's foot his daily study.

It is said that a coloured hoof wears better than a white one, and that the hind hoof is smaller than the fore, and more upright, and longer than it is wide. The hind shoes are invariably worn out before the front ones.

In ancient times shoeing with metal was not known; therefore, a hard strong hoof was considered one of the best features or qualities of the horse.

The Greeks and Romans were the first to attach a kind of leather protection to the horse's foot, and afterwards a few iron plates, and sometimes silver and gold were used, as illustrated in the life of Nero. Seathes, the celebrated horseman of old, said :—" The first part of the horse to look at is the foot, for no matter how beautiful the upper house is decorated, all is failure if the foundation be not secure." The Arabs seldom have the hind feet of their horse's shod, which is likewise the rule in many parts of Germany.

The stable should by no means be damp, and it is strictly necessary that the harness room should be perfectly dry, and kept clean and free from dust. Suitable pegs, harness brackets, cases and drawers, &c., should be properly fitted for each article. A fire place is necessary for drying and warming clothing, and, if adjoining the stable, assists ventilation, and is likewise handy for boiling water, making bran mashes and poultices.

The harness room should be liberally supplied with everything for the use of the groom, and all should be strictly kept in order. The stableman's motto should be—" A place for everything, and everything in its place."

The Author has recently introduced a new Saddle Stand, which is considered a decided improvement upon the old-fashioned and awkward saddle horse, which has been the cause of so many broken trees, from being tipped over. The new stand combines the necessary drawers for girths, bridles, extra stirrup leathers, silk cords, thongs, &c., takes up very little space, and being upon four invisible wheels can be moved to any part of the room. It is strong enough to hold any quantity of saddles, and keeps the flaps in proper position throughout, the original advantage being that the top is made the same form and size as a hackney saddle, and is of reasonable height, so that a gentleman can cross it and try the easy seat and fit of a new purchase without girths, thus saving time and inconvenience. It is particularly adapted for saddlers' shops, for showing saddles off to the best and safest advantage. A model* may be seen at the Author's establishment, supporting the "Original Self-coloured Saddle," as exhibited by him at the Birmingham Horse Show, in 1871-72, and London, 1882, at which latter Exhibition the Author was awarded the "First Prize Medal" and a "Special Certificate of Distinguished Merit" for his general display of Harness and Saddlery, and for his book "CENTAUR,"† which honours were presented to him by H.R.H. the Duke of Teck as the "First Highest Award."

It may be well to give a few general instructions with reference to the selection of fittings for the stable. In the first place, the Author would remark that, owing to the perfection to which iron fittings are now brought, they are certainly the best. They are made with the mash trough, &c., enamelled inside, so that it can be kept as clean as a china basin. The iron fittings being almost indestructible, make really durable work, while neither the kicking nor biting of vicious horses can have the least effect on them. The crib-biter is also deprived of his solitary enjoyment, as with properly formed iron work he cannot lay hold of it with his teeth. A great difference of opinion seems to exist with reference to the suitability of stalls and loose boxes for general use, and it would be impossible to lay down an universal rule applicable in all cases, but it will be sufficient to say that there is no place where the tired hunter so soon recovers his wonted energies as in a comfortable box. This is not at all times available, owing to limited space in stables, especially in towns, where it is found difficult to accommodate the requisite number of horses in boxes.

The length of a stable, divided into 12-ft. spaces, will show the number of loose boxes that can be put in it,

---

* The Author will supply one or more on application.
† Vide Certificates.

while if divided into 6-ft. spaces it will show about the number of stalls that can be erected.

In dividing the stable into stalls, the use of an open railing between the horses is strongly recommended. Horses, being of a very sociable disposition, greatly relish the companionship of their stable associates; and often a horse has been known to go down seriously in condition when removed from his companions to a separate place.

Stables are divided, according to requirements or convenience, into stalls, or loose boxes. Their size is the first consideration. For carriage horses they must not be smaller than 6' 0" wide, but where possible 6' 3" or even 6' 6" should be provided, as being much better. For cart or dray horses they must not be less than 7' 0" wide. The length from the wall varies from 9' 0" to 10' 0". For loose boxes, where the horse has full liberty of action, 12' 0" × 12' 0" is an average size, but this depends upon the form of building.

In advising the most suitable designs it is necessary to take in detail, and properly consider, each individual part.

We would draw attention to the divisions between the stalls, which, for carriage horses, should be open wrought-iron panelling above the boarding; but, for cart or dray horses, solid divisions of hard wood, well strengthened with iron cross-rails, are preferable.

As illustrating two, which we consider are the best we have seen of their respective classes, we give the following divisions (see Illustrations on pp. 112, 113), manufactured by Messrs. Hassall and Singleton, of Phœnix Foundry, Birmingham, and the Author thinks it well to fully describe them.

Fig. 1 is suitable for carriage horses, having open wrought-iron panelling above the boarding. At the head or manger end it is solid, to prevent the horses seeing each other when feeding. It is also provided with double-sliding barriers, which, used at night, prevent the horse leaving his own stall, in case he breaks away from his tying.

For cart or dray horses Fig. 2 represents a division of great strength. The heel-post is carried up to support a beam. It is fitted with one or two sliding barriers, as required.

In each of the above, the heel-post, if fixed with the improved self-fixing base in concrete bed, is much firmer.

112   CENTAUR;

The manger fittings should be carefully selected to suit the requirements of the horse, and the kind of food given him. For carriage horses whose consumption of food is not large, moderate-sized mangers and racks are sufficient, but for cart and dray horses they should be larger.

The subject has been fully entered into by the beforementioned Firm, from whose large number of designs the Author has selected Figs. 3 to 9 as being worthy of notice.

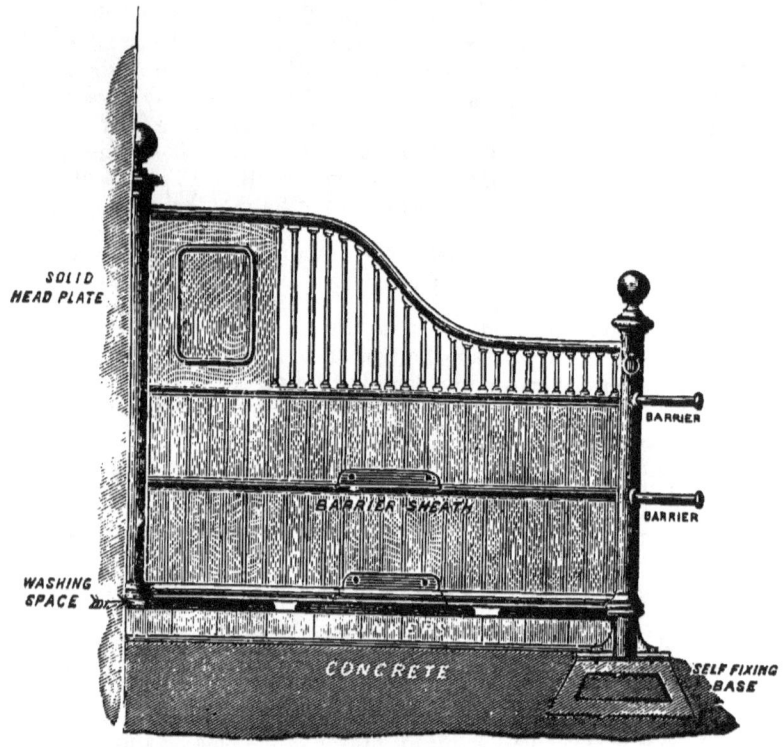

Fig. 1.

The front (Fig. 3) is very massive, and effectively prevents crib-biting. The manger trough, which for cleanliness is enamelled, is constructed so as to allow free access to the food, and is fitted with guard-bars to prevent waste. The hay rack is on a level with the manger, which is considered most suitable to the natural habits of the horse, and to prevent waste, which has formerly been an objection to this form of rack, it is fitted with a hinged hay-grid on top, which falls as the hay is consumed. The water-pot may or may not have a fixed basin, but where it is preferred it is of the form shown, having an enamelled tip-up basin with receiver underneath. This receiver is connected by a pipe to the stall drain, and when the contents of the basin are discharged into it, assists in flushing. This basin

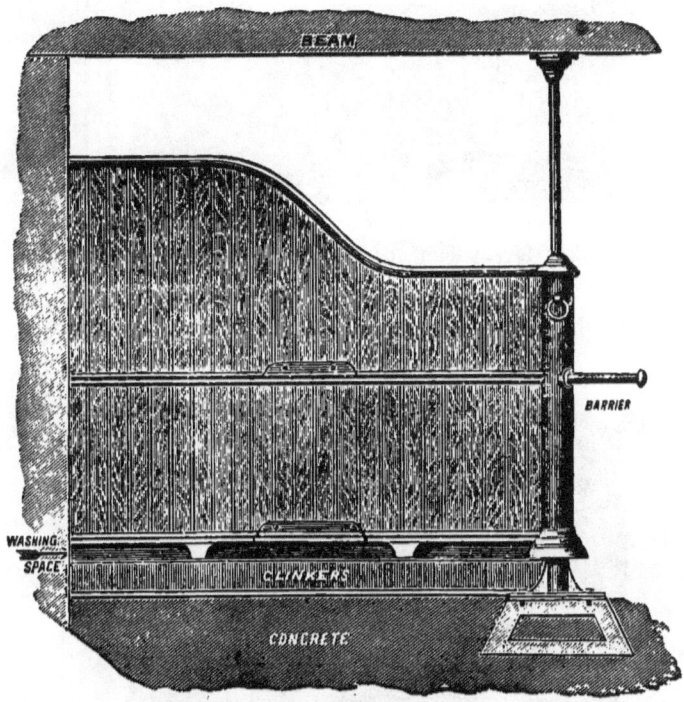

Fig. 2.

may be connected either to a permanent and self-acting water supply or a tap.

For cart horses this has a very large manger-trough, provided with guard-bars (Fig. 4), and has the same massive front. The hay rack being flush with the wall, and the hay shaft from loft, being carried up in the wall itself, has less disadvantages than top racks generally.

The floors should be paved with a hard and moderately rough material of a non-absorbent nature, and the adaman-

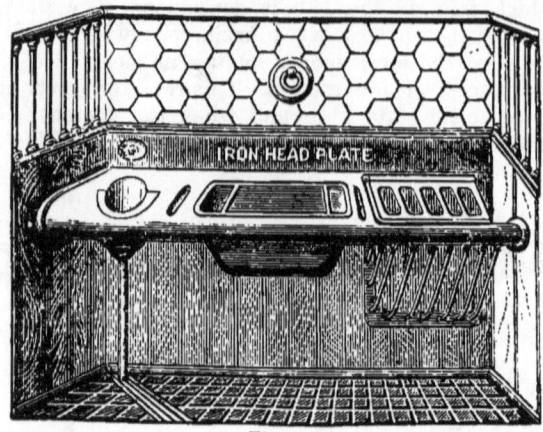

Fig. 3.

tine clinker is superior for this purpose, on account of its brightness of colour and great hardness. It is made in

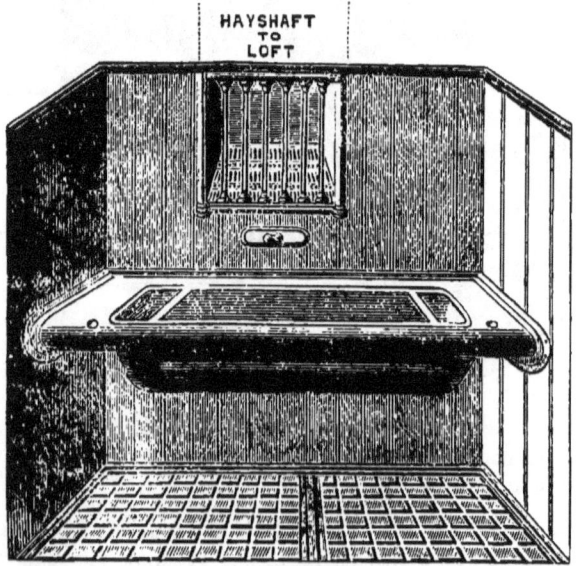

Fig. 4.

suitable shapes. Sloping floors are objectionable and injurious to the horse, as before mentioned; but how to make them quite flat, and, at the same time, effectively drain them, has not hitherto been fully considered. Messrs.

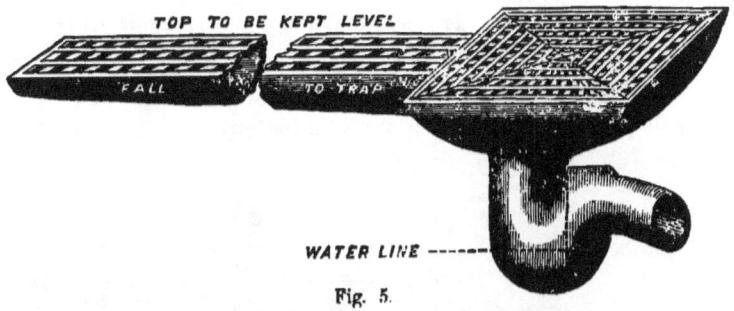

Fig. 5.

Hassall and Singleton, however, provide us with a gutter which answers this purpose admirably (Fig. 5).

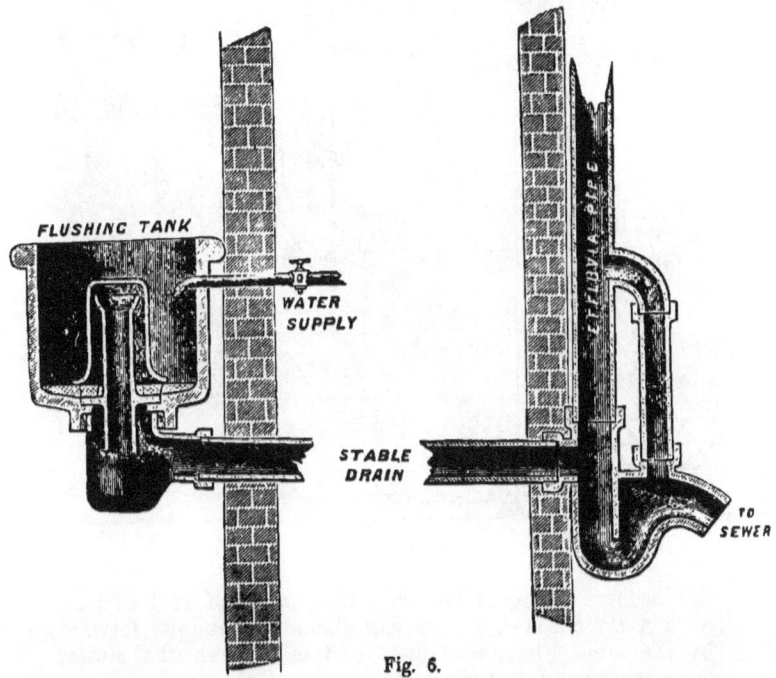

Fig. 6.

It is a covered gutter, with strong loose top-plate, intended to be fixed quite level on the surface, the necessary fall for drainage being constructed in the gutter itself. It is connected to a trap in passage behind stalls. Both gutter and trap are of such construction that, presuming by accident the cover-plates are left off, no injury would come to the horse through stepping into them.

The effective and regular cleansing of drains, as well as their proper ventilation, is most important, and, as regards

Fig. 7.

the former, it should be self-acting to be of real service. Such a system is shown in Fig. 6, and is brought forward by the same Firm, who have certainly given the matter their most careful study and attention.

A self-acting flushing tank, which is supplied with water direct from the main, and regulated by properly constructed

OR, THE TURN OUT. 117

valves, discharges its full contents, at stated fixed periods, into the drain. It is connected to the end of the main drain, thoroughly flushing it of all impurities in its action. At the opposite end, at the connection of drain to sewer, proper trap and ventilation pipes are provided, as shown.

The fittings for loose boxes should be very strong, and the doors should be framed in wrought iron. Where space is limited, convertible loose boxes and stalls are very

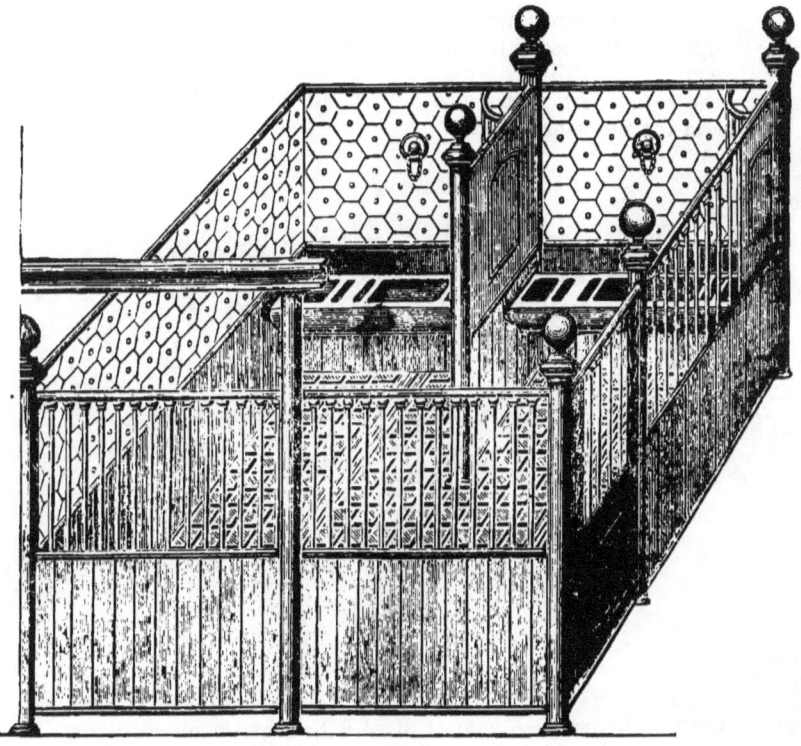

Fig. 8.

desirable. A good plan is shown by Messrs. Hassall and Singleton for converting a loose box into two stalls (Figs. 7 and 8).

It consists of a movable central division, revolving on a central pillar, secured at top and base with suitable sockets. It is well made, all the wearing parts being of gun metal.

Light and ventilation are matters for careful consideration. As regards the latter, no special rule can be laid down, much depending upon the buildings themselves; but, to perfectly carry off all foul air, and introduce sufficient fresh, without draught, is essential.

For the former plenty of light, but subdued in tone, is necessary, and this can be assisted by a judicious selection of the head linings. Tiles of neutral tints are preferable.

For inlet ventilators Fig. 9 shows a very good method of opening or closing them, which is simple, nice looking, and combines with it a head-ring for stall. It can be had from the same Firm, who also supply all classes of ventilators and the necessary fittings.

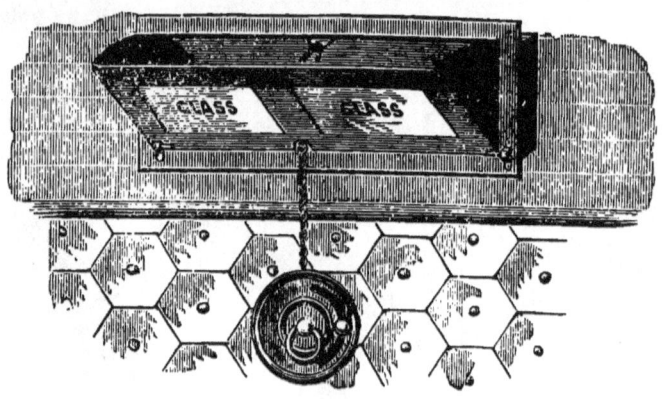

Fig. 9.

The tyings for the stalls should be noiseless, should have the weights encased, and, if fitted with brass-mounted cords, are preferable to chains, as before mentioned.

The Author would here say that he hopes, by the time this popular Edition of "CENTAUR" is issued, to have his Model Stable and Coach-house completed for the inspection and guidance of his readers; and he will be pleased to supply and superintend the fixing of Stable Fittings generally, on the above principle.

Before dismissing the subject of modern Stable Fittings, we would associate the ancient surroundings; by referring to the unique and highly-educational display of trappings and accoutrements as preserved and shown to the world in the Horse Armoury of the Tower of London. For the inspection of which—"at his leisure"—the writer is favoured with special privileges, through the considerate courtesy of the Governor of the Tower, Lieutenant-General C. Maitland, C.B., who, in 1880, generously commanded* the Chief Warder (Mr. T. Bunyan), "to give the Author every facility for studying the Tower and its antiquities"— thus coupling the public and the reserved sights; which order, it is unnecessary to say, we have many times appreciated as a privilege and honour indeed.

In recording the name of Mr. H. Hughes, who holds the office of "Headsman" of the Tower, and is known as the Yeoman—or Gentleman—Gaoler, we think and speak of him as a very dear friend, whom we cannot sufficiently thank for his oft-repeated kindly assistance and information, added to careful and punctual attention to the most minute wishes and requirements during our researches; the result of which we purpose giving in another volume.

We would say, in passing, that our friend the "Headsman's" residence (or "quarters"), is the actual old house in the second storey of which Lady Jane Grey was imprisoned, and from the window saw the headless body of her husband (Guildford-Dudley) carried across the Court-yard (or Green) the same day as she herself was beheaded.

It may not be generally known (and the Author cannot find it anywhere recorded in history) that the head of the father of Lady Jane Grey (Henry Grey, Duke of Suffolk), after being severed from the body, was exposed for some days upon a spike†, and afterwards secretly preserved in a glass casket, carefully concealed under the pulpit of the Minories Church, near the Tower, where it can be seen to this day. The sensations and emotions one experiences on beholding this, the greatest historical antiquity in existence of its kind, may be better imagined than described.

But the above is only one of the many vivid illustrations of the past the reader will meet with on a more minute and extended examination and inquiry.

---

* As shown in Mr. Bunyan's letter to the Author, August 14, 1880.
† In the Author's possession.

Therefore, the Author trusts he will be readily forgiven by the reader, and at the same time understood, whilst interesting himself in the horsemanship of the past, diverging as it were, somewhat, by blending his feelings with his country's history. And it will be always interesting for the reader in learning of the best and most modern appliances, to study at the same time the various systems and complications of the olden days.

The Writer does not intend in these final lines to this chapter to refer so much to the Stable Fittings in use centuries ago as to the equipments for horse and rider, but when the latter were used the *former* must, in some shape or other, have existed.

The principal study in connection with the trappings and harness for man and horse in those days, was the many complications, and peculiarities and fixings, for the different parts; their uses, the materials of which they were made, who made them, and the great weight to be carried.

The ancient records of England contain many documents relating to the stores used in times of peace and in times of war, specimens of which stores are still in existence, and can be seen at the Tower of London. Such a display of historical associations does not exist elsewhere, hence the pride all Englishmen feel in their national Institution; and the great interest taken in the Tower by foreign visitors, particularly the millionaires of America, who can and do afford special trips for the purpose of visiting the sights of the Old Country, and the Tower of London in particular.

The original Horse Armoury is taken down, and the armour is now placed in the White Tower.

Life-sized equestrian statues of our Kings and Queens are ranged in proper historical order, which most minute detail fully endorses the pages of history, commencing with the period of the Norman Conquest; when the body armour of the warriors was made of leather, and beautifully painted in various colours.

It is said that the plated armour of the time of Edward III. became so splendid that the knights were killed for the sake of their spoil, instead of being taken prisoners.

Among other relics, is an elaborately carved German saddle, made of bone.

There are several equestrian figures representing knights of the time of Henry VI., Edward IV., and Richard III., showing the actual saddles and bridles of that period.

Among the ancient swords, spears, daggers, tilting lances, helmets, gauntlets, and chain mail, are a curious collection of ancient spurs, a battle axe attached to the bow of the saddle, and a complete suit of horse armour.

One of the most prominent life-sized figures is that of Henry VIII., wearing the actual suit of armour, &c., known to have belonged to and been worn by that monarch. It consists of tilting helm, gorget, back and breast-plates with placcato; garde de reins; panedrons, with passe gardes (for turning away the thrust of a lance); rear and van braces; gauntlets, the left a tilting one; tassets; demicuisses; genoullieures; jambs; and square-toed sollerets. In the right hand is a mantel-de-fer, and a long sword is worn at the waist.

During the reign of Queen Mary the weight of the armour became so great that the knights (giants as they were) used to faint (and the horses to fall down with the lumber of their trappings) under it, and when unhorsed could not rise.

The reader may view the suit worn by the Earl of Leicester, 1560, showing his initials, R. D. (Robert Dudley) on the knee-guards, and the family badge; and also the suit of armour presented to Henry VIII., on his marriage with Catherine of Arragon, which suit is considered to be one of the most curious in the world. Likewise is shown the suit of armour worn by that King when he was only 18 years of age, the weight of which was 92-lbs., and is described as being "rough from the hammer." There is likewise an equestrian statue representing James II., showing the genuine dress and armour of that King, also the saddle, bridle, reins, stirrups, &c., of his horse.

In Queen Elizabeth's armoury is shown, among the various weapons of that time, the military fork,* used for cutting the horse's bridle reins. At the end of the room

---

* Specimen of which the Author has in his collection of antiquities.

is a life-size figure representing Elizabeth, mounted on a carved horse, the statue showing the State costume and trappings of that time.

With other items are shown the stirrups worn by the Founder of the Tower—William the Conqueror; and in a glass case are also curious specimens of the horse armour of that period.

To enumerate all the beauties, and interesting relics associated with our subject would take a volume of itself.

The Author strongly advises all readers of "CENTAUR" to complete the circuit of the Horse Armouries of the Tower of London.

DOCKING AND NICKING.

"He jests at scars that never felt a wound."

THE above are very cruel operations, and at a not very remote period were almost universally practised, but of late years, regular feeding, properly filled harness,* and kind treatment have been found by humane horse owners to be excellent substitutes.

Docking is nothing more nor less than cutting off the horse's tail, and is often attended with danger.

The operation—if permitted at all—should be performed by a professional man, who uses an engine or machine made for the purpose.

After the tail is taken off, the raw stump is seared with a hot iron to stop the bleeding, and the part is powdered with resin, likewise touched with a hot iron, to melt and run it over the wound.

This is the general process of docking, and the operation is attended with the greatest risk, particularly when it is performed by a careless, unskilful, and unfeeling operator (who generally acts on the impulse of the moment, using his pocket-knife or the first handy weapon), especially if the horse is fat or fleshy, and the tail be cut or chopped off too near the rump.

Nicking means cutting four or five gashes across the under side of the tail, for the purpose of giving the horse an "elegant appearance," by causing the tail to curve.

---

* See "Crupper Dock," in Article "Fitting the Harness."

The first nick, as it is called, is started, say three inches, from the rump, and the others at equal distances according to the length of the tail.

The most cruel part of the operation consists in taking or drawing a portion of the tendons out of the tail.

The amount of pain which the horse endures during the process of docking and nicking, rests more or less with the operator; but in any case it is extremely painful, so much so that many proprietors of horses have feelingly determined to set their faces against the system altogether; in fact, the very cruel and unnecessary practice we hope will soon be fast dying out, and happily become the exception, not the rule.

We give an extract from the *Midland Evening News*, October 20th, 1884:—

> DOCKING HORSES.—The fashion of mutilating horses tails has now become so common that for the heavier kinds of horses required in the army it is sometimes almost impossible to procure a sufficient number without taking some which have been submitted to the injurious operation of "docking." The military authorities have been advised to reject all such mutilated horses, as horses with short tails are practically unfit for service in the field, where flies are troublesome.

From the following illustration it will be seen that the practice of "docking" is not only cruel, but illegal:—

> DOCKING A HORSE'S TAIL.—At the Bridgnorth Petty Sessions, recently, T. H—— and J. J. W——, horse dealers, and J. H——, were charged with cruelty to a horse, by "docking" its tail with a butcher's knife.—J. H—— said he "docked" the animal himself, and was in the habit of doing so to other horses, but did not consider it cruelty.—Mr. Cann, Veterinary Surgeon, was called, and gave it as his opinion that, according to the evidence, the horse had been cruelly illtreated.—The Chief Constable remarked that after the horse was "docked" it was immediately harnessed and driven about the town.—The Bench said the case against H—— and W—— would be dismissed, as there was not sufficient evidence to convict them: but J. H—— would be fined 15s. and the costs, making a total of £2.

CART, FARM, AND PIT GEARS;
SHOEING AND ROUGHING.

"As easy as an old shoe."

HE above adage does not at all times apply to the make or fit of the heavier class of harness; yet the very fact of the extraordinary weight of leather, wood, straw, and iron that some horses are condemned to carry, independent of the loaded cart or wagon, is sufficient of itself to suggest that every part of the set of gears, whether shafter or leader, should at least be a perfect and easy fit.

It will be plain to every considerate mind that the horse should be measured for his suit; but even this is not sufficient in itself to ensure the comfort of the horse and the security of the team, without proper judgment on the part of the saddler in each particular case, and the discretion of the horse owner as to the make and form he has decided upon having.

The latter should at all times avoid cheap, low-priced, or auction goods.

It is, and long has been, the Author's opinion that cart gears are made up far heavier and more lumbersome than is necessary, and he considers the example set by London carriers generally—Pickford's, Sutton's, and Railway Companies in particular—a step in the right direction towards bringing about a complete alteration throughout the country, and revolutionize in favour of less weight, not only for the horse's back, but, in fact, all over his body, and in the future it is to be hoped the large housings, savors, and winkers which are, to a certain extent, adhered to by the country saddler, as he is termed, will become "a thing of the past."

The breech-band is of necessity required to be strong and specially safe, but the writer is of opinion that there is not the slightest occasion for a 5-inch breech-band, or crupper, or back-band, in cart harness; and he contends that breech-bands $3\frac{1}{2}$ and 4 inches wide are strong enough, if well made and stitched by hand with strong threads, a small awl used, and plenty of wax; particularly if, after the first row is sewn, a strong filling of solid mill banding —either old or new—be inserted under the lay, and with the ends of the lay carried round the ironwork. The stitching should be four straight rows or slight waves; fancy work, such as diamonds, points, or crosses, in stitching is calculated to cut and weaken the leather, and will at times break off, or through, at those particular filagree patterns. The piece or pieces of leather above referred to as "filling" are better if old and firm, but must be sound and free from cracks. It is not necessary to pare or shave down the edges for rounding; simply wetting and hammering flat each side before inserting between the top lay and breech-band body is sufficient.

The shaft crupper, belly-band, and cheeks of the bridle should be made on the same principle.

The housings of the saddle and collar are better glued together when lined, instead of being pasted.

The firmness of a set thus built will be beyond all comparison with the wide over-loading and flimsily made old pattern harness. All the stitching should be carefully rubbed down at the bottom side, and if the top is hammered it should be done very lightly, and only for the purpose of rounding the work off after wetting; if the mark of the face of the hammer is left it indicates hurried or careless workmanship.

The hurried manner in which the shaft horse is sometimes forced down hill plainly indicates the necessity for a safe breech-band and hip straps.

The most important part of the cart-set, for the comfort of the horse, is the collar; and the only portion of it that can be reduced in weight is the housing. The old-fashioned monster housings never ought to be revived, and the writer thinks they can never be forgotten.

Some say they had their uses in "keeping the wet off;" but that local remedy was a poor and lumbering substitute for the horse-cloth.

It is extremely important that the collar be lined with best check, and faced between the straw and the check with good, clean wool, and the shape of the collar fitted exactly to the form of the horse's neck. Open topped collars must be strapped perfectly tight—in fact the top strap in all open collars, whether for use on the surface or under ground, should only be punched one hole; this will ensure the shape and firmness of the collar being kept as much as possible.

A cruel practice has been known to be indulged in for the purpose of showing a cheap job in repairing,—which is done at the expense of the horse, particularly in contract work,—by simply covering the old and dirty lining with new check, and passing the same off for "re-bodying and fresh strawing and wooling," when, at the same time, the old filling has neither been disturbed nor renewed in any way. Such disgraceful workmanship is nothing more nor less than a wicked robbery to the customer, and torture for the horse, and would not be permitted in the workshop of any respectable and conscientious saddler; but it is a well-known fact, that, in addition to the above, nails and tacks have been substituted for stitches by the unprincipled and cheap contractor, and when it has become an absolute necessity for re-wooling, the very cheapest, knotty, and dirty flocks have been used, without the slightest consideration for the horse or the reputation of the workman.

In easing cart or other collars, holes should by no means be cut into them, but the lining opened at the side piece, turned back, and thus hollowed, as marked where the wound lies, and made to miss the tender parts, faced with clean wool, and quilted down, particularly in a cart collar or saddle; but if leather lined, as in stage or harness collars, the part, after easing out, simply requires a wet sponge rubbed over the leather and slightly malleted, and it will then lie in the form desired.

The saddle tree should be made sufficiently wide to allow the pad to fit, and not to stand up or pinch the back.

There is no real necessity for the saddle housings and savors to be large or heavily lined.

If ornaments or plates are desired, the smaller they are the more neat and tasteful they will appear, besides being lighter for the horse to carry.

Double girths are at all times necessary, and should not be supplied less than 1½ inch wide for an average sized horse.

It is important that the belly-band should be the same strength as the breech-band, and that all the ironwork throughout the set be perfectly sound, well made, and of best material.

The foregoing rule as to substance and workmanship applies particularly to cart, farm, pit, and boat gears, the making or repairing of which should not be done "slop," or in a careless and common way, for the sake of price or other ulterior motives, but in the best and most efficient manner possible, as this class of harness is constantly exposed to the roughest possible wear and tear in all weathers and almost all atmospheres, and is generally worn by strong and well corned animals.

If it is the farmer's rule to have his gears repaired at the farm, say once a year, none but good, practical, and sober workmen should represent the saddler. More mischief has been caused to the horse's back and the good name of the tradesman through complaints, justified too frequently by the carelessness of some journeyman, than is pleasant to either the customer or the trade. Frequently the man has been dissatisfied with the food, and the quantity or quality of beer supplied him, or complaints are made by the farmer of his horses being injured through bad workmanship; and no wonder, for cases have occurred in which the hand-iron or other tools have been stuffed with the wool into the lining by the thoughtless workman. If it is mutually understood that food and refreshments shall be supplied by the farmer, the quality should by all means be good, and the quantity of the latter regulated according to the ability or disposition of the workman and the hours of labour. This alone will command a fair day's work, reasonable charges, and no complaints or dissatisfaction on either side.

Pit Gears require an equal amount of care in making and repairing, and a careful selection of material at all times. The argument that the work is "going under ground" and " out of sight " does not alter the fact that some horses in the mines are as massive and good looking, and as well fed, and in many cases better cared for, than many horses above ground; therefore it is really necessary that none but the best leather, check, wool, laces, and ironwork, be used in the making up and repairing of all gears worn under ground.

The Split Crupper and Hip Straps—used for boating purposes—should likewise be firm and carefully made, the side pipes true, and the collar bodies full and easy in the draught. The housing should not be fixed upon the collar to stand up, but to lie nearly flat, for the purpose of missing the bridges when passing under them.

The Hames should be shorter in the top than the ordinary cart hames, for the same reason, as regards the roofing.

The Boat Bridle is not required to be heavy—in fact, the lighter the better, and should be made with a narrow noseband. Boatmen, as a rule, take great pains with the horses entrusted to their care; the writer has frequently heard boatmen speak of the horse as their most constant and only companion, which is easily accounted for when the fact of their long and solitary journeys together is considered.

On questioning a driver—who was jocularly shouting to his horse—upon one occasion, as to why he had forgotten his whip, the answer was, "My hoss wants no whip, I carries my pipe instead, and keeps the whip in the manger."

Nose-tins and Nose-bags should be made with judgment, and as light as possible consistent with their use; the bottom of the bag should be solid leather, and the sides porous, for ventilation.

The Heavy Harness, used for dray work—say that used by Brewery and Railway Companies—is, as a whole, above the average in make and quality, for the principal reason that a good price is paid and a good pattern adopted; and the care bestowed to keep it and the horse clean and in good condition is extremely creditable to the draymen, which system must be a source of great satisfaction to the horse owners, who are very proud of and are known to pay long prices for their steeds.

The general system adopted by the Midland Railway Company in permanently dispensing with winkers to the bridles throughout their whole system is a very humane and truly laudable act, there being less weight for the horse to carry, and the open cheek gives him every opportunity of seeing his way; and it likewise means economy in the first cost and after repairs.

In the saddlery trade, the repairing department is a very important one, and, as before intimated, should command the special attention of both mechanic and principal. Good workmanship, with economical views as to cost and promptitude, should be the constant effort.

Men without reason and forethought have been found in all businesses, but the man who would substitute nails for stitches—where sewing is absolutely recognized as the only legitimate end—is not a fit associate for good workmen.

The Author has—in his travels and valuation engagements—heard of serious results that have arisen from such carelessly executed and bad workmanship. If steady, honest, and sober journeymen could be guaranteed to employers, they would be stimulated and encouraged to pay good wages for a reasonable amount of work; and it is very desirable that workmen, without distinction being made, should prove themselves conscious of doing justice both to employers and their customers.

In contracting to keep gears and harness in repair all the year round, no matter whether the work is done on or off the premises, the best and cheapest way in the end is that the workmen should be instructed to do every job as well and promptly as possible, and should be provided with proper materials for that purpose. The old saying, "Once well done is twice done," strictly applies to the contract department of the saddlery trade, and s generally acknowledged by the trade; and the Author has no hesitation in saying that his experiences among business men lead to the firm conviction that no profession, trade, or calling requires more care or thought; and, as a rule, no tradesman is more succesful in giving good value and satisfaction to his customers than the conscientious saddlery and harness manufacturer.

Under the title of "Stable and Stable Fittings, &c.," the subject of Shoeing and Roughing has been noticed; still, in closing this article on "Cart, Farm, and Pit Gears," it may not be out of place to state that what is there set forth in reference to the shoeing of saddle and carriage horses, is equally applicable to draught horses, on the feet of which it is highly essential that as much care and attention should be bestowed as upon those of the hackney or hunter; indeed, seeing the heavy loads the waggon horse has to draw suggests for itself that every means, consistent with efficiency, should be adopted for reducing as much as possible the weight of iron upon his feet, and guarding against his being unskilfully or improperly shod; and the more so considering the fact that the great weight he has behind him increases his torture when pricked by a carelessly driven nail. This adds to the difficulty of keeping him upon his feet in slippery weather, particularly when the roughing is neglected, or improperly done; because, in the first instance, the substance of the shoe adds to the pressure upon the nail and forces it into the sensitive part of the foot, while in the latter, when once the animal slips, the weight of the load forces it down; whereas a horse with a light load and safe shoes might, if he stumble, recover his footing without falling, in which case the bearing-rein has nothing to do with the question.

The foot-gear of the horse should—as the motto heading these lines expresses it—"fit as easy as an old shoe," and in the event of its being otherwise, the results to both the animal and the man may be, and oft-times are, serious.

The following excellent notice appeared in one of the local papers, and was enclosed to the Author. It is here given with the view to, if possible, "drive the nail (or argument) further home":—

HORSE-SHOES AND HORSE-SHOEING.—On an average, horses require shoeing once a month. The length of time a shoe will wear depends much on the kind of service a horse is doing, and on the kind of road he is daily travelling. A team horse in heavy draught does not wear out as many shoes as one used in a hack; quick motion grinds shoes down more rapidly. Wooden pavement is but a little saving to the wear and tear of shoes, for the grit and dust, which become impacted in the interstices of the wooden block, grind away shoes like the friction of an emery wheel. The hind shoes wear out first, and there is more strain and friction on them than on the forward shoes. It is impossible and improper for a horse to wear shoes more than six weeks, for the growth of the foot shortens the shoe, as well as changes the shape otherwise. The neglect will cause the shoe to encroach upon the soft textures of the foot and produce lameness. There are but few practical mechanics who have sufficiently studied the foot of the horse. It is not enough to know the anatomy of the foot, and where to insert a nail not to cause pain, but the foot should be studied in the state of nature, before the mechanism of man has, by artificial appliances, distorted it. The shape of the hoof of the wild horse, or of one which has never been shod, should be taken as a model. The foot is then properly balanced, neither too long nor too broad, but it has adjusted itself to nature, and the muscles and tendons are not strained by travel. Confinement and unskilful shoeing change the anatomical relations of the foot, and the best judgment of the mechanic is often taxed to correct the growing deformity—from unskilled shoeing. When a reasoning, skilful mechanic is found, the horse is safe in his hands, for he only preserves the normal shape of the hoof, and adjusts the shoe to protect it. The frog in the hoof of a horse is placed there for a particular purpose, and should not be cut by the shoer. If this is allowed, contraction and lameness will follow. The shape and weight of the shoe should be accommodated to the purpose for which they are designed. The tram horse requires a shoe lighter and without corks, while the draught horse must have a heavy, broad shoe, with corks, to enable him to obtain foothold, and travel with the least possible strain.

Therefore, the simple rule to be laid down as requiring punctual attention in horse-keeping, in addition to the feet and shoes, is—

  AIR,

    LIGHT,

      LITTER,

        GROOMING,

          EXERCISE,

            FOOD,

              and WATER.

EFFECT OF MUSIC UPON THE HORSE.

"Hark! 'tis the Indian drum."

EVERYWHERE the horse is recognized as the most useful of the servants of man, and it yields in intelligence to the dog alone

In the early ages of the world, the horse seems to have been devoted to the purposes of war and pleasure; but its beauty and strength and tractability have now connected it, directly or indirectly, with all the purposes of life. If it differs in different countries in form and size, it is from the influence of climate and cultivation, but otherwise, from the war horse—as it is depicted on the friezes of ancient temples—to the stately charger of Holsten, or from the fleet and beautiful Arabian to the diminutive Shetlander, there is an evident similarity of form and origin.

Of course, in training the horse for military purposes, it is necessary that it should understand the various bugle sounds or calls, and it is astonishing how quickly these are recognized and understood by the horse, who appears never to forget them.

It is related that a milkman once stepped from his cart to supply a customer with milk, and just as he did so the bugle of a cavalry regiment that was being drilled in a public park near, sounded, and away bolted the horse, drawing cart and milk cans behind it. In vain the milkman screamed and yelled, and in vain the pedestrians attempted to stop the runaway, but its martial ardour, having been inflamed by the well-remembered bugle call, it brooked no opposition, and suffered no obstacle to impede its course, till it found itself in the ranks of its old companions-in-arms, where its comical appearance, with accoutrements not exactly according to regulation pattern, excited considerable amusement. On inquiry it was found the animal had formerly been a cavalry horse, and hearing the well-known sound to which in former years it had bounded with pride and pleasure, the animal, despite its age, could not resist the enchanting influence of the music.

It is known that horses readily understand a few notes of music, but cases can be cited in which they have been trained to keep time to some very complicated compositions.

Some time ago the Author had occasion to call upon a friend, who takes a great pride in his stud. Just as he arrived, his friend and good lady were about to proceed to the court-yard to inspect a new addition to the stable in the shape of a young colt. It need scarcely be added that the writer gladly accepted an invite to accompany them. The animal—a fine looking creature—was trotted out; but it had never been broken, and had just been shod for the first time that morning; and like "Fear," it "started at the sounds itself had made," and as the metal rang upon the pavement it became quite nervous. The lady seeing this, stepped forward and commenced patting and stroking his mane, and while she was so engaged, a band of music at a short distance struck up a plaintive air, and the lady—quite mechanically—commenced to hum the tune. No sooner did she begin than the colt placed its head upon the lady's breast, when she called her husband's attention and that of the Author to the occurrence; but the moment she ceased singing the animal raised its head, but replaced it when the singing was repeated. This proceeding, which was done several times, leads one to think that music might be advantageously used in the training of horses, especially those of a sensitive or timid nature.

And we are reminded of tales once heard of the "Horse Charmers" in Ireland, who were said to be able, by merely humming or singing some words or notes close to the animal's ear, to tame the most vicious or restive horse that could be brought to them.

The Author has personally tried several experiments with his own steeds at various times and places, which conclusively prove the theory propounded above, and corroborates the experience just narrated. For instance, he has on several occasions, while his animal was cantering round the field in which it was turned out to graze, commenced playing upon a cornet, when the animal would suddenly stop and prick up his ears as though listening most attentively to the strains of the instrument; he has also, when the animal—a beautiful bay mare—was in her loose box in the stable, caused the stable door to be thrown open and at the same time has opened his sitting-room window, and commenced playing an air upon the pianoforte, when the mare would immediately leave the stable and come trotting and neighing directly to the window whence the sounds emanated; an illustration which goes far to prove that music, which is said to possess "charms to soothe the savage breast," has a wonderful and lasting effect on the equidæ.

NATURAL CLEANLINESS OF THE HORSE.

> "But he was fastidious as a lord,
> And particular about bed and board;
> But spirited and docile too,
> Whate'er was to be done, would do."

ERHAPS no animal is so fastidious about its food and drink as the horse, which is naturally an herbivorous animal; hence its thin and muscular lips, its firm and compressed mouth, and its sharp incisor teeth, are admirably adapted to seizing and cropping the grass; while the peculiar construction of some of the bones of the face enable it to grind down its food as perfectly as it could be ground in the best constructed mill.

The olfactory nerve of the horse is more than four times the size of that in man. Hence the horse can detect smells that might escape the notice of man, and an effluvia that did not attract his attention might be a source of great annoyance to the horse.

It is a well-known fact that horses will not eat food that has been breathed upon and left in the trough or manger; consequently care should be taken never to pack or put more food in the manger than can be readily disposed of.

The horse is as particular about the water it drinks as the food it eats; and it is asserted by some authorities that the quality of the water supplied has a peculiar effect upon the animal. Thus, hard water, freshly drawn from the well causes griping and roughens the coat of the animal. The temperature of the water given to a horse is a matter of very great consequence. Water taken from a running stream will rarely harm; but if drawn from a well, by its coldness, not unfrequently produces colic, spasm, and even death.

The horse that is not properly groomed, and carefully stabled, soon begins to exhibit the results of inattention; it becomes dispirited, rejects its food, and loses flesh. So well aware are those who take a pride in their horses of this fact that the utmost care is bestowed upon the ventilation and drainage of modernly constructed stables.

A curious case occurred recently in Birmingham which clearly illustrates the sensitive nature of the horse and its susceptibility to the effects of effluvia. A manufacturer engaged in the metal trade, but who resides at some distance from the town, owned a very valuable horse, which he kept for the purpose of riding to and from his place of business, where, as he was sometimes detained for hours, he had a stable erected for his horse. He had not long had the animal when it became languid and ultimately unfit for work. A veterinary surgeon was consulted, and for a time he was completely at a loss to account for the symptoms; from which, however, the animal recovered after a short residence at the country house of his owner; but no sooner had it commenced its visits to the town stable than the symptoms returned. The veterinary surgeon was again called in; but this time he paid a visit to the stable, which was in close proximity to a casting shop, the fumes from which reached the stable and were the cause of the animal's illness. A new stable was erected in a more healthy part of the works, and the result was most satisfactory.

WONDERFUL HORSES.

"So meekly docile thou art, in leed."

WORK like the present would scarcely be complete were it to pass unnoticed some of the fabulous species of the horse tribe.

A few years ago there was exhibited in Walsall a very curious animal—one side of which resembled a very finely developed horse, while the other possessed all the characteristics of a cow, even to the cloven hoof, and the rudimentary formation of a horn.

Now, as Dr. Gray observes, the horse family is distinguished from all others by its undivided hoof. That the above animal was a cross between the horse and a Gnu—which is a species of wild ass, and is called by the Dutch settlers at the Cape, the "Bastard Wild Beast"—was considered by some very probable. If so, that would account for the cloven hoof and the horn, as the Gnu has both; but although the cloven hoof and the horn might be accounted for upon that supposition, yet that could not account for the flank and shoulder, which resembled those of a cow, as the Gnu, although possessed of horns and cloven hoofs, has a body resembling that of the horse.

Some of the ancient writers describe a species of horse with a mane extending the whole length of the animal, from head to tail.

Some authors have depicted horses with a unicorn-like horn in their forehead.

And among the collection made by Aldrovandus, is a horse with a human head and face (Centaur); and another with hands instead of fore-feet, which he tells us belonged to Julius Cæsar, and would suffer no one else to mount him. "*Caius Julius Cæsar utebatur equo insigni pedibus prope humanis et in modum digitorum ungulis fissis,*" &c.—as a writer in Knight's Cyclopædia very justly observes—this may have only been some malformation of the hoof, like that in the case of the animal exhibited in Walsall; but whether it was merely a malformation or not, the painter has represented the animal with two human hands, having on each four fingers and a thumb, and also nails.

WILD HORSES.

> "He looked as though the speed of thought
> Were in his limbs; but he was wild,
> Wild as the deer, and untaught,
> With spur and bridle undefiled.
> With flowing tail, and flying mane,
> Wide nostrils—never stretched by pain,
> Mouth bloodless to the bit or rein;
> And feet that iron never shod,
> And flanks unscarred by spur or rod;
> A thousand horse, the wild, the free,
> Like waves that follow o'er the sea."

IT is very doubtful whether at the present day any true descendants of an original wild stock of horses exist.

Dr. Gray observes that the wild horse, as depicted by Gmelin, very much resembles the ponies left at liberty on the commons of Cornwall, and on the mountains of Scotland, and are rather domestic animals which have become deteriorated.

The wild horses of America, although they retain their size and form, and have not deteriorated, are the descendants of the domestic horses taken to America by the Spaniards.

Horses were first landed at Buenos Ayres in 1537, and that Colony having been for a time deserted, the horses were allowed to run wild. In 1580, forty-three years afterwards, they were found wild at the Straits of Magellan. In the Pampos they abound, but these are not descendants of horses that had never been subjugated to man.

HORSEY PHRASES, SLANG TERMS, AND RACY REMARKS.

"Be thou familiar, but by no means vulgar."

IN order to render this work as acceptable to all classes of readers, and as easily understood as possible, all technical phraseology, cant language, slang terms, or stable expressions have been studiously avoided. As, however, our readers may meet with such terms in other works, or in the periodical literature of the day, or hear them at auctions, fairs, and other public places, and may be at a loss to understand their meaning, it has been considered that an exposition of some of the more frequently used terms and phrases may be of service. A selection of these has therefore been made by the Author from memory, and such explanations given as will enable anyone to understand their meaning, whether on the turf, in the auction room, or in the stable.

Amble—A peculiar kind of pace, wherein a horse's two legs, of the same side, move at the same time.

Aubin—A broken pace, between an amble and a gallop; a defect

A Mark—A ninny; to take advantage of; good impression; "made his mark."

A Pony of Beer—Small glass.

Bars—The fleshy rows that run across the upper part of the horse's mouth.

Bay—A bay horse is the colour commonly called a red, inclining to chesnut. This colour varies in several ways; thus— "a dark bay," or light bay.

Bishoper—One skilled in horse dentistry (but not for the general weal).

Bots—Short, thick grubs, which trouble horses in the beginning of summer.

Beaning—Placing a pebble between the shoe and the sole of the foot of the horse.

Boar—A horse that tosses its nose in the wind.

Copped—Caught.

Crib-biter—Horse that gnaws its manger.

Crick—In the neck; a stiff neck; the horse cannot take its meal from the ground.

Chipped the bark off—Has been down.

Curb—A tumour caused by hard riding, blows, and kicks. Curb—A chain to the bit.

Catch a Weasel Asleep—Off one's guard.

Casting—Overthrowing.

Down in the Mouth—Low spirited.

Dead Nail—A sharper.

Eye Openers—Early drinks.

Ease him—To take the weight off his back; to relieve of money.

Feel—To feel the horse in the hand by the reins; that the horse is obedient to the wish of the rider.

Film—Upon the horse's eye.

Fiver—Bank note.

Fire—Life; energy; go; "got some fire in him."

Faked up—Doctored with intent.

Frenzy—Madness; excitement.

Fullock—Used in speaking of accidents.

Glums—A deep indentation over each eye of the aged horse.

Gall—Sore back.

Goer—Very speedy horse.

Gait—Pace.

Goes Freely—Without effort.

Gullett—Passage for food.

Gulp—To swallow eagerly.

Gumption—Shrewdness; understanding.

Gyve—Fetters for legs.

Good Worker—Will pull at anything.

Hand—Four inches; bridle-hand; sword-hand; hand high; all hands.

Horse Coper—A dealer in stolen or "picked-up" horses; a buyer of wids, whistlers, roarers, pipers, crib biters; one who gets his money any way he can; and is sometimes known as a "flatcatcher."

Horse Chaunter—Gentleman cheat.

Half-Bull—Half-crown.

Hollow-Backed Horse—Weak spine.

Hush Money—Bribing to secrecy.

Humour—Disease; out of sorts.

Humbug—An impostor.

Horse Power—Expressive of a steam engine.

Horse Leech—A leech that bites horses.

Hitch—Failure or break down; to hitch, fasten, or buckle to.

Hissing—To make sibilant sound.

Hock—The joint between the knee and the fetlock.

Hobby—A strong nag.

Hobble—To walk lamely.

Hollowness—Insincerity.

Honest—Upright in dealing; good value

Hoodwink—To blind; to deceive.

Hoof—The horny part of horse's feet.

Hopple—To tie the feet, but not closely.

Hoy—To stop; halt.

Hide Bound—Tight skin.

Hard Horse—Insensible to whip; hard mouth; no control.

Hernia—A rupture.

Hip-shot—A disorder of the horse.

Hie—Hasten; hurry up.

High Flyer—Lofty carriage.

Hack—Horse for riding and driving.

Hackneyed—Much used.

Heigh-oh—An expression of langour.

He "runs the show"—Finds the money.

High Stepper—Showy.

Hurry-up—Make haste; quicken your hand

In Form—Good condition.

Jade—Old and worn out horse.

Jibber—Horse that will not pull.

Jaw-knotted—Inflated kernels.

Jerk—Strike, or fling and kick with the hind quarters.

Kicked—To stand treat.

Kup-Kup—Come, come.

Kid—Joke.

Look Alive—Be active.

Mark—Black spot which shows the age of the horse.

Make-up—Assumed dress.

Mash—A drink given to a horse; a bran mash; "he's a masher."

Monkey—Five hundred pounds.

Moon—A disorder in the eyes of the horse.

Morfoundering—Cold upon heat; overridden and heated, and too suddenly cooled.

Nice Mouthed—Over choice in eating.

Not in the Hunt—No chance.

Near Side—Left side.

Nag—A neat, small horse.

Off Side—Right side.

Off his Feed—Cannot enjoy food.

On Tick—On credit.

Overdone—Over-ridden; over-worked; wind and strength exhausted.

Puffing the Glums—Disguising the glums by perforating the skin with a pin, and blowing up the cavities with air.

Palate—The upper part, or roof, of the mouth.

Pony—Twenty-five pounds.

Part—To pay; full speed of the horse

Puller—Horse that requires no traces; will pull by the reins.

Pace—Motion; walk; trot; gallop.

Pricked—Negligence of the farrier in driving the nails.

Punch—Well set; well knit horse.

Pie-Bald—White spots upon a coat of another colour.

Quid—Sovereign.

Rig-Out—Suit of clothes.

Rise in the Barometer—Kicked out of the stable.

Spin—Ride or drive of a few miles; a sharp trot.

Stayer—Long-winded horse.

Slink—To sneak away.

Snort—To force air through the nose.

Set-up—To complete.

Stag-evil—A cramp or convulsion.

The Rhino—Coin of the realm.

Tether—To tie a horse by the leg.

To Crab—Spoil the sale.

That's off—The deal is over.

The Straight Griffin—Direct information.

Tips—To hint or inform.

Tit—A little horse or nag.

"*Turn Out*"—Horse, harness, and vehicle.

Turned-up—Sure footed; done with it.

Thrape—To thrash; to chastise.

Tall-Talk—Self elevation.

Ticklish—Tender.

Trot him out—Show him up.

Vault—To spring into the saddle.

Vice—A fault.

Vives—A distemper.

Welsher—One who leaves the betting ring to get a biscuit and glass of sherry, and forgets to return to pay his debts.

Wid—A broken-winded horse.

Warbles—Small, hard tumours.

Whistler—Horse that roars, and so termed on account of short wind.

Wheezing—Blowing.

Well-up—Plenty of money; a good mount.

Wants no Whip—Free, easy action.

White-face—White mark down the horse's face.

White Lie—Told as an excusable falsehood.

Wolves' Teeth—When they prick or wound the tongue or gums.

Wet both Eyes—Two drinks.

Whoa—Stop, stand.

Yap—Pay.

Yap-up—Pay up.

HORSE SHOWS, AND MAY-DAY CELEBRATIONS.

'Twas morn—a most auspicious one;
From the golden East, the golden sun
Came forth his golden race to run;
    Through clouds of most splendid tinges,
Clouds that lately slept in shade,
But now seem'd made of gold brocade,
    With magnificent golden fringes:
In short 'twas the year's most golden day,
By mortals called the "FIRST OF MAY."

HE defenders of horse racing tell us that the so-called sport was instituted with a view to improve the breed of horses. Granting this to be the case, it could only improve them in one direction— that of swiftness. How far the institution has succeeded would be rather difficult to say.

But whatever may have been the necessity for fleet horses in olden days, when the only messengers were the "couriers" and the "carrier pigeons," the necessity for developing swiftness at the expense of other qualities of the horse now no longer exists; for the electric telegraph far outstrips the swiftest pigeon, and the express train can distance completely the fleetest steed.

Seeing, then, that speed merely is no longer a desideratum in the horse, and seeing also the evils arising from and associated with the "turf," would it not be better to substitute some more rational mode of encouraging the improvement in the breed of horses in their training and management? With a view to carrying out this idea, the Author introduced an exhibition of draught-horses on May-day fifteen years ago; and speaking from his own experience he can safely say the results have been most satisfactory, as the prizes offered have had the effect of inducing the wagoners and carters to bestow more care and attention upon the animals placed under their care; for they have learned the very useful lesson, that if they desire to present their horses in a condition necessary to ensure their taking a prize, they must attend to their animals and groom them regularly and well all the year round, and not merely dress them up for the Show.

The Author feels confident that if what he has done on a small scale were carried out in every locality throughout the kingdom upon a larger scale, much good would be accomplished and the breed of horses considerably improved; for when a horse is kindly treated and properly attended to, its temper is improved, and the improvement is transmitted.

The writer of the "*Russo-Turkish War*" informs us that no people on earth excel the Turks in their tender care and regard for the lower animals, and it is well-known that the Arabs bestow the utmost affection upon their horses, and the result is that the horse of the Arab is most docile—indeed, so much so, that the children may be seen fondling and playing with them. The Arab being passionately attached to his horse, the horse becomes so to its master.

It is related that on one occasion an Arab was taken prisoner and carried to a considerable distance from the encampment of his tribe, and having been bound hand and foot was placed in a tent a short distance from where his steed was picketed with a number of others. During the night the horse, with its teeth, bit the rope with which he was tied, and making its way to where its master lay bound, it seized the silk scarf or sash which was tied round his body and dashed off across the plain, and never halted till it placed its master safe at his tent, and then fell down exhausted, and expired.

Such devotion, such affection, could not have been developed by the whip or the spur of the jockey, but only by that kind treatment which the Author advocates.

He is of opinion, if, in addition to the May Shows, prizes were offered for the best kept and most orderly arranged stable, and judges appointed to visit and inspect the stables of the competitors periodically during the year, the owners of horses would find their animals better attended to, and their stables more orderly kept and economically managed.

Fully impressed with these views, the Author seriously appeals to noblemen, private gentlemen, railway companies, brewery companies, agriculturists, tradesmen, and others, to take this matter up, with a view to something practical being done.

> Hast thou given the horse his might?
> Hast thou clothed his neck with the quivering mane?
> Hast thou made him to leap as a locust?
> The glory of his snorting is terrible.
> He paweth in the valley and rejoiceth in his strength;
> He goeth out to meet the armed men;
> He mocketh at fear and is not dismayed,
> Neither turneth he back from the sword.
> The quiver rattleth against him,
> The flashing spear and javelin.
> He swalloweth the ground with fierceness and rage;
> Neither believeth he that it is the voice of the trumpet.
> As oft as the trumpet soundeth he saith, Aha!
> And he smelleth the battle afar off,
> The thunder of the captains and the shouting.
>
> *From the new revised edition of the Bible.*

THE FREE REGISTRY SYSTEM.

"Honesty is the best policy."

HEN the land had become desolated through the Wars of the Roses, and England lay half unpeopled by the feuds of York and Lancaster, labourers were few, and, as a consequence, higher wages were demanded; but the Government stepped in and declared the wages of labourers, artificers, and others should be the same as they were before the Civil Wars; and by the Act of Parliament, 5 Elizabeth, cap. 4, sec. 5, it was enacted:—

"That the justices of every shire, riding, and liberty, or the more part of them, being then resident within the same, and the sheriff, if he conveniently may, and every mayor and other head officer within any city or town corporate * * * * shall yearly in Easter sessions, or within six weeks next after, assemble and call unto them such discreet and grave persons as they shall think meet; and having respect to the plenty or scarcity of the time, and other circumstances, shall have authority to limit and appoint the wages as well of such of the said artificers, handicraftsmen, or any other labourer, servant, or workman whose wages in time past have been by any order or statute rated and appointed, as also the wages of all other labourers, artificers, workmen, or apprentices of husbandry which have not been rated, as they shall think meet by their discretion to be rated, limited or appointed."

By the 6th section of the same Act the rate of wages fixed was to be proclaimed, and by the 18th section it was enacted:—

"That any person giving more wages than that fixed was to be imprisoned for 10 days, and to forfeit £5, one half of the penalty to go to the King, and one half to the informer. And any person accepting more than the wages fixed, was by the 19th section to be imprisoned for 21 days."

This, then, was the origin of the "Statutes" or hiring fairs, to which all servants repaired annually to be engaged for the ensuing year, and the party hired received a retainer, or hiring fee.

This is still done in the enlistment of soldiers, the summoning of witnesses, and in securing the services of counsel, and did very well when the servants to be hired were few; but after the Labour Laws were amended, and the Statutes referred to were repealed, then servants were no longer compelled to remain in their own parish, but moved from place to place; and it became a common thing for unprincipled servants to take hiring fees from different masters and get drunk with the good conduct money.

Consequently these "mops," "fairs," and "statutes," became such nuisances, that in many places they have been entirely abolished, and those who wish to find good servants never think of going to such places for them.

But the "Statutes" being abolished the question comes, "Where are employers to find servants to suit them, and servants employers requiring the labour they have to dispose of?" This is one of the difficulties that naturally result during a transition state. The old institution has been swept away, but where is the new and better one to be found?

The Author, seeing the dilemma in which both masters and servants have been placed by the altered circumstances of the times, has—and he believes successfully—found the desideratum so anxiously desired, and so much needed by the public, and that is a Free Registry, where servants can record their wants, and employers their requirements, and both can be accommodated without trouble or expense.

To illustrate the benefits of a Free Registry to both employers and employés, let us suppose a gentleman wants a groom. Well, he does not know all the localities where grooms "most do congregate," and if he did he cannot go and question all and sundry as to whether or not they are "out of livery" and wish to don the buttons. But he can call at the Free Registry and state what he requires; and a groom desiring a re-engagement also calls, and the keeper of the Registry offices finds by investigation that the groom is just the individual required, and at once takes the necessary steps for securing for him the vacant situation. Here, then, both these parties have been spared loss of time, loss of money, and a vast amount of anxiety, which they would have had but for the Free Registry system, for without it they might never have met, and if they had there might have been delays and questionings that would have resulted in each forming of the other an unfavourable impression, which, even had an engagement taken place, would have marred their mutual respect for one another.

But the keeper of the Registry, by procuring all the necessary information, saves both parties the trouble and worry of character hunting and certificate finding. He knows his men and the situations they are qualified to fill—for the applicants know it will answer their purpose best to be explicit, and therefore communicate freely to him all that it is requisite for him to know, in order to enable him to form a correct estimate of the applicant's talents and abilities; and hence he has no difficulty in putting the right man in the right place.

EXPLANATION OF ILLUSTRATION.

BITS, MUZZLES, Etc.

———•———

1. Plain riding and driving bradoon, suitable for racing, hackney, and hunting purposes.
2. Hackney or riding bit.
3. Stage bit for buss or van.
4. Breathing bit.
5. Branch cheek lady's bit, with solid shell.
6. Revolving mouthed guard bit.
7. Pelhams.
8. Jointed mouth colt snaffle with one player.
9. Elbow carriage bit, to prevent horse biting rein billets.
10. Globe cheek cab or van bits.
11. Swivel or running bradoon.
12. Liverpool loose mouthed guard bit.
13. Bentinck bit.
14. Plain riding snaffle.
15. Loose mouth Buxton carriage bit.
16. Easy mouth riding bit.
17. Radical snaffle for riding, and much used in racing.
18. Gag bit (Instrument of Torture).
19. Riding snaffle.
20. Flat-ringed Wilson snaffle for riding and driving.
21. Round ringed Wilson snaffle for riding and driving.
22. Racing snaffle.
23. Stallion snaffle.
24. Breathing bit.
25. Double mouth snaffle.
26. Horse muzzle, solid leather.
27. Poultice boot.
28. Horse muzzle, wire.
29. Cavinson irons.
30. Horse muzzle, straps.

BITS MUZZLES &c.

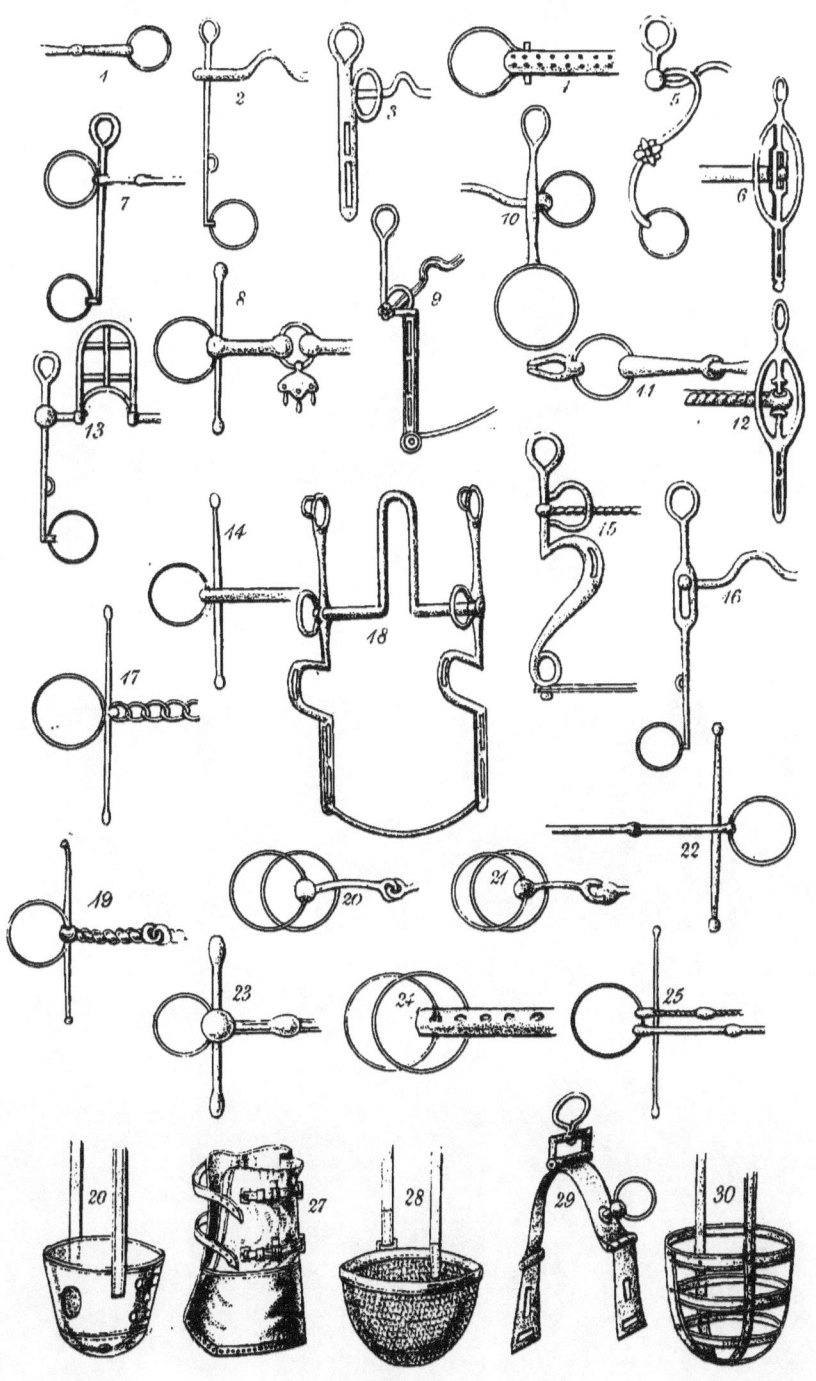

SADDLERS' SHOPS.

CONSIDERING the variety of articles and the diversity of colours to be met with in the Saddlery and Saddlers Ironmongery Trade, wonder has often been expressed that saddlers' shops do not present a more attractive appearance. In this respect they seem, as a rule, far behind the age. Of course there are in this, as in every other case, honourable exceptions; but still it must be admitted that, generally speaking, a saddler's shop presents a very dull contrast to either a draper's, or even an ironmonger's establishment. Now, why should it be so? The various coloured leathers used in modern saddlery are as bright and lively as are those of the choicest silks; and if displayed to advantage, and interspersed with made-up articles, plated-goods, gold and silver spurs, and ornaments—such as harness mountings—a very pleasing effect would be produced; and where there is room the whole might be rendered more attractive by equestrian models, in military uniforms, riding habits, and hunting costumes. The addition of hand and travelling bags, purses, and other fancy goods, would enhance the display, and impart an important feature to the stock. Horse cloths, rugs, and railway wrappers, might also be displayed in a manner that would be attractive; instead of being, as they may sometimes be seen, piled in a heap like a lot of soiled linen ready for the wash. Drapers know better how to show off their goods to advantage. They have lay figures, on which their dresses, shawls, jackets, and wraps, are artistically and gracefully displayed. Why should not saddlers do the same? For instance, why should not these two lay figures—one representing a lady, the other a gentleman, occupying the compartment of a railway carriage, with their wraps, rugs, and bags, all displayed to the best advantage, as for a journey? Such figures would be an excellent substitute for those live mechanics, sometimes found occupying the principal and prominent positions in saddlers' front shops.

SADDLERS' GUIDE.

IN here introducing a Harness Maker's Guide—or aid to the memory—in the form of a list in detail of the different parts of the various makes of harness, showing at a glance the *average* lengths and widths of strappings, as "cut out" and when "made up," the Author believes—and is advised—that he is satisfying or supplying a long felt requirement, not only to the trade in particular, but by rendering reliable assistance to the consumer and harness purchaser. Thus, the private gentlemen will be enabled, by referring to these pages and comparing the size of his horse and make of the vehicle, to describe his requirements correctly, either by post or otherwise, which alone will tend to facilitate matters and give satisfaction to all parties concerned. For instance, buyers are not all acquainted with the technical terms, sizes, and proportions of harness, the knowledge of which, with the aid of a tape-measure, or rule, will be found invaluable, particularly in buying ready made harness.

The practical harness maker will find these pages both useful and interesting, as a ready key and assistant, at times of pressure or otherwise, in the production of leatherwork. The new beginner in the trade, apprentice, and articled improver will thus be enabled to grasp, as it were, a life's difficulty, in a comparitively short period, after a careful perusal of and occasional reference to these pages, by catching the plot of the whole trade, and retaining the picture in his mind's eye without effort, fear, or the usual feeling of over responsibility. Not only will the apprentice, by digesting this guide, be perfecting and improving himself, but he will be enabled to show himself as a reliable source of profit to his master, whose best interests he is at all times and under all circumstances expected to have at heart, and thus it is hoped he will be enabled to use from the start that unusual expression in the early stages of adapting a calling for life, "I like the trade," and by his readiness in turning all materials to the best, quickest, and most profitable account, to blend all with that great desideratum, viz., smooth temper and willingness to learn.

In assisting the memory we economise time, and thus reduce the cost of production, which must tend to ensure the fair amount of profit due to the manufacturer, and which has not been always assured him.

Should any solitary item be omitted from among the many here given, the reader can easily supply the information required by comparing the other parts named, and with the aid of care and judgment he will find this Guide sufficient to answer every purpose.

The Author feels satisfied that the manufacturer will appreciate the extent of labour involved in this portion of the work, which sympathy will fully compensate the writer, whose original anxiety was simply (in adding to the literature of the trade) to fill the gap too long vacant.

To give everybody's system and measurements is an impossibility, therefore the following is offered as a fair and thoughtful *average for the manufacture of the best quality of harness only.*

AVERAGE MEASUREMENTS, "CUT OUT," AND "MADE UP," OF THE LEATHER WORK FOR THE VARIOUS PARTS OF HARNESS,* &c., &c., &c. :—

BRIDLE.
(GIG.)

	Pony.	Cob.	Full Size.
Head (cut out)	$20'' \times 1\frac{1}{4}''$	$21'' \times 1\frac{3}{8}''$	$22'' \times 1\frac{1}{2}''$
,, (made up)	$20''$	$21''$	$22''$
Split each end	$5\frac{1}{2}'' \times \frac{5}{8}''$	$6'' \times \frac{5}{8}\,\&\,\frac{3}{4}''$	$6\frac{1}{4}'' \times \frac{3}{4}''$
Noseband (cut out)	$27''$	$30''$	$32''$
,, (made up)	$25''$	$28''$	$30''$
,, Point	$5''$	$5\frac{1}{2}''$	$6''$
,, Middle	$10\frac{1}{2}''$	$11''$	$11\frac{1}{2}''$
,, Billet Spaces	(2) $1''$ each	(2) $1\frac{1}{8}''$ each	(2) $1\frac{1}{4}''$ each
,, Buckle End or Back	$7\frac{1}{2}''$	$9\frac{1}{4}''$	$10\frac{1}{4}''$

* In the following Measurements it is as well to point out that (′) indicates feet, (″) inches, and (×) by, thus $20'' \times 1\frac{1}{4}''$ means 20 inches by 1¼ inches.

BRIDLE—*(continued).*

	Pony.	Cob.	Full Size.
Cheek and Billet, all round (cut out)	26" × ⅝"	28" × ¾"	31" × ¾"
Cheeks (made up)	6"	7"	8"
From Billet point to top of cheek, centre of buckle, punch hole or crue	17"	18"	19"
From centre to centre of cheek crue holes	6½"	7½"	8½"
Billets	9"	9½"	10¼"
Winker Straps, round (made up)	12"	13"	14"
Winker Straps (plain)	11"	12"	13"
" " (points)	5"	5½"	6"
Face Piece	10½"	11½"	12½"
Throat-band, plain (cut out)	20"	22"	23"
Made up	17"	18"	19"
Throat-band, with swivels (cut out)	23"	25"	26"
Made up	17"	18"	19"
Bearing Rein (flat part, cut out)	48"	54"	60"
Bearing Rein (round part)	20"	21"	22"
Bearing Rein (prepared buckle end)	3"	3¼"	3½"
Bearing Rein (prepared ring end)	4"	4¼"	4½"

BRADOON BEARING REIN.[*]
(CARRIAGE.)

	Full Size.
Centre (cut out)	6' × ¾"
Round parts (2)	2' 6" each.
" " (made up)	1' 10" each.
Billet for centre of Bridle Head (cut out)	7" × ⅝"

Sewn on head, leaving 6" from centre of split.

SHAFT TUGS.
(SPRING CART OR CAB.)

Tops (cut out)	2' 6" × 1¾" or 2"
" (made up)	1' 2"
Lining (cut out)	1' 1½"

[*] The Author thinks there is a good opening for improvement in Bearing Reins; a hidden spring (india-rubber or otherwise) would meet the case.

SHAFT TUGS.

(GIG.)

	Pony.	Cob.	Full Size.
Top (cut out) ...	2' 0" × 1¼"	2' 2" × 1⅜"	2' 4" × 1½"
" (made up, hole to hole ...	11"	1' 0"	1' 1"
Lining (cut out)...	10½"	11½"	1' 0½"

HAME TUGS.

	Pony.	Cob.	Full Size.
Lay or Body (cut out)...	1' 4" × 1⅜"	1' 5" × 1½"	1' 6" × 1⅝"
" " (made up)	8"	8½"	9"
Safes	10½"	11"	1' 0½"

BREECHBAND.

(SHORT.)

	Pony.	Cob.	Full Size.
Body (cut out)	6' 4" × 1¼"	6' 7" × 1⅜"	7' 4" × 1½"
" (made up)	3'	3' 2"	3' 6"
Hip tugs (cut out) ...	8½" × ⅝"	9" × ¾"	9½" × ¾" & 7⅞"
Hip tugs (made up)	4¼"	4½"	4¾"
Shaft straps (cut out)...	2' 6" × 1"	2' 8" × 1⅛"	3" × 1¼"
Shaft straps (made up)	2'	2' 4"	2' 6"

If full lined, double this length, in one piece.

	Pony.	Cob.	Full Size.
Hip strap ...	3' 10" × 1¼"	4' 0" × 1½"	4' 2" × 1⅝"
Split (each end)	1' 3" × ⅝"	1' 4" × ¾"	1' 5" × ¾" & ⅞"

BREECHBAND.

(LONG.)

	Pony.	Cob.	Full Size.
Body	8' × 1⅛"	9' × 1¼"	10' 6" 1 × ⅜"
Tapered at each end, average...	2' × ⅞"	2' × 1"	2' 1⅛"

BREECHBAND.

(BROUGHAM.)

	Full Size.
Body	7′ × $1\frac{3}{8}$″
Tapered	1′ 10″ to $1\frac{1}{8}$″ point.
Two Slip Tugs (cut out)	2′ × $1\frac{1}{8}$″
" " " (made up)	9′

Remaining length to loose out or take up; surplus points not shown.

Patterns supplied by the Author.

BREECHBAND.

("EXTENSION.")

Suitable for Gig, Tandem, or Brougham. The neatest and most useful Breechband made.

Body (full size, cut out) 3′ × $1\frac{3}{4}$″, $1\frac{1}{4}$″ lay on top all through, punched at end for buckle (roller preferred) to lie on the body, sufficient space left for loop front and back of buckle.

Hip Tugs (ordinary length), sewn $5\frac{1}{2}$″ from each end of body.

Two 12″ points by $1\frac{1}{4}$″ sewn on $1\frac{7}{8}$″ ring for buckling to breechband body.

Two Hip Tugs on rings (usual make).

Breechband Straps (required less than ordinary length).

Patterns supplied by the Author.

BREECHBAND.

(CARRIAGE.)

To connect to Hame Tug.

	Pony.		*Cob.*		*Full Size.*
Body (end to end, made up) ...	7′ 6″ × $1\frac{1}{8}$″	...	8′ 6″ × $1\frac{1}{4}$″	...	9′ 6″ × $1\frac{3}{8}$″
First Hip Tug (from centre of seat	1′ 4″ × $\frac{7}{8}$″	...	1′ 5″ × 1″		1′ 7″ × $1\frac{1}{8}$″ or $1\frac{1}{4}$″
Second Hip Tug (from other tug) ...	$4\frac{1}{2}$″ × $\frac{7}{8}$″	...	$5\frac{1}{2}$″ × 1″		$6\frac{1}{2}$″ × $1\frac{1}{8}$″ or $1\frac{1}{4}$″
Trace Carrier (made up, sewn in bottom row, centre of tugs)	$5\frac{1}{2}$″	...	6″	...	$6\frac{1}{2}$″

Punch first hole of Breechband 5″ from end, and 5 holes each end, 2″ apart, for buckling to Hame Tug.

KICKING STRAP.
(FOUR WHEELER.)

Pony.	Cob.	Full Size.
4′ 9″ × 1⅛″	5′ 6″ × 1¼″	6′ 2″ × 1⅜″

KICKING STRAP.
(DOG CART OR GIG.)

Pony.	Cob.	Full Size.
4′ 4″ × 1⅛″	5′ × 1¼″	5′ 6″ × 1⅜″

KICKING STRAP TUG.

	Pony.	Cob.	Full Size.
Made up	1′ 0½″	1′ 1″	1′ 1½″

HAME TUG.
(CARRIAGE.)

	Pony.	Cob.	Full Size.
Cut out	2′ 3″ × 1⅜″	2′ 7″ × 1½″	3′ 0″ × 1⅝″
Made up	1′ 1″	1′ 3″	1′ 6″
Safe	1′ 4½″	1′ 7″	1′ 10″

The pipe loop and sewing of the lay should be equally divided in length.

All loops should be well clear of the buckles to facilitate the unbuckling, which saves time and wear.

	Pony.	Cob.	Full Size.
Short Tug or Bearer (cut out)	8″ × 1″	8½″ × 1⅛″	9″ × 1¼″
Short Tug (made up)	4″	4¼″	4½″
Bellyband (off-side, made up)	1′ 10″ × ⅞″	2′ 0″ × 1″	2′ 4″ × 1⅛″
Bellyband (near-side, made up)	1′ 0″ × ⅞″	1′ 2″ × 1″	1′ 4″ × 1⅛″

HAME STRAP.
(CARRIAGE.)

Pony.	Cob.	Full Size.
1′ 8″ × ⅝″	1′ 9″ × ¾″	1′ 10″ × ¾″

Roller Buckles.

MARTINGALE.

	Pony.	Cob.	Full Size.
Body (cut out)	2' 6" × ⅞"	2' 9" × 1"	3' 2" × 1⅛"
Billet (cut out)	1'	1' 1"	1' 1½"
Patent Tab	5¼"	5½"	6½"

To Pattern.

CRUPPER.

(GIG.)

	Pony.	Cob.	Full Size.
Body	1' 5" × 1⅜"	1' 8" × 1½"	1' 10" × 1⅝"
Split	5½"	6½"	7½"
Strap	2' 10" × ⅞"	3' 3" × 1"	3' 6" × 1⅛"

CRUPPER.

(CARRIAGE.)

	Pony.	Cob.	Full Size.
Body	1' 7" × 1⅜"	1' 9" × 1½"	2' 0" × 1⅝"
Split	5½"	6½"	7½
Strap	2' 10" × ⅞"	3' 3" × 1"	3' 6" × 1⅛"

Pipe Loop and Winker Patterns sent on application.

HIP STRAP.

(CARRIAGE.)

With Off-side and Near-side Trace Carrier.

	Pony.	Cob.	Full Size.
Off-side Strap	3' 8" × 1"	3' 10" × 1⅛"	4' 2" × 1¼"
Off Carrier	1' 2" × 1"	1' 3" × 1⅛"	1' 4" × 1¼"
Near Carrier	1' 0" × 1"	1' 1" × 1⅛"	1' 2" × 1¼"

GIRTH.

(GIG.)

	Pony.	Cob.	Full Size.
Body (off-side)	$1' 10'' \times 1\frac{5}{8}''$	$2' 0'' \times 1\frac{3}{4}''$	$2' 2'' \times 2''$
Point (near-side, or strap)	$1' 4'' \times 1''$	$1' 5'' \times 1\frac{1}{8}''$	$1' 6'' \times 1\frac{1}{4}''$
Chape (if not all through)	$10\frac{1}{2}'' \times 1''$	$11\frac{1}{2}'' \times 1\frac{1}{8}''$	$1' 0'' \times 1\frac{1}{4}''$

Three loops, equal distances, the first well away from the buckle.

Girths, as a rule, are cut too wide, hence the many jibbing and rearing horses. Wide and clumsy girths chafe, irritate, and punish the horse; all girths should be cut out of prime pliable leather, and if for best harness (full lined) a stiff lay should be run from end to end, nicely rounded, and half the width of the body.

A short strap or large loop attached to the girth for the backband to run through, protects the forelegs of the horse.

All girths and straps should be fitted well up into the saddle, thus strengthening the flap.

GIRTH.

(CARRIAGE.)

	Pony.	Cob.	Full Size.
Body, plain or patent (off side)	$2' 8'' \times 1\frac{1}{2}''$	$3' 0'' \times 1\frac{5}{8}''$	$3' 3'' \times 1\frac{3}{4}''$
Body, plain or patent (near side)	$1' 1'' \times 1\frac{1}{2}''$	$1' 0'' \times 1\frac{5}{8}''$	$1' 2\frac{1}{2}'' \times 1\frac{3}{4}''$
Strap	$1' 4'' \times 1''$	$1' 5'' \times 1\frac{1}{8}''$	$1' 6'' \times 1\frac{1}{4}''$

If straight pads, "pad tops" should be cut $\frac{1}{4}''$ wider than the girth body.

PAD TOPS.

Pony.	Cob.	Full Size.
1' 4"	1' 5"	1' 6"

Patterns forwarded.

Apply to the Author—

E. W. GOUGH, Walsall.

PAD-END POINTS.

Pony.	Cob.	Full Size.
8″ × 1″	9″ × 1⅛″	10″ × 1¼″

DOCK.

Pony.	Cob.	Full Size.
1′ 3″ × 2¼″ tapered to 1⅜″	1′ 4″ × 2½″ tapered to 1½″	1′ 5″ & 1′ 6″ × 2¾″ tapered to 1⅝″

All Docks should be large and stuffed with linseed, the latter being of a moist and healing nature, thus preventing wounds under the tail, and displays of bad temper in both horse and driver.

A complete set of patterns for above, and pipes, winkers, &c., &c., forwarded on application to the Author.

HAME STRAPS.
(GIG.)

	Pony.	Cob.	Full Size.
Top (roller buckle)	1′ 6″ × ⅝″	1′ 7″ × ¾″	1′ 9″ × ¾″
Bottom	1′ 7″ × ⅝″	1′ 8″ × ¾″	1′ 10″ × ¾″

Hames should be carefully fitted to each collar by the hame maker, thus ensuring attention to the chief points, viz., top, bottom, and draft.

FLAT DRIVING REINS.
(GIG.)

	Pony.	Cob.	Full Size.
Black part	5′ 6″ × ¾″	6′ 0″ × ⅞″	7′ 0″ × 1″
Hand part	5′ 6″ × ¾″	6′ 0″ × ⅞″	6′ 6″ × 1″
Middle splices (nicely rounded)	3½″	4″	4½″
Billets	11″ × ¾″	1′ 0″ × ⅞″	1′ 1″ × 1″
Sewn on, one loop (clear of buckle)	2¼″	2½″	2¾″

REINS.
(CARRIAGE.)

	Pony.	Cob.	Full Size.
Draft part	5' 6" × 3/4"	6' 6" × 7/8"	7' 6" × 1"
Coupling	4' 6" × 3/4"	5' 6" × 7/8"	6' 6" × 1"
Billets	1' 1" × 3/4"	1' 1" × 7/8"	1' 2" × 1"
Hand parts	5' 6" × 3/4"	6' 0" × 7/8"	6' 6" × 1"
Lined draft	1' 7" × 3/4"	1' 9" × 7/8"	2' 1" × 1"

THE "CENTAUR" SAFETY PATENT BILLETLESS REINS.

(Invented, Patented, and Manufactured by the Author.)

No Buckle—Are absolutely safe for general wear.
No Chain—Horse cannot bite them at the bit.
No Loop—Perfectly simple, being without complication.
No Tong—Leather cannot be ripped in wear.
No Punch-Holes—To weaken the leather.

The advantages of the above reins are palpable at the first glance—

1. Are fixed in much less time.
2. Better appearance—The perfection of neatness.
3. More durable—Will wear three times as long as the ordinary billets: in fact, can scarcely wear out.
4. Can be adapted to any existing reins.
5. Are cheaper.
6. For trotting purposes, they are simply invaluable.

The reins being the most important item of the "Turn Out," we have no hesitation in predicting that the *trade* will specially value the principle of the above, and private gentlemen will indeed feel, from the moment the Patent is attached, that they have the horse "well in hand." The Author will adapt any existing reins as above at a nominal cost. The principle can be fitted to hackney reins, pillar reins, coupling reins, dog leads, dog couples, dog slips, and other analagous purposes.

TRACES.
(CARRIAGE.)

	Pony.	Cob.	Full Size.
Gig	4' 8" × 1 1/4"	5' 4" × 1 3/8"	5' 9" × 1 1/2"
Phaeton	5' 0" × 1 1/4"	5' 10" × 1 3/8"	6' 2" × 1 1/2"
Carriage	5' 6" × 1 1/4"	5' 10" × 1 3/8"	6' 2 1/2" × 1 1/2"
Hand leather or Draw (made up)	4"	4 1/4"	4 1/2"

Trace rings extra.

BACKBAND.
(GIG.)

	Pony.	Cob.	Full Size.
Made up	7' 2" × $1\frac{1}{4}$"	7' 7" × $1\frac{3}{8}$"	7' 9" × $1\frac{1}{2}$"
Point	1' 4"	1' 5"	1' 6"
Middle	2' 11"	3' 2"	3' 6"

3 loops—1st loop well clear of buckle, to facilitate buckling and unbuckling; last loop 9in. from buckle, in full size; other sizes in proportion. All loops equal distances.

BACKBAND.
(TILBURY.)

	Full Size.
Made up to buckle at each side	7' 6" × $1\frac{1}{2}$"
Bellyband, roller buckle each end, and 3 loops each side	2' 10" × $1\frac{1}{2}$"
Backband middle	3' 0"
Point each end of same	1' 6"
Reverse sewing	0' 9"

BACKBAND.
(CAB.)

Made up	8' 0" × $1\frac{3}{4}$" or $1\frac{5}{8}$"
Middle	3' 2"
Point	1' 7"

Sewn 4 rows all through. 2' in centre sometimes not sewn.

BACKBAND.
(CAR.)

Made up	8' 0" × $1\frac{3}{4}$" and $1\frac{5}{8}$", sometimes $1\frac{1}{2}$"
Middle	4' 0"
Point	1' 7"

TRACES.
(CAB.)

	Full Size.
Made up	4' 6" × $1\frac{3}{4}$" or $1\frac{5}{8}$" and upwards.

Swivel and chain 1' 1", at end 5 links.

TRACES.
(CAR.)

	Full Size.
Made up	5' 0" × 1$\frac{3}{4}$" or 1$\frac{5}{8}$"

Chains 1' 1", at end 5 links.

TRACES.
(TANDEM.)

Pony.	Cob.	Full Size.
6' 6"	... ... 7' 6"	... ... 8' 6"
7' 6" × 1$\frac{1}{4}$" ...	... 8' 6" × 1$\frac{3}{8}$" ...	... 9' 6" × 1$\frac{1}{2}$"

With spring hooks.

REINS.
(CAB.)

Each side	19' 6" × 1"

REINS.
(CAR.)

Each side	12' 0" × 1"

REINS.
(TANDEM.)

Made up each side ... 20' × $\frac{3}{4}$" ... 22' × $\frac{7}{8}$" bare, 25' × $\frac{7}{8}$" full.

Spliced and made as best gig reins.

POLE STRAPS.

Pony.	Cob.	Full Size.
4' 0" × 1$\frac{1}{4}$" ...	... 4' 6" × 1$\frac{3}{4}$" ...	... 5' 2" × 1$\frac{1}{2}$" or 1$\frac{3}{4}$"

Sewn four rows all through (on the bend). Bend sometimes not sewn.

BREAST COLLARS.

	Pony.	Cob.	Full Size.
Body (end to end)	$3' 0'' \times 2''$	$3' 6'' \times 2\frac{1}{4}''$	$4' 2'' \times 2\frac{1}{2}''$

Should at all times be sewn on the bend, and made firm in centre, say 16, 17 or 18in., so as to prevent "break or pinch in the body." Lining should be fixed after body is sewn, and being a selected piece of bag hide, spotted on top and left loose at bottom prevents friction.

2 carrier tugs ... ... $5'' \times 1''$

Made up for gig size. Others in proportion.

Wither strap (made up) ... ... $2' 10'' \times 1''$

Small pad in centre and 1" rein dee or swivel each side. Carriage breast collars have 4 carrier tugs $5'' \times 1\frac{1}{4}''$, bellyband $2' 4'' \times 1\frac{3}{8}''$, and points $1' 4''$, made as above.

AVERAGE WEIGHTS OF THE LEATHER WORK, "CUT OUT" FOR SET OF SINGLE HARNESS:—

	Pony.	Cob.	Full Size.
Plain	$8\frac{1}{2}$lb	10lb	$12\frac{1}{2}$lb
Part lined	$9\frac{1}{2}$lb	$11\frac{1}{2}$lb	$13\frac{1}{2}$lb
Full lined	12lb	$13\frac{1}{2}$lb	$15\frac{1}{2}$lb

Including pipes and loops.

VAN OR SPRING CART.
(YORKSHIRE.)

Bridle. Full Size.

Head $2' 0'' \times 2''$, split 7" each side, leaving straps or points 1" wide.

Cheeks and Billets all round $2' 7'' \times 1''$.

Cheek $8\frac{1}{2}''$.

Billet $1' 0''$.

Throat band, $2' 2''$ cut out, made up $1' 8''$.

Noseband, cut out $5'$ double $\times 1\frac{3}{8}''$, made up $2' 6''$; point $6''$, two $1\frac{1}{4}''$ spaces; middle $1' 0''$, one loop on each space; one loop (stout) at buckle (well away).

Front $1' 1\frac{1}{2}'' \times 1\frac{1}{4}''$, clear centre.

Winker straps $1' 4'' \times 1\frac{1}{4}''$, split $9''$.

Round ditto, $1' 4''$ and $1' 2''$ face piece.

BREAST PLATE.
(VAN.)

Cut out ... ... 3' 2" × 1⅛" ... 1' 1½" billet × 1¼"
Patent leather tab, cut to pattern, 6".

GIRTH.
(VAN.)

Body (cut out) ... 2' 6" × 2¼"—good selected leather.
Lay ... 1¾"—all through girth—well into saddle.
Point or strap (near side) 1' 6" × 1⅜".

BACKBAND
(VAN.)

Made up ... ... 9' 0" × 1¾" or 2"

SHAFT TUGS.
(VAN.)

Top (cut out) ... ... 2' 8" × 1¾" or 2"
Linings .. .. 1' 2½" × 1¾" or 2"

(3 good metal loops.)

CRUPPER.
(VAN.)

Strap ... ... 3' 6" × 1¼"
Body ... ... 2' 0" × 2¼" split 8"
Lay ... ... 1' 2½" × 1¼"
Dock* ... ... 1' 5" × 3" middle

* Tapered to 1", stuffed with linseed.

BREECHBAND.
(VAN.)

Body (made up)	$3'\ 8'' \times 2\frac{1}{2}''$	(ring to tug $8\frac{1}{2}''$)
4 Tugs	$6'' \times 1\frac{1}{4}''$	
2 Hip straps	$4'\ 2'' \times 1\frac{1}{4}''$	each, stout
2 Shaft straps	$3'\ 0'' \times 1\frac{3}{8}''$	each, stout

HAME STRAPS.
(VAN.)

Bottom strap	$2'\ 0'' \times 1''$	(roller buckle)
Top strap	$1'\ 10'' \times 1''$	(roller buckle)

No Traces. Hames with chain and spring hook preferred to all Van sets.

REINS.
(VAN.)

$15' \times 1''$ each side ... ...   Billets $1'\ 0'' \times 1''$

AVERAGE WEIGHTS OF LEATHER WORK AS "CUT OUT" FOR SET OF VAN HARNESS, 16℔. (SOLID). LESS HAND PARTS AND TRACES, AS ABOVE:—

TROTTING HARNESS.

($4\frac{1}{2}$℔., including leather work and furniture.)

Breast collar made up—

Body, $3'\ 0'' \times 1\frac{1}{2}''$; traces run round same and spliced in centre, $4''$ traces rounded $5'$ from end of breast collar, with buckle at end, and $1'\ 10'' \times 1''$ billet.

Wither strap, sunk stitches, $2'\ 8'' \times \frac{7}{8}''$ tapered to $\frac{5}{8}''$

Martingale, crupper split $8''$, and made $3'\ 10'' \times 1\frac{1}{4}''$ tapered to $\frac{3}{4}''$, well tapered down, linseed dock sewn on end, thick in centre.

Pad, all in one piece, $3'\ 8'' \times 1\frac{3}{8}''$ (known as a leather plate), no tree or plates. Pad consists of a stout piece of leather through which the backband runs, backband hole being $8''$ each side of centre socket; terrets are sewn on top lining and well blocked up; point sewn on each end of flap $12'' \times \frac{3}{4}''$; good loose girth, buckle at each side, $1'\ 7''$ long $\times 1\frac{1}{4}''$; bridle, no winkers; all strapping $\frac{1}{2}''$ wide reins; strong $1''$ and $\frac{1}{2}''$ strip run through; hand parts under side as connected loops for grip. Average weight of ordinary trotting harness, 6℔.

The Author will supply any patterns desired, in either zinco, leather, or paper, or will send by post a model set, as above.

FOUR IN HAND.

(FULL SIZE HARNESS.)

The foregoing pages will give details for strapping, &c.

Bridles, same as full size gig.

The wheeler horses have centre territt in head extra.

Leading traces are 4' 6" made up, exclusive of cockeye or spring-hook.

Wheeler traces, same as carriage.

Leading pads somewhat lighter than wheeler.

Leading reins 24' × ⅞" full each side.

CART HARNESS, &c., &c.

(SHAFT SET.)

	Full Size.
Bridle head (cut out)...	1' 10" × 1½"
Made up ...	1' 10"
Front (cut out) ...	1' 4½" × 1½"
Made up ...	1' 3"
Ear pieces (cut out) ...	8" × 1½"
Made up ...	4"
Winker straps ...	1' 4" × ⅞"
Cheek ...	2' 6" × 1½"
Made up ...	1' 2"
Noseband ...	1' 10" × 3¼" centre
Made up ...	1' 3"
Throat band ...	3' 11" × 1¼"
Made up ...	3' 8"
Near side rein ...	2' 3" × 1¼"
Made up ...	1' 8"
Off side rein ...	5' 3" × 1¼"
Made up ...	5'
Reins* (cut out) ...	25' 0"
Made up ...	24' 0" × 1"

*Average 12' each side.

HOUSINGS FOR SADDLE, COLLAR, AND WINKERS, AND SAFE LEATHERS.

To Patterns sent, on Application.

GIRTHS.

Cut out, 1 front ... 5' 6", Made up ... 4' 10" × 1½"
Ditto 1 back ... 5' 8",   „   ... 5' 0" × 1½"

GIRTH STRAPS.

Cut out (2) ... 1' 11" × 1½", Made up ... ... 1' 11"

SAFE LEATHERS.

Cut out (2) ... ... 10" × 8½", Made up ... 10" × 8½"

CHINE STRAPS.

1' 1½" × 1½", Made up ... ... 10" × 1½"

CRUPPER.

Body, cut out ... 2' 6", Made up ... 2' 2" × 3½" or 4"
Lay or top, cut out 2' 0",   „   ... 1' 8" × 2¾" or 3"
Rounded.

HIP STRAP.

Cut out ... ... 2' 6", Made up ... ... 2' 2" × 1½"

CRUPPER STRAP.

Cut out ... ... 1' 3", Made up ... ... 1' 3" × 1¾"

COLLAR.

To measure.

BREECHBAND.

Body, cut out 5′ 8″, made up 4′ 8″ × 3½″ or 4″.
Lay, or top, cut out 4′ 6″ × 3″ or 3½″, to run round ends to underside.
Tugs, cut out 1′ 10″, made up 7″ × 1½″.
Hip strap, cut out 4′ 3″, made up 4′ 0″ × 1½″.
Safe leathers, made up 1′ 0″ × 3″.

BELLYBAND

Cut out ...   ... 3′ 8″ made up ...   ... 2′ 10″ × 3″ or 3¼″

HAME STRAP.

Cut out   ... 2′ 10″, made up   2′ 7″ × 1¼″, roller buckle.

CHAIN OR LEADER SET.
BRIDLE.

If with narrow noseband, cut out 1′ 10″ made up 1′ 3″ × 1¾″, other parts same as shaft bridle, or less winkers, according to order and pattern.

CRUPPER.

Body, cut out 4′ 0″ × 4″ or 4½″, made up, split at each end.
Dock, 1′ 5″ × 3″, made up, 6″.
Chapes 7″ × 1½″.
Hip straps, cut out 2′ 6″, made up 2′ 2″ × 1½″.
Lay, cut out 9″, made up 6″ × 3¾″ or 3½″.
Loose hip straps, made up 2′ 9″ × 1¾″.
Hip strap tugs, made up 5″ × 1½″.
Loose tugs, cut out 1′ 8″, made up 1′ 5″ × 1½″ or 1¼″.

BACKBAND.

Cut out 3′ 4″, made up 2′ 10″ × 4½″ or 4″, safe leathers each end 11″ × 8½″, loops 1′ 0″ × 2¼″.

BOW BACKBAND.

From eye to eye ... 4' 0" Made up ... ... $4\frac{1}{2}''$ or 4"

PLOUGH BACKBAND.

Made up 4' 0" × $3\frac{1}{4}''$, safes 7" × 5" each end, and hooks.

BELLYBAND.

Cut out ... ... 3' 2" Made up ... ... 2' 8" × $2\frac{1}{2}''$

LEADING REIN.

Cut out ... ... 7' 0" Made up ... ... 6' 6" × $1\frac{1}{4}''$
Billet 1' 0".

COUPLING REIN.

Cut out   ... ... 2' 8" Made up ... ... 2' 6" × $1\frac{1}{4}''$
Billet   ... ... 1' 0"   "   ... ... 1' 0" × $1\frac{1}{4}''$
Short side ... ... 1' 4"   "   ... ... 1' 0" × $1\frac{1}{4}''$
Billet   ... ... 1' 0"   "   ... ... 1' 0" × $1\frac{1}{4}''$

CART HEAD COLLARS.

Head (cut out) ... 4' 9" Made up ... ... 4' 4" × $1\frac{3}{4}''$
Nose   ... ... 3' 9"   "   ... ... 3' 4" × $1\frac{3}{4}''$
Stays   ... ...   9"   "   ... ...   9" × $1\frac{3}{4}''$
Throat band ... ... 1' 11"   "   ... ... 1' 8" × 1"
Throat strap ... ...   8"   "   ... ...   8" × 1"

NECK STRAP.

Cut out ... .. 4' 3" Made up ... 3' 6" × $1\frac{3}{4}''$ or 2"
Cow strap (kicking) 3' 6" × $1\frac{3}{4}''$, made up with bottom square.

BREAST PLATE.

3' 9", made up 2' 10" to pattern.
Billet 10", made up 10".

LENGTHS AND PARTS.

Measurements and Patterns of Hackney head collars, bridles, girths, chapes, &c., &c., sent on application to the Author.

Address—E. W. GOUGH,
"CENTAUR" Harness and Saddlery Works,
Walsall.

HOODWINKS.

Sacking ... ... 2' 0" × 1' 4" made up ... ... 1' 8"
(With or without eyes).

NOSEBAGS.

Sacking, or cocoa matting 3' 4" all round, for 1' 0" bottom.
Solid leather, 3' 3" all round, for 1' 0" bottom.
Straps, off side, made up 3' 6" × 1¼"; near side, made up 11" × 1¼"

SHAFT CLOTH

(OR WHEELER.)

Oilcloth, titling, or felt (full size) ... ... 5' 0" × 3' 0"

CHAIN CLOTH

(OR LEADER.)

Oil cloth, titling, or felt (full size) ... ... 5' 0" × 5' 0"
(Required extra long if to cover collar).

PIT GEARS.

Cap, made up (average full size)	1' 6" × 9½"
Backband	2' 8" × 3½"
Crupper	3' 10" × 3½"
Ditto, with dock and hip straps, made up	2' 0" × 1¼"
Bellyband	2' 6" × 2"
Loose hip straps (made up)	2' 6" × 1¼"
Ditto tugs	1' 0"

Collar, Hames, Chains, &c., to measure.

LOOSE HIP STRAPS.

(FOR LEADER OR CHAIN GEARS.)

Body (made up)	1' 10" × 1½"
Billet	2' 6" × 1½"

Sewn on ring, with hook for attaching to dee or triangle.

A complete set of trade patterns, suitable for all kinds and sizes of harness, and the different parts, including Housings, Side Pieces, Side Pads, Loops, Pipes, Safes, Docks, Winkers, Face-pieces, Breast-plates, Hame-covers, Lays, Chapes, &c.; and of all classes and makes of Leggings, Leglets, Overalls, and Footballs.

Sample specimens of all the various makes and metals comprised in the harness and furniture of every design or pattern; complete advice, lists and prices of saddler's tools; monograms and crests from customers own seal, *sent to any part of the world, on application.*

The Author is now perfecting a complete set of safety light harness made up *entirely without buckles*, and which will be on view at his show rooms. Pattern set forwarded on application.

WEB HARNESS.

The joint production of the Author and Arthur Hart, Esq. (proprietor of the celebrated Viney Bridge Mills, Crewkerne, Somerset)*. The above Harness is made entirely throughout

---

* The Viney Bridge Mills and Web Manufactory claim to be the oldest of the kind in the Kingdom, and the Author can speak from long experience of the productions that are turned out being SECOND TO NONE. The above Firm

the whole set of Web, which web has been specially invented and manufactured for the purpose by Mr. Hart. It is made of fawn, white, and various coloured circular web, woven together, which, having a round selvedge edge, cannot cause the least possible friction or pain to the horse. It is made in all widths, suitable for the different parts of harness, and the whole set is made up extremely light, so that an invalid can lift it on and off the animal. The above Harness is intended for *Country Residences, Convalescent Homes, Homes for Incurables, Hospitals, &c., &c.*, and will be found very suitable for Circus use, Public Processions, and Horsebreakers.

Its advantages are—*Lightness, Cleanliness, Durability,* and *Cheapness,* and it will be found extremely *Humane* for trade purposes (occasional use), where the horse is suffering from tender skin, and is not bad enough to be idle. In fact, the "Humane Web Harness" will be most useful and handy in a variety of ways, and no stable should be without it.

For particulars and price of a complete set of Web Harness, send size of horse, and description of vehicle used, to the Author. Address—

E. W. GOUGH,

"CENTAUR" Harness and Saddlery Works,

Walsall.

---

was established in 1789, therefore it is nearly 100 years old, which fact must speak for itself, and indeed recommend itself to all users of Web, which article alone is a most important item in the Saddlery business, and the Author feels it his duty to render the Trade all the assistance in his power by calling attention to so important an item as WEB, AND WHERE TO GET IT. The Crewkerne Works, or Mills as they are properly called, are very extensive in both plant and machinery, and the whole is most admirably situated and convenient for the production and delivery of every article in that class of business; in fact, many of the newest productions emanate from the Crewkerne (Viney Bridge) Mills, where the reader can see the perfection of Spinning Machinery in full motion, can go through the weaving sheds, drying sheds, bleaching sheds, bleaching grounds, stores, and twine walks, and can study the departments specially devoted to saddlery productions—those connected with upholstery and kindred trades. To enumerate the whole of Mr. Hart's specialities would almost command a chapter of itself, but the Author will confine himself to the principal items manufactured, viz.—Chair Webs and Cocoa Bindings; Upholstery and Packing Twines; Girth, Roller, Brace, Body-belt, Straining, Rein, Halter, Tent, Tray, Pack, Packing, Circular, Kersey, Elevator, &c., Webs of every description in Jute, Cotton, Linen, Wool, and Union, for Saddlery, Upholstery, and other purposes. Mr. Hart also manufactures Girths, Rollers, Surcingles, Braces, Body-belts, Halters, &c. He is at present very busy with large Government orders, which fact speaks or itself **as to the extent of the establishment.**

A FEW NECESSARY HINTS AND RECEIPTS.

Not intended for encroaching upon the sphere of the horsebreaker or Vet.

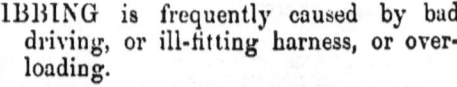JIBBING is frequently caused by bad driving, or ill-fitting harness, or overloading.

STUMBLING arises sometimes from having picked up a stone, or weakness and over-work; at all times the blacksmith or vet. should be consulted; rest and bandages are good treatment.

SHYING is often caused by nervousness; the horse should never be thrashed, but coaxed, and gradually brought up to the object shied at; or hand the animal over to a horse-breaker for a time.

BITING is sometimes the result of teazing in the stable or general careless treatment, and when once acquired by the horse, is seldom, if ever, cured. The muzzle or other protection should be in constant use.

RUNNING AWAY.—If it is a known fault, care must be taken respecting the kind or make of bit used. If the habit be acquired by a high-spirited horse, the animal should never be left alone in the street.

KICKING.—The kicking horse must be mastered by stratagem; sometimes it arises from playfulness, and sometimes from abuse. Good sound harness, and an experienced driver, are absolutely necessary.

REARING.—The rearer should never be struck on the top of the head, but turned round, or its leg strapped up.

CANKER IN THE MOUTH is often caused by a rusty bit. Use a weak solution of lemon, or gargle with white wine vinegar ½ pint, burnt alum 1 oz., common salt 1 oz., Bole armenic ½ oz., mix and shake in bottle for use. Mop the mouth all round morning and night; let the horse fast for one hour after each dressing.

For Blain.—Veterinary surgeons lance freely and deeply, and administer aperient medicines. Washing is a good thing, but time must be taken over it.

Barbs or Paps should never be touched by any instrument; cooling medicine removes them.

Lampas.—The roof of the mouth may be slightly lanced, or aperient medicine administered; but heated irons should never be applied on account of destroying the sensibility of the mouth.

Spasmodic Colic.—The horse should be walked about and friction used to the belly. The advice is—two ounce doses of spirit of turpentine, with an ounce of laudanum and spirit of nitrous æther in warm water or gruel. In the event of the above failing, the animal is bled and warm injections are administered. The long continuation of the spasmodic action is liable to produce entanglement of the bowels, then the case is hopeless.

Worms may be cured by small doses of tartar emetic, or calomel with a little ginger being given to the horse half-an-hour before his first meal, and worked off with linseed oil or aloes.

Catarrh or Cold can be removed by a few mashes and a little medicine.

Scabby Itchiness on the edge of the eyelid is cured by diluted nitrated ointment of mercury.

Warts are cut off with the scissors, and the roots touched with lunar caustic.

Hoof Ointment.—The following simple but useful prescription was given to the Author on board the "Australasian" steamship by an old bushranger, viz.:—Stockholm, or Archangel tar and mutton suet melted together, to be brushed round the hoof every day.

Surfeit is often caused by indigestion; slight bleeding is serviceable—good food indispensable.

MANGE requires thorough dressing with Barbadoes tar one part and linseed oil two parts, with internal medicines.

GREASE is cured in the first stage by bran, or turnip, or carrot poultices, and moderate physic.

SPLINTS are cured by a simple operation, and sometimes by the application of blister ointments.

SPRAINS require rest and warm fomentations. Receipt (for outward application)—Boil two ounces saltpetre in one pint of vinegar until reduced to $\frac{1}{3}$ pint, when cold add $\frac{1}{4}$ pint of oil of hartshorn and $\frac{1}{2}$ pint of spirits of turpentine.

OVER-REACH sometimes requires the attention of the blacksmith, and at other times Friar's Balsam will effect a cure.

SORE BACKS AND WITHERS should be promptly attended to with water dressing and poultices; if the wounds are raw and open the animal must have rest.

TO PROTECT WOUNDS FROM THE FLY.—Keep the part moist with a rag dipped in a solution of tar.

TO ASSIST THE GROWTH OF HAIR.—Hog's lard and mercurial ointment, mixed in equal parts with finely powdered burnt leather, by way of colouring.

TO MAKE GRUEL.—1 lb. oatmeal to a quart of water mixed in a pan to 3 quarts of boiling water, stir on the fire until it thickens, then cool for eating.

TO MAKE A POULTICE.—Bran or linseed meal, to be made with boiling water and as hot as can be borne; should be applied to the feet with a leather poultice boot, as shown in the illustration, bits, &c.

FOR HORSES THAT TURN ROUND IN THE STALL.—Use two reins.

All enquiries, orders, &c., should be addressed direct to—

E. W. GOUGH,
Author of "CENTAUR,"
Walsall.

VARIETIES OF THE HORSE.

"In truth he was a noble steed,
A Tartar of the Ukraine breed."

IN former times horses were known in classes, such as "The English War Horse;" and even now we hear of "The German Horse," "The French Horse," "The Danish Horse," "The Norwegian Horse," "The Lapland Horse," "The Swedish Horse," "The Russian Horse," "The Circassian Horse," "The Turkoman Horse," "The Turkish Horse," "The Indian Horse," and those of the Eastern Archipelago.

Richard Cœur-de-Lion purchased two Cyprus horses for his own use, and they were celebrated for speed and beauty.

The following are the varieties of the horse, and the writers by whom they are mentioned, as given by Dr. Gray, in the catalogue of the British Museum :—

The Parameros of Peru	H. Smith.
The Tarpan Wild Horse (primeval bay stock)	"
The Andalusian Horse	"
The South American Horse	"
The Mexican and Seminole Horse	"
The Feral Horses of America	"
The English Race Horse	"
The Barb of Morocco	"
The Race of Africa	"
The Persian Race	"

The Toorkee Races ... ... *H. Smith.*
The East Indian Races ... ... "
The New Holland Horse ... ... "
The Transylvanian Horse ... ... "
The Moldavian Horse ... ... "
The Greek Horse ... ... "
The Spanish Horse ... ... "
The Villous Horse (primeval of the white stock) ... "
The White or Grey Horse ... ... "
The Marengo ... ... "
The Black Horse ... ... "
The English Draught Horse ... ... "
The Dun or Tan Horse ... ... "
The Decussated Horse (or the Eelback Dun Horse of
    Ukraine) ... ... "
The Myautzee (or the Pied Horse of China) ... "
The Bhooteahs Ponies ... ... "
The Pickarrow Ponies ... ... "
The Yaboos or Afghanistan Ponies ... ... "
The Hungarian Horse (with slit nostrils) ... ... "
The Common Bashkir Horse ... ... "
The Morea Ponies ... ... "
The Swedish and Norwegian Ponies ... ... "
The Shetland Ponies ... ... "
The Galloway ... ... "
The Dartmoor and Exmoor Ponies ... ... "
The Sardinian Wild Horse ... ... "
The Tattoo or East Indian Pony ... ... "
The Tangum, Piebald, or Skewbald Horse *(Equus varens)* "
The Skewbald of Achin (in Sumatra) ... ... "
The Koomrah or Equus Hippargions ... ... "
The Koomrah or Equus Lalisi ... ... "
The Kuda or Saran Horse ... ... "
The Javan Horse ... ... "
The Tambora or Birma Horse ... ... "
    Equus antiquorum ... ... *Gener.*
    Equus Cabullus ... ... *Linnaus F. Cuvier, Fischer, Gray.*

The Equus Equa	*Pliny.*
Generous Horse	*Pennant.*
Cheval	*Buffon, Cuvier.*
Pferd	*Redinger.*
Ross	*Schrank.*
The Arabian Horse	*B. wick, Low, Smith.*
The Race Horse	*Bewick, Low.*
The Hunter	*Bewick.*
The Irish Hunter	*Low.*
The Connemara Horse...	"
Old English Black Horse...	"
The Cleveland Bay Horse	"
The Suffolk Punch	"
The Clydesdale Breed	"
Black Horse	*Bewick.*
Old English Road Horse	"
Common Cart Horse	"
Improved Cart Horse	"
The Bornou	*White.*
Cheval d'Islande-var., Islandicus... ...	*Gaim, Lesson.*
Equus Monogicus...	*Lesson.*
Equus Cabullus frisius	"
Thibet Horse	*Hodgson.*
Cheval a Port Frisses, E. frissus...	*F. Cuvier.*
Tutto, or Maharatto Pony (sedulously propagated in the Deccan, is much used to transport luggage, and is very vicious)	*Sykes.*
Tattoo (a Hack Pony of Calcutta)	*Hardwick.*
Tangham of China	*Hodson.*
Hubstec of Deo Harmad...	"
Tangham of Lhassa	"
Tangham of Gyanche	"
Hippargus...	*Oppian.*
Boryes	*Herodotus.*
Bourra of Koldagi	*Rüppell.*
Horse of Asiatic Russia, with a curled moustache on the upper lip	*Falk. Pallas.*
Naked horse, of a beautiful form, of Asiatic Russia	*Pallas.*

The Argamaki, of Bockaria, Asiatic Russia (a white Horse, with very close minute articulated brown spots) ... ... *Pallas.*
The Tangum or Tangham, (primeval Piebald stock of Thibet) ... ... *H. Smith.*
    Bonaparte's Arab (Marengo) ... ... ,,
    Crisp-haired Horse (primeval of the Black Stock) ,,
    North Africa (not gregarious) ... ... ,,

IRON HORSES: CYCLES.

ALTHOUGH the bicycle is not immediately connected with the horse and its belongings, still it is an institution of the road, and a popular machine alike with horsemen and athletes, and will continue to be so with the general public as a means of locomotion, both for long and short journeys.

Therefore, the "Rule of the Road" becomes a more important item, and the writer is advised that it will not be out of place to devote a Chapter to the consideration of the Bicycle, and its associate, the Tricycle.

We believe the origin of the bicycle has been attributed to parties who were only improvers or perfecters of the rude and imperfect machines in use for many years past as mere toys.

But, like many other useful inventions, the bicycle owes its origin to a very humble individual, one Gavin Dabzell, a cooper, of Lanarkshire, in Scotland, who, in the year 1836, constructed the first bicycle that ever proved successful for business and pleasure.

Dabzell, to his profession of cooper, added that of tea dealer, and used to travel from village to village selling tea. Of course, his first machine was a rough production compared with the beautifully finished and perfected machines of the present day.

But, although his was a clumsy and awkward specimen, Dabzell managed to travel with considerable speed, and it is remembered that on one occasion he actually beat the mail coach, which was bound to keep up a speed of 10 miles an hour, and he ran round it three times during the journey, to the great amusement and delight of the passengers, and the disgust, and annoyance, and irritation of the driver and guard.

Dabzell's machine had the smaller wheel in front. But there can be no doubt that this was the first bicycle, and another quaint story is told about it. Having learned to manage his machine, Dabzell started one evening down the village at considerable speed, when an old woman, who happened to be standing at the cottage door as the thing rushed passed her, ran into the house, exclaiming, "Oh! come out! come out, quick! here's a cart wheel running away with a man."

The tricycle is simply the adaption of three wheels to the machine instead of two, this form being preferable for business purposes and for riders of maturer years. If electricity can be applied successfully as a motive power to the tricycle, there remains no doubt but that a great future is before the new and useful branch of industry—the manufacture of bicycles, tricycles, sociables, tandems, and like machines. The duty remains for the Author to strongly advise care and wide-awake caution and unselfish consideration on the part of all travellers on the road, whether horsemen or cyclists.

The strict observance of the following "Rules of the Road," as laid down and published for the special use of Midland machinists, will be found both pleasurable, safe, and economical :—

No. 1.—A person shall not ride or impel any bicycle, tricycle, velocipede, or other similar vehicle, upon any footway, pavement, or causeway, made or set apart for the use and accommodation of foot passengers.

No. 2.—Every person riding a bicycle, tricycle, velocipede, or other similar vehicle, who overtakes any wagon, wain, cart, carriage, or other vehicle drawn by animal power, or any horse, mule, or other beast of burden, or any foot passengers proceeding along the carriage-way, shall, when within a reasonable distance from and before passing such wagon, wain, cart, carriage, or other vehicle drawn by animal power, horse, mule, or other beast of burden, or such foot passengers, by sounding a bell or whistle, give audible and sufficient warning of the approach of his bicycle, tricycle, velocipede, or other similar vehicle.

No. 3.—A person shall not ride a bicycle, tricycle, velocipede, or other similar vehicle during the hours between one hour after sunset and one hour before sunrise, unless he shall carry attached to such bicycle, tricycle, velocipede, or other similar vehicle, a lamp which shall be so constructed and placed as to exhibit a white light in the direction in which he is proceeding, and shall be so lighted and kept lighted as to afford adequate means of signalling the approach or position of such bicycle, tricycle, velocipede, or other similar vehicle.

No. 4.—Every person riding a bicycle, tricycle, velocipede, or other similar vehicle, who overtakes and passes any wagon, wain, cart, carriage, or other vehicle drawn by animal power, or any horse, mule, or other beast of burden, shall keep his bicycle, tricycle, velocipede, or other similar vehicle to the right or off side of the carriage-way.

No. 5.—Every person when riding a bicycle, tricycle, velocipede, or other similar vehicle, shall. when meeting any wagon, wain, cart, carriage, or other vehicle drawn by animal power, or any horse, mule, or other beast of burden, keep his bicycle, tricycle, velocipede, or other similar vehicle to the left or near side of the carriage-way.

No. 6.—In every case where a person riding a bicycle, tricycle, velocipede, or other similar vehicle, meets or overtakes any wagon, wain, cart, carriage, or other vehicle drawn by animal power, or any horse, mule, or other beast of burden, and where by reason of such meeting or overtaking any animal drawing such wagon, wain, cart, carriage, or other vehicle drawn by animal power, or such horse, mule, or other beast of burden, such animal, horse, mule, or other beast of burden may become restive or alarmed, or may cease to be under the due control of the person for the time being in charge of such wagon, wain, cart, carriage, or other vehicle drawn by animal power, or of such horse, mule, or other beast of burden, he shall dismount as speedily as possible, and shall continue dismounted so long as may be reasonably necessary.

No. 7.—Every person who shall offend against any of the foregoing Bye-Laws, shall be liable, for every such offence, to a penalty of forty shillings. Provided nevertheless, that the Justices or Court before whom any complaint may be made or any proceedings may be taken in respect of any such offence, may, if they think fit, adjudge the payment as a penalty, of any sum less than the full amount of the penalty imposed by this Bye-Law.

A CHAPTER OF ACCIDENTS.

IT is difficult nowadays to take up a daily or weekly journal without seeing one or more reports of Accidents, such as "Run Over," "Upset," "Thrown in the Hunting Field," "Sad Collision with a Steam Tramcar," "A Careless Horseman," "A Drunken Driver," "Overloading," "Wrong Side," "Furious Driving," &c., &c., whereby serious, and in many cases, fatal injuries have been inflicted upon either the animal or the people, or both.

It is hoped the careful perusal of, and attention to, the foregoing Chapters and rules, will at least reduce the number of such notices, and the *risks of the road* in particular, to the permanent comfort of the horseman and the general safety of the public.

The following Extracts, taken from the daily journals, we give by way of practical illustration, and the more forcibly to *drive* our arguments home. The "cuttings," we trust, will point their own moral to the reader :—

CARRIAGE ACCIDENTS.

While the Prince of Wales was driving to a *fête* given by Lady Murray, at Cannes, the carriage ran against a heap of stones. One of the shafts was broken, but no further damage was caused, and another carriage having been sent for, his Royal Highness proceeded to the *fête*.

The Empress Eugénie visited the Imperial tomb at Chislehurst. Whilst alighting from her carriage the Empress fell and rather seriously injured her right leg.

As Dr. Norris was being driven down Newhall Hill in a brougham, the horse fell, and Dr. Norris was thrown out. He fortunately escaped without any serious injury, though the coachman received a severe shaking. The shafts and wheels of the carriage were broken and the knees of the horse were cut.

A serious carriage accident occurred at Barham, near Ipswich. A brougham containing Sir William and Lady O'Malley and General and Mrs. Percival was overturned through the bolting of the horse, and all the occupants thrown out, Lady O'Malley receiving such severe injuries as to necessitate the immediate amputation of her left arm.

ACCIDENTS IN THE HUNTING FIELD.

While hunting with the Kilkenny Hounds, Lord Clifden met with a very serious accident during a spanking run over a rough country. The field, a very large one, became scattered, and Lord Clifden's horse, which was tired at the time, came to a double-ditched embankment. His lordship put his horse to the jump, but it stumbled on the embankment, and threw his lordship, who sustained a severe fracture of the collar bone. Doctor Mourgan was next up, and knowing nothing of the accident, jumped the embankment, and narrowly escaped coming down on Lord Clifden as he lay helpless on the other side. His lordship, who was suffering intense pain, was driven to Kilkenny Castle.

The Earl of Ravensworth was out riding, and while in the act of leaping a hedge near Ravensworth his horse stumbled and threw him forward. His lordship fell upon his head, and suffered from a slight concussion of the brain.

Whilst hunting with the Albrighton Hounds near Shareshill, Lady Boughey met with a slight accident. Her ladyship was encouraging her horse to leap a fence with a dry ditch on the other side, when she accidentally slipped off the saddle on to the ground, fortunately without sustaining anything further than a slight shaking.

Lieut.-Col. Thornycroft (Tettenhall) came to grief at a fence, unhappily with serious consequences. His horse slipped in attempting to jump the fence, and the colonel was thrown forward on to his left shoulder, dislocating the shoulder bone, and otherwise shaking him. On returning home medical advice was at once obtained, and the injuries attended to. After a quiet night's rest the gallant colonel felt better, but his medical adviser informs him that it will be some little time before he will be able to hunt again.

Alderman F. D. Gibbons met with an accident whilst out with the Albrighton Hounds at Ryton, about three miles from Shifnal.

He was riding his horse at a fast pace, and was just about to put the animal at a boggy ditch, when, owing to the steed stumbling, the rider came a cropper to the ground. To make matters worse, the horse, it is stated, rolled right over him, and he was hurt very much. Mr. B. W. Lamb, surgeon, happened to be near at the time, and he at once attended to Mr. Gibbons' injuries. After a brief rest he was able to return home. It is understood no bones were broken.

The Household Brigade Draghounds met at Wraysbury, and ran over a stiff line of country, finishing at Datchet pump, about two miles from Windsor. During the run, Lieutenant Pereira, of the Grenadier Guards, fell heavily in taking a fence, his hunter rolling over him. When picked up he was found to be much injured, and was immediately conveyed to his quarters at the Victory Barracks, Windsor. Here he was attended by the regimental surgeon, Dr. Cross, and other medical gentlemen. The young officer passed a restless night, and lay in a very precarious state.

Sir Charles Mordaunt met with a severe accident while hunting with the Warwickshire Hounds. It appears that the pack found on Shuckburgh Hills, and at almost the first fence in the valley Sir Charles came to grief. The horse, his favourite grey, rose well at the ditch and hedges, but failed in clearing the ditch beyond, throwing its rider upon his shoulder, and breaking his collar bone.

Mr. Wickham, who married Lady Ethelberta Gordon, wa thrown from his horse while hunting near Peterborough. He broke his collar bone and sustained other serious injuries.

Colonel Lister, a Monmouthshire magistrate, was killed while hunting with the Llangibby Hounds.

Lady Theodore Guest, sister of the Duke of Westminster, broke her leg whilst hunting.

The Hon. G. Douglas Pennant met with a serious accident whilst hunting with the Grafton Hounds near Lillingston Dayrell, he being thrown on to his head. The wound bled freely, and Mr. Pennant was taken home to Wicken Park.

General Sir Charles Staveley, whilst hunting with the Avon Vale Harriers at Road, near Bath, was thrown from his horse and sustained concussion of the spine.

A serious accident occurred at Syston, Leicestershire. The Quorn Hounds were moving out of paddock, when Mr. Trew, of Baggrave Hall, riding with Lord Manners, the master, was thrown, and his horse fell upon him. Mr. Trew's feet were entangled in the stirrups, and he was dragged some distance along the ground. Eventually the horse was stopped, and on Mr. Trew being picked up it was found that he had sustained serious injuries to the spine.

Mr. Harrison, of Esher, was thrown from his horse whilst hunting with the Queen's Hounds, and sustained a concussion of the brain. He died at the Royal Hotel, Ascot.

FATAL ACCIDENTS.

A fatal accident occurred at Bridgnorth, to a man named Mason, 96 years of age. A horse in the shafts of a four-wheeled carriage, having taken fright, bolted down High-street, and on arriving at Listley-street corner came in contact with Mason, who was knocked down with great violence. The deceased was as quickly as possible removed to the surgery of Dr. Mursfield, life being apparently extinct. On examination it was found that one of his legs was broken, and that he had received a very bad wound in the back, in addition to which his thigh was shockingly cut. The deceased expired between six and seven the same evening. A man named Downes, who was driving the vehicle when the animal bolted, was thrown from his seat, but escaped with only a few bruises.

A wagoner named George Nott, in the employ of Mr. Boulton, farmer, Codsall, was attending to a colt in his master's stab'e, when the animal kicked him in the face, smashing his jaw into two or three pieces, in addition to inflicting other injuries in various parts of the body. The poor man managed to crawl out into the fold, and, as best he could, called out for assistance. His cries being at length heard by some passers by, he was removed to Mr. Boulton's house. He died shortly afterwards.

Henry Batchellor, of Witley, died from injuries received at the Corngreaves Works, Cradley. While engaged in shunting operations he was knocked down by a horse, and trampled under foot. His ribs were fractured, and he sustained internal injuries.

George Savage, a wagoner, in the employ of Mr. Wells, of Ascot, whilst engaged in his duties, was run over by a horse and cart. His injuries were so serious that medical attention proved of no avail, and he expired in great pain.

A boy about eight years old, son of the Rev. Bermin Cassin, rector of St. George the Martyr, Southwark, was killed in Old Kent Road, London. A slight commotion was caused in the thoroughfare by the passage of a fife and drum band, and as the boy attempted to cross the road he was knocked down by a loaded van and his back completely broken.

John Tanner was run over and killed by a cart driven by John Sayce, of Orton.

CAB ACCIDENTS.

Colonel W. R. Newton, the celebrated American biologist, was riding a tricycle in Aldersgate Street, London, when the machine collided with a cab. Colonel Newton was thrown violently to the ground, sustaining a fracture of the skull, from which he died two hours afterwards.

An inquest was held on the body of J. B——. The deceased and G. L—— were crossing the road, when they were both knocked down by a cab. L—— escaped unhurt, but the deceased was so severely injured that she had to be removed to the hospital, where she died from the injuries received.

J. C——, cab proprietor, was admitted into the hospital suffering from concussion of the brain. He was driving in Birmingham in a gig, when by some mischance he fell out and sustained the injury.

Two women, one in Camberwell, the other in Westminster, were killed by being run over, the one by a cart, and the other by a cab; and in each case a verdict of manslaughter was returned against the driver.

A cab accident occurred to a woman named S. S——, wife of one of the warders of Winson Green Gaol, which terminated fatally.

A van belonging to the commissariat and transport goes round Aldershot camp daily to collect the officers' children who attend the camp school. When at the top of the main road the horses bolted and dashed down an incline. About twenty children were thrown violently out, all being more or less injured. No death occurred.

An inquest was held on the body of Mr. Robert Augustus Aspinall, aged 77, a Middlesex county magistrate. He had just left the Carlton Club, in Pall Mall, London, and was crossing the road, when he was run over by a four-wheeled cab. He died in the hospital from his injuries.

Ellen Scanlan was run over and killed on Christmas Eve by a cab, at Pimlico, London. The driver's cab rolled in a peculiar manner, and he drove a spirited horse which bolted and caused the accident.

OMNIBUS ACCIDENTS.

An omnibus was overturned in Liverpool Road, Islington, London, and several persons were injured, one seriously. It appears that the omnibus was being driven too sharply round a corner when it was overturned. Four persons who had received injuries were conveyed to the Great Northern Hospital, Caledonian Road. Three of them were permitted to leave after having their injuries attended to, but one young man was insensible and had to be detained.

An alarming accident, attended with serious injuries to two persons occurred on the road between Penn and Wolverhampton, being caused by an omnibus coming into collision with a heavy lorry. The 'bus, to which, as usual, three horses were attached, was driven by the proprietor of the vehicle. As the two vehicles approached each other the horse attached to the lorry appears to have first shyed at the 'bus, and then to have made an attempt to bolt. The wagoner, who it is supposed was seated on the front of the lorry, tried to govern his horse with the reins, but, notwithstanding his endeavours, the animal dashed into the right side of the omnibus. By the force of the collision one of the shafts of the lorry was driven right through the panel of the 'bus beneath the windows, a portion of the woodwork being forced clean out, and some of the ironwork displaced. The driver of the 'bus, at the time of the accident, was enabled to keep his seat and to maintain control over his horses.

STABLE ACCIDENTS.

A man named Handley, of Toll End, was engaged dressing two horses with some oils for a disease called the riff, when he accidentally put the candle too near the animals. The oils caught fire, and the animals were soon in a blaze. The unfortunate animals being maddened with pain rushed out of the stable Great alarm was occasioned in the streets by the appearance of burning horses, but, fortunately, no mishap occurred.

STREET ACCIDENTS.

Major Adams, of the Royal Artillery, while proceeding from Woolwich in charge of an exercise battery, was thrown from his horse at East Greenwich, and seriously hurt. The animal had become restive, and bolted, but the major succeeded in pulling it up, when it stumbled, and, falling, rolled over its rider, who sustained a fracture of the skull, besides other injuries.

Sir William Muir was thrown from his horse whilst riding to the India Office and was severely shaken.

While proceeding home from court in a hansom cab, in consequence of the harness breaking, Lord Justice Baggallay was nearly thrown out of the vehicle, and sustained a severe shaking.

Whilst William Bowden, of Lower Street, Tettenhall, was driving a horse and trap, the animal took fright and ran away. Bowden was thrown out of the vehicle, and the side of his face bruised.

While a young horse was being driven in an empty wagon belonging to an iron merchant of Willenhall, it became frightened and bolted down the street. A man who had been standing at the animal's head was knocked down, and the wheels of the vehicle passed over him, inflicting serious bruises. The animal afterwards ran into the window of a public house, breaking it, and from thence into the yard of a chemist, where it was secured.

A number of persons returning from a football match at Perry Barr had a narrow escape. They were riding in a wagonette along the Birchfield Road, but as the vehicle was too full on one side, it turned over, the whole party being thrown into the road. The accident caused some excitement, but beyond a few scratches and bruises no injuries were sustained, but the vehicle was very much damaged.

Florence Baker was playing in the road at Deritend, when she was knocked down and run over by a cart. It was found that one of her legs was broken.

A man was driving a furniture van, near Sparkbrook, Deritend, when, in endeavouring to recover the reins, which had slipped, his legs became entangled in them, and he was thrown under the vehicle, the wheels of which passed over his leg, breaking his ankle and injuring his knee.

A boy named George Hill was knocked down and run over by a heavy coal cart, at Cheapside, Deritend. Besides several internal injuries, one of his legs was severely crushed.

A little boy named Eli Taylor, whose parents reside at Merridale Street, Walsall, was playing in the street, when he accidentally ran against the fore legs of a horse drawing a ginger-beer wagon. The boy was knocked down, and two of the wheels of the vehicle went over his body, injuring him seriously.

A groom named Farmer, in the employ of a Derby veterinary surgeon, was riding out a spirited horse, when the animal slipped and threw him. Farmer's foot became entangled in the stirrup, and, the animal starting off at a furious pace, he was dragged for some distance before the animal was caught. The unfortunate young man's head was terribly injured by repeatedly coming in contact with the macadam road.

Andrew Brookes was driving a horse and trap across the Five-ways, Wolverhampton, when the shaft caught Mr. Joseph Banner, of Heath Town, in the side, knocking him down, injuring his ribs, and cutting his forehead.

TRAMWAY ACCIDENTS.

A butcher's cart was standing near the Cross, at Rocky Lane, Birmingham, when it was passed by a steam tram. The horse became unmanageable and ran down Rocky Lane at a furious rate. An old woman was in the middle of the road wheeling a perambulator, and, being deaf, did not hear the shouts of the driver. The horse threw her with great violence to the ground. She was removed to premises near in an unconscious condition.

A steam tramway engine was running from Birmingham, and came into collision with a cab containing four passengers. The cab horse was knocked down, the cab overturned, and the passengers were severely shaken, whilst the driver was somewhat seriously injured. No car was attached to the engine.

A cart laden with iron was being driven up Soho Hill, West Bromwich, when one of the wheels became fixed in the tram line, and the axletree broke, letting the body of the cart down. The driver was thrown from his seat and sustained a fracture of one of his thigh bones, and the horse's near hind leg was also broken. The animal had in consequence to be slaughtered.

Recently, the first team of the West Bromwich Albions were in danger of losing the services of their noted goal-keeper, Bob Roberts, and the second team ran some risk of being annihilated altogether. During the afternoon they were playing, and on their return home in a three-horse brake the leader shyed at a tramcar. The brake was placed across the tramway, with a similar result to that which attended the notorious effort of a cow to stop an express train. The steam engine caught the brake in the centre, and a general smash-up followed. All the occupants were pitched out and more or less damaged. Fortunately no serious injury was sustained by any one.

A serious trap accident occurred at Wolverhampton. A licensed victualler, accompanied by his two children, was driving a trap, when the wheels of the vehicle became entangled in the tram rails and the horse fell down. All the occupants were thrown out, each being severely shaken.

A carter, in the employ of a maltster, of West Bromwich, was engaged in unloading some malt, when his horse took fright at a tramcar which was passing, and bolted. The man was thrown down, and the horse trod upon him, inflicting severe injuries.

At York County Court, a widow, named Harney, sued a Tramway Company for £12 12s. damages, sustained through the negligence of the defendants or their servants. The plaintiff took a tramcar, and a second car was following, and when it was a little behind the one in which the plaintiff was, the driver looked behind him. On re-directing his attention to his horses he found he was very near upon the first car. He applied his brake, but as he saw that this would not avoid a collision, he pulled his horses off the track, and his car ran into the one in which plaintiff was. She was standing ready to get out, and was thrown by the concussion violently upon the floor of the car. In consequence of this accident she was unable to follow her occupation, and had to obtain assistance. Verdict for the plaintiff for the full amount claimed, with costs.

H. H——, in the employment of Mr. V——, was driving a one-horse omnibus, at Wednesbury, when the vehicle came into collision with the engine of a passing tramcar. The omnibus was considerably damaged, and H—— was thrown from his seat, and so much injured that he was detained at the Hospital.

J. R—— was driving a horse and cart laden with ten people, at Walsall, when his horse shyed at an approaching tramcar. The horse swerved to one side, and the cart came in contact with the car, and was overturned, the axle being broken, and three or four of the occupants of the car injured, one of them seriously.

Mr. Wainwright, farmer, of Crow Greaves, Bridgnorth, was out driving with a horse and trap, when one of the wheels of the vehicle caught in the tram rail, and skidded along, causing the horse to fall down. One of the shafts was broken, and Mr. Wainwright was thrown out, but was not injured.

As a dray was being driven down Tipton Road it was run into by the engine of one of the tramcars plying on the road. The wheel of the dray was knocked off, and the vehicle was otherwise damaged; but no one was hurt. This was the second accident of a similar character in the same neighbourhood, in both instances brewers' drays coming to grief.

At Wednesbury, a Tramway Company's engine and car collided with a wagon. The wagon was broken in two, and the man in charge of the horse and wagon was badly injured, both his legs being broken. The horse was also injured.

Mr. and Mrs. Pankhurst were returning home, when the horse attached to the trap in which they were riding became startled at the steam tram, and bolted. Both lady and gentleman were thrown out with great violence, and were seriously injured.

One of the spare tram horses used to assist in drawing the tramcars at Walsall was being taken back to the company's stables, when the animal became restive and commenced rearing, and swerving across the footpath, backed right into one of the windows of a shop. The horse backed against the window with such violence that a large pane of glass, quite half an inch thick, was completely shattered. The damage done to the window and goods inside is estimated at not less than £20.

An action was recently tried at Dudley, before Sir Rupert Kettle, in which J. G—— sought to recover from a steam tramways company the sum of £5 10s. damages sustained by a collision between a steam tramcar and a horse and cart driven by the plaintiff's servant. For the plaintiff it was contended that as he was driving up the road his horse became restive at the approach of a tramcar, which was alleged to be drawn at the rate of 10 miles an hour. Plaintiff put up his hand as a signal to stop the car, but as the engineer was then stooping down, no notice was taken of the signal, and the engine ran into the horse. For the defendants it was urged by the driver of the engine, several witnesses, and the manager to the company that the car was travelling at a speed of between four and six miles an hour, and that plaintiff contributed to the accident by his inefficient control of the horse. His Honour said the case was of so much importance to the travelling public that he should take time to consider his judgment. This has now been given, and is as follows:—
1. I find that the driver endeavoured to bring the engine to a stand still within the meaning of bye-law III., as soon as he became aware of impending danger. 2. I find that the driver of the engine was guilty of negligence in not keeping a sufficient look out to have seen that the plaintiff's horse, by his restiveness, caused an impending danger, and thereupon bringing his engine to a standstill. 3. The immediate cause of the accident was the swerving of the plaintiff's horse towards the approaching tram. 4. It was known to the plaintiff's driver that his horse shyed at

tramcars, but no extra means of controlling him were provided. There was no evidence that the defendants' car driver had knowledge that the horse was a shyer. It was the duty, under these circumstances, of the plaintiff's driver, when his horse became restive, pranced and jumped about, to have promptly signalled warning to the engine driver by some more efficient means than holding up his hand; or that he should have used some more efficient means to restrain his horse than pulling the reins. Upon these facts my judgment is for the defendants by reason of the contributory negligence of the plaintiff's servant. Costs to follow. (Defendants' costs—£5 8s.; taxed at £4 1s.)

On this subject the *Midland Evening News*, of January 12th, 1885, has the following severe comments, which we re-produce without remark:—" The perils of the road to drivers of spirited or restive horses have always been numerous, and in most cases unavoidable, but when to these are superadded the graver perils arising from the introduction of 'steam tramcars' on the public highways of the district, it may easily be conceived that the life of an owner of a vehicle is by no means 'a happy one.' A case which was heard in the County Court some time ago, in which a grocer sued a steam tramway company for damages sustained by a collision between a steam tramcar and the plaintiff's horse and trap, forcibly illustrates the imminent danger to life and limb which every driver of a vehicle has to brave in his daily occupation. The plaintiff alleged that as he was driving along the road his horse became restive at the approach of a tramcar, which he calculated was going at a speed of 16 miles an hour. He signalled to the engineer to stop the tram, but as the latter was stooping down at the time the signal was unnoticed, and the tram, therefore, ran into his horse. For the defence it was alleged that the car was only travelling at a speed of between four and six miles an hour, and that the plaintiff contributed to the accident by his inefficient control over his horse. Sir Rupert Kettle said the case was of so much importance to the travelling public that he should take time to consider his decision. That decision has just b en given, and we anticipate that vehement exception will be taken to it by the 'travelling public' If the decision had been given at the conclusion of the evidence it would still have been open to objection, but it would have escaped the animadversions which will be passed upon it now that it has been pronounced after deliberate consideration. Sir Rupert Kettle first of all finds that the engineer endeavoured to bring the engine to a standstill within the meaning of the byelaw III. *as soon as he became aware of impending danger*; and next that he was guilty of negligence in not keeping a sufficient look out to have seen that the plaintiff's horse, by its restlessness, caused an impending danger, necessitating the bringing of the engine to a standstill. So far, then, it is clear that the engineer

was seriously at fault, inasmuch as he had not kept a sufficient
look out as he was bound to do in order to prevent an accident;
and every ordinary individual would at once jump to the conclusion that as negligence was proved on the part of the defendants
the verdict would be for the plaintiff. Not so, however, for, with
all the force of an antithesis, Sir Rupert Kettle proceeds to show
that the defendants were, if not in the right, at any rate not in
the wrong, but that the plaintiff himself was the cause of the
accident, and deserved, therefore, not only to lose his horse and
imperil his life, but to bear the costs of the action into the
bargain—a conclusion which the unfortunate owner of the restive
horse will no doubt regard as equivalent to adding insult to injury.
The decision proceeds to point out that it was known to the
plaintiff's driver that his horse shyed at tramcars, but no extra
means of controlling him were provided; that the defendant's
engineer had no knowledge that the horse was a shyer; it was,
therefore, the plaintiff's duty, when his horse became restive, to
have promptly signalled warning to the engineer by some other
means than holding up his hand, or used more efficient means
to restrain his horse than pulling the reins. Upon these facts
judgment must go for defendants by reason of contributory
negligence. Now 'contributory negligence' is a very good legal
phrase to conjure with, but it seems to us to be of questionable
appropriateness in the present instance. First of all, it has
nothing to do with the question that the plaintiff knew his horse
shyed at steam tramcars. If all the horses that shyed are to be
kept off the roads on this account, then one half of them would
have to be shot as useless. True his Honour points out an
alternative, for he refers to more efficient means of controlling a
horse than the reins. But what are these 'more efficient means?'
Because if there are any such, drivers of horses would be very
glad to know them in order that they may be employed for the
safety of their own necks and their property. It is perfectly well
known to owners of spirited horses that once these animals come
into close contact with one of these road engines their terror
places them beyond all control, and they either make a sudden
swerve round in front of the car or dash on to the footpath, at the
imminent risk of coming into contact with a lamp post or other
obstacle. It follows, therefore, that if there are no means of
controlling a horse beyond the reins, the judgment is based upon
a wrong conception of the situation. Besides, there are some
portions of the roads over which the tramcars run so narrow as
to render it extremely perilous for the owner of a frightened
horse to attempt to pass one of these cars, and yet the speed at
which the cars travel make it impossible to get out of the way in
time to avoid a collision. This question of speed would of course
be an important one in case of a fatality, but when a company's
officials swear that the speed, as in the case under review, was
only between four and six miles an hour and are believed in

preference to the assertion of the plaintiff that it was sixteen miles
an hour—though the former estimate means that the car was
going at a snail's pace, it argues badly for the chances of a widow
getting damages in case of a fatality. As to the question of
signalling, the driver of the tramcar was, on the judge's own
showing, more in the wrong than the plaintiff, for while the latter
did signal (though insufficiently, as Sir Rupert Kettle assumes) the
former was not keeping the necessary look-out, and, therefore, the
fault of the collision lay with him. The graver negligence was
on the part of the defendants, particularly if it is borne in mind
that these 'steam trams' are a recent innovation, and have
brought the danger upon owners of horses by turning the highways into railroads. Neither has it anything to do with the case
that the engineer had no knowledge that the plaintiff's horse was
a 'shyer,' except to make the case worse for the defendants.
The engineer had no right to cease for a second a watchful
look out for restive horses, because the existence of the bye-law,
requiring him to bring his engine to a standstill in face of
impending danger, pre-supposes this very restlessness on the part
of horses. Moreover, the restlessness on the part of spirited
horses is notorious, and, being the aggressors on the road, the
defendants were bound to use every precaution against accidents.
If steam tram drivers are to be permitted to cut people down at
their pleasure, the roads had better be resigned to them altogether.
This is clearly one of those cases, judging from the facts, as
reported, which ought to be carried to a superior tribunal, for it
is evident that a vast number of commercial travellers, tradesmen,
and professional gentlemen, driving in the tram districts, will be
exposed to the gravest risks if engineers of tramcars can be guilty
of negligence and the company in spite of it escape 'scot free.'
Further, these 'iron horses' do not fight fair. The advantage in
a collision is all on their side, and the reckless engineer has no
fear of a severed limb or a broken neck to sober him into a
suitable frame of mind. Not so the driver of a horse. His life
and that of his horse are in great jeopardy, and it is, therefore,
the imperative duty of the law to protect the weaker against the
stronger in all cases in which, as in this, negligence on the part
of the tramway company is admitted."

TRAP ACCIDENTS.

A fatal trap accident happened to Mr. John Brawn, limemaster,
Rushall. The deceased was on his way home, when some
wagoners or market gardeners drove past him at a furious pace
and shaved his wheel ; and, afterwards, a man who had annoyed
him and others in the same way on previous occasions raced past
him, the two vehicles very nearly coming into collision. Being

over-cautious and desirous of avoiding an accident, he walked his horse until past the last-named man's horse, and afterwards kept on at a rate of six or seven miles an hour, with his wheel in the channel, until he reached Shelfield. There his wheel caught against the end of a pipe which had been laid in the channel to carry the water under the margin of the footway. He himself and his horse were startled, but his horse at first half stopped in obedience to his call, and then dashed off at a rapid pace. He was tossed out of the gig, his leg getting entangled in the wheel, and locking it, and finding as he was being dragged along that his head was striking the ground, he, by a desperate effort, grasped the spokes. On reaching his home his brother went for a doctor, but death took place the same evening.

A serious trap accident took place at Chapel Ash. A horse and trap belonging to Mr. ·T—— were standing opposite the shop of Mr. W——, Mr. T—— and his daughter being in the vehicle, when a collision took place between the trap and the horse and trap of Mr. A——, who was driving towards his home. Mr. and Miss T—— were thrown out of their vehicle, both of the shafts of which were snapped off. The horse bolted off at a rapid pace, dragging the broken shafts with him, but was eventually stopped. Mr. and Miss T—— escaped with a severe shaking, though a bank note and some gold and silver fell out of Mr. T——'s pockets and were lost. By the force of the collision Mr. A—— was thrown from his vehicle and sustained a cut on his head.

Two young men were driving a small pony and trap, when the animal became restive and rushed into a wagon. The pony was badly cut by the collision.

G—— P—— was admitted to the hospital, suffering from a severe scalp wound. He was driving in a trap, when the horse took fright and ran away, the man being thrown out.

R—— H—— was driving along in a trap with another man when, nearing the corner, the trap went into a rut, and threw both men out. H—— sustained a severe scalp wound. The other man was uninjured.

Mrs. B——, publican, was driving in a high trap, when the horse slipped and fell, and Mrs. B—— was thrown with great violence to the ground. She sustained a severe wound on the temple, and was greatly shaken.

A horse in a trap took fright and rushed into the shop of Mr. R——. The horse sustained severe cuts about the head and chest from the glass, and the whole of the window of the shop was knocked in. No one however, was injured.

WAGON ACCIDENTS.

A serious accident occurred in Waterfall Lane, Old Hill. Two men in charge of a wagon and four horses were conveying an iron roll, weighing upwards of five tons, from Messrs. Guest and Silvester's Victoria Ironfoundry, West Bromwich. to the Corngreaves Ironworks, Cradley. When descending Waterfall Lane, which is very steep, the slipper came off the wheel, and the wagon commenced to run down the incline at a fearful rate. The front horses swerved, and the trace chains fortunately became disconnected, the leading horses being liberated. The wagon shafts and the shaft horse were driven with great violence against the house of a miner named Clark, the lower portion of the premises and the furniture being completely demolished. The wagon was also wrecked and the horse killed. The damage was estimated at £120.

Henry Bachelor, horsedriver, died from the effects of shocking injuries received when following his employment at the New British Iron Company's Works, at Corngreaves. The deceased was in charge of three horses in shunting tracks on a railway in the Corngreaves Works. The middle horse became very restive, and kicked deceased twice on the left side, which caused him to fall. Whilst on the ground deceased was trampled upon by two of the horses. When picked up it was ascertained that the poor fellow was badly injured, and he was removed to his home, where he died.

A Midland Railway Company's wagon, laden with heavy girders, and drawn by three horses, was proceeding along Lodge Road, when the front packing blocks slipped, causing one of the heavy girders to fall upon the back of the rear horse. This caused the horse to plunge, and when opposite a shop occupied by a greengrocer the wagon swerved round, and completely knocked out the window with the whole of the brickwork. The long girders projected five or six feet into the shop, and it was some hours before the wagon and its freight could be removed. Fortunately no one was in the shop at the time of the accident. A little girl was knocked down by the shaft and sustained a scalp wound.

William Griffiths, a wagoner in the employ of a hay and straw dealer, of Cheslyn Hay, met with an extraordinary accident whilst in Wolverhampton. In the mouth of what is said to be an old pit shaft, which had been filled up to within about fifteen feet from the surface, two horses were lying, attached to a wagon that was completely overturned, the wheels being in mid-air, and underneath the body of the wagon, entirely shut in, was Griffiths, who had been in charge of the team. A police-officer and those with him at once extricated Griffiths from his perilous position, and he was taken to the hospital, where it was discovered that he had sustained a broken collar bone and other injuries to his chest. It appeared that he had been with a load of hay, and in returning had lost his way in the darkness and driven his horses some 600 yards out of the beaten track over the waste mounds, until both driver and team were abruptly precipitated into the shaft from which they were rescued. Had the horses by any means avoided the pit and travelled 10 yards further in the same direction they must have walked into an old "swag" containing a depth of about 10 feet of water. The horses seemed little the worse for the accident.

ACCIDENTS THROUGH DRUNKENNESS.

T—— B—— was fined 20s. and costs for being drunk whilst in charge of a horse and cart at Wolverhampton.

T—— P——, a groom, was charged with being drunk whilst in charge of a horse and trap. Prisoner was driving when he overtook and ran into a tricycle on which a young man was riding; the machine was upset, and damage done to the extent of 35s. The man was fined 20s. and costs, with the alternative of one month's imprisonment, for being drunk.

B—— S——, of Dudley Port, was charged with being drunk whilst in charge of a horse and cart. He was seen by an officer driving furiously. The shaft of his cart ran into the brisket of a horse attached to a Midland Railway Company's dray, inflicting so serious a wound as to cause its death. He was fined 20s. and costs.

D—— L——, a cab and car driver, was summoned for being drunk whilst in charge of a horse and cab. The prisoner was obstructing the road. When ordered to move on he refused, and he was drunk. The prisoner, a very violent man, was sent to gaol for a month.

J—— R—— was charged with being drunk whilst in charge of a horse and trap. The man was found quite incapable of taking care of the vehicle and horse. Defendant, who said he was sorry for what he had done, received a caution, and was discharged.

FURIOUS DRIVING.

R—— M——, a fruiterer, of Birmingham, was charged with causing the death of a man named Wood. The deceased was crossing Corporation Street when a horse and cart driven by the prisoner turned the corner and knocked him down. The wheels passed over his body, and he was taken to the hospital, where his injuries were found to be serious. He died in the hospital. The Coroner before whom the inquest on deceased was held, addressing the man, said it would never do to let the public go unprotected in the streets, and he was found guilty of 'great negligence,' and discharged with a caution.

An inquest was held relative to the death of Mrs. S——, wife of a teacher of music. She was knocked down by a horse and cart driven at a furious rate, and died from the injuries received. The jury returned a verdict of manslaughter against the driver.

A similar verdict was returned against a cabman for running over and killing a woman in Pimlico, London.

J—— B—— sued C—— B—— and his daughter A—— for £25, damages sustained through his child having been injured by the negligence of the female defendant. It was alleged that while the plaintiff's child, aged two years, was walking across the street the female defendant drove furiously and negligently along, with the result that the child was knocked down and the wheel of the vehicle passed over its head. For eight weeks the child's life was despaired of and it was said to have been permanently injured. Judgment was eventually given for the defendants, but without costs.

RUNNING DOWN.

E—— G——, widow, of Wolverhampton, brought an action to recover £500 damages from J——. W——, butcher, and J—— A—— butcher, who were alleged to have caused the death of her husband, by running him down. The deceased was in the habit of going about the district with a pony and trap. He and his wife were returning through Compton to Wolverhampton. The wife was in the pony-trap driving, and the deceased was walking behind the cart talking to a man. As they approached the Post Office the defendants, who were each driving a horse in a trap at a fast pace, coming abreast, and A—— got first past the deceased's cart on the proper side, but W——, it was alleged, passed on the other side. Deceased was knocked down and both his legs were broken. He was removed to the Infirmary, where he died.

ON THEIR WRONG SIDE.

A collision took place at Lozells. A milk cart and a butcher's cart—both on their wrong side of the road—were turning the corner, when they came into violent collision. Both the drivers were thrown from their seats and severely bruised, the milk cart driver being so badly shaken that he could not proceed further. The horses also were much cut and bruised, and the contents of the carts were scattered.

SUDDEN DEATHS WHILE DRIVING.

A horse and trap, the occupant of which was a gentleman, was found wandering aimlessly along the road. On stopping the vehicle a police officer ascertained that the gentleman in it was insensible. He conveyed him to the hospital, where he died. The deceased was Charles E. Champion, brewer's agent, Harborne, and the cause of death was apoplexy.

A man named Frederick Crimpton took a load of hay to Mr. J. Riley's, of Tottenham Wood. The rain was falling heavily at the time, and consequently he hurried on the work of unloading. Mr. Riley's groom had just been talking to him, and then turned away to go to another part of the yard, and on returning in about a minute, Crimpton was found lying on his back. The groom at first thought he was in a fit, and called for assistance, but it was found that he was dying. An attempt was made to administer brandy to the poor fellow, but without success, and he died shortly afterwards.

The object of the Author in recording so fully the above "Chapter of Accidents" is to draw the reader's attention particularly to the many dangers he is liable to either in the hunting field or the streets, and to bring home to him the great necessity of avoiding as far as possible those obstacles to safety which are therein dwelt upon. This advice applies more particularly to the "steam tramcar" and the "traction engine," which, as will be seen, have proved a fruitful source of danger. Of course, many of the incidents recorded are accidents pure and simple, but, on the other hand, a large number of them would never have happened if the advice so persistently given by the Author in the preceding pages had been accepted and acted upon.

SHAKESPEARE A HORSEMAN.

"And speak his very heart."—*Winters Tale*, Act iv., Scene iii.

E would still further "CENTAUR'S" cause by holding up a few of the pictures drawn by the great master.

Of Shakespeare's knowledge, experience, and love for the horse, and good feeling and kindness towards the dumb creation generally, there can be no doubt; in fact it is said that Shakespeare's earliest occupation in London was the care of horses outside the theatres, and in his writings for the play the horse is frequently introduced and enlarged upon, and its trappings and surroundings most vividly described in poetry and prose. We have noticed that it is, and has been for years past, the one great study and pleasure of many students of Shakespeare to associate his name and writings with all trades and professions, and their own in particular. Much instruction as well as amusement is derived from the various lines of argument laid down in the quotations selected from his works. We have spent many happy evenings listening to "Shakespeare, a Surgeon," "Shakespeare, a Lawyer," &c., &c., by those whose ambition has been to connect the great poet with their particular trade or profession.

Our most prominent and permanent experience being a paper written and read by a well-known gentleman in Birmingham, viz., "Shakespeare, a Builder;" and a builder he was made to all intents and purposes, though not in the sense intended by this section of his worshippers. Were it not a known fact that Shakespeare was nothing of the kind, really the arguments laid down, and the selections from his writings brought so vividly and continuously to the front and so strongly to bear, one would be inclined to feel that, if Shakespeare was not apprenticed to a builder, he must

The Author's Centaur

have been in some way connected with that particular craft, or was greatly interested in bricks and mortar all his life. Be that as it may, the Author of "CENTAUR" would say Shakespeare was a horseman; not a horse doctor, nor a horse dealer, but one who had a thorough knowledge of, and interest in, the horse and its surroundings. His description of a "screw" and bad "Turn Out," as quoted from "Taming of the Shrew," could not be better or more truthfully pictured by any harness maker, horse breaker, or veterinary surgeon.

TAMING OF THE SHREW.
ACT III. SCENE II.

BIONDELLO. His horse hipped with an *old mothy saddle*, the *stirrups* of no kindred, besides possessed with *glanders*, and like to mose in the *chine*; troubled with the *lampass*, infected with the fashions (farcy), full of *wind-galls*, sped with *spavins*, raied with the yellows, past cure of the *fires* (vives, "*staggers*"), stark spoilt with the *staggers*, begnawn with the *bots*, swayed in the back and shoulder-shotten, *near-legged* before (foundered in the fore feet), and with a *ha'f-checked bit*, and a *head-stall* of *sheep's leather*, which, being restrained to keep him from *stumbling*, hath been often burst, and now repaired with knots; one *girth* six times pieced, and a woman's *crupper* of velure (velvet), which hath two letters for her name, fairly set down in studs, and here and there pieced with *pack-thread*.

And again what wonderfully expressive words are put into the mouths of the Constable of France, the Duke of Orleans, the Dauphin, and others, in the late Charles Calvert's favourite play:

HENRY V.
SCENE VII.

CON. Tut! I have the best *armour* of the world.
—— 'Would it were day!
ORL. You have an excellent *armour*; but let my *horse* have its due.
CON. It is the best horse of Europe.
ORL. Will it never be morning?
DAU. My Lord of Orleans and my Lord High Constable, you talk of horse and armour,—
ORL. You are well provided of both as any prince in the world.
DAU. What a long night is this! I will not change my horse with any that treads but on four *pasterns*. Ca, ca! He bounds

from the earth as if his entrails were hairs: *le cheval vo'ant*, the Pegasus, *qui a les nar.nes de feu !* When I bestride him I soar; I am a hawk. He *trots* the air; the earth sings when he touches it; the basest *horn* of his *hoof* is more musical than the pipe of Hermes.

ORL. He's the colour of the nutmeg.

DAU. And of the heat of ginger. It is a beast for Perseus; he is pure air and fire, and the dull elements of earth and water never appear in him. He is, indeed, a horse, and all other *jades* you may call beasts.

CON. Indeed, my lord, it is a most absolute and excellent horse.

DAU. It is a prince of *palfreys*; his *neigh* is like the bidding of a monarch, and his countenance enforces homage.

ORL. No more, cousin.

DAU. Nay, the man hath no wit that cannot, from the rising of the lark to the lodging of the lamb, vary deserved praise on my palfrey. It is a theme as fluent as the sea; turn the sands into eloquent tongues, and my horse is argument for them all; 'tis a subject for a sovereign to reason on, and for a sovereign's sovereign to ride on; and for the world (familiar to us, and unknown) to lay apart their particular functions, and wonder at him. I once writ a sonnet in his praise, and began thus:—

"Wonder of nature,"—

ORL. I have heard a sonnet begin so to one's mistress.

DAU. Then did they imitate that which I composed to my courser; for my horse is my mistress.

ORL. Your mistress bears well.

DAU. Me well; which is the prescript praise and perfection of a good and particular mistress.

CON. Ma foy ! the other day methought your mistress shrewdly shook your back.

DAU. So perhaps did yours.

CON. Mine was not *bridled*.

DAU. O ! then belike she was old and gentle, and you rode like a Kerne of Ireland, your French hose off and in your straight trossers.

CON. You have good judgment in horsemanship.

DAU. Be warned by me, then, that they who ride so, and ride not warily, fall into foul bogs. I had rather have my horse to my mistress.

Thus we see the expressions, titles, and terms, used by Shakespeare nearly 300 years ago are still in vogue to day, and in many instances cannot be improved upon. Anyway, his love for, and kindness to the horse is a great example and lesson for the present generation; and not only for the horse do his sympathies extend, but for the meaner beasts, such as the mule, ass, dog, &c. See—

MERCHANT OF VENICE.

ACT IV. SCENE I.

SHY. What judgment shall I dread, doing no wrong?
You have among you many a purchased slave,
Which, like your asses, and your dogs, and mules,
You use in abject and in slavish parts,
Because you bought them. Shall I say to you,
Let them be free?

TROILUS AND CRESSIDA.

ACT V. SCENE I.

THER. With too much blood and too little brain these two may run mad; but if with too much brain and too little blood they do, I'll be a curer of madmen. Here's Agamemnon—an honest fellow enough, and one that loves quails; but he has not so much brain as ear-wax; and the goodly transformation of Jupiter there, his brother, the bull—the primitive statue and oblique memorial of cuckolds; a thrifty shoeing horn on chain, hanging at his brother's leg—to what form but that he is, should wit, larded with malice, and malice, forced with wit, turn him to? To an ass, were nothing; he is both ox and ass. To be a dog, a mule, a cat, a fitchew, a toad, a lizard, an owl, a puttock, or a herring without a roe, I would not care; but to be Menelaus, I would conspire against destiny.

MEASURE FOR MEASURE.

ACT I. SCENE III.

CLAUD. A horse whereon the governor doth ride,
Who newly in the *seat*, that it may know
He can command, lets it straight feel the *spur*.

COMEDY OF ERRORS.

ACT III. SCENE II.

DROS. Such claim as you would lay to your horse.

MUCH ADO ABOUT NOTHING.

ACT III. SCENE V.

DOGB. Well said, i' faith, neighbour.
VERGES. Well, God's a good man; an two men ride of a horse one must ride behind.

LOVE'S LABOUR LOST.

ACT IV. SCENE I.

PRIN. Was that the King, that *spurred* his horse so hard against the steep uprising of the hill?

ACT I. SCENE II.

MOTH. The dancing horse will tell you.

MIDSUMMER NIGHT'S DREAM.

ACT III. SCENE I.

As true as truest horse that yet would never tire.

AS YOU LIKE IT.

ACT III. SCENE V.

CEL. Yes, I think he is not a pickpurse, nor a *horsedealer*.

CEL. . . . . As a puny tilter, that *spurs his horse but on one side*.

ACT V. SCENE III.

2nd Page. I' faith, i' faith, and both in a tune, like gipsies on a horse.

TAMING OF THE SHREW.

ACT III. SCENE II.

BION. O, sir, his *lackey*, for all the world caparisoned like the horse, with a linen stock on one leg, and a kersey boot-hose on the other, gartered with a red and blue list, an old hat, and "the humour of forty fancies" pricked in't for a feather; a monster, a very monster, in apparel; and not like a Christian ootboy, or a gentleman's lackey.

BION. No, sir, I say his horse comes with him on his back.

ACT IV. SCENE I.

GRU. First, know my horse is tired; my master and mistress fallen out.

CURT. How?

GRU. Out of their *saddles* into the dirt, and thereby hangs a tale.

GRU. . . . . . we come down a foul hill, my master riding behind my mistress——

CURT. Both on one horse?

GRU. What's that to thee?

CURT. Why, a horse.

GRU. Tell thou the tale; but hadst thou not crossed me thou shouldst have heard how her horse fell, and she under her horse;

thou shouldst have heard in how miry a place! how she was
bemoiled; how he left her with her horse upon her; how he beat
me because her horse *stumbled*; how she waded through the dirt
to pluck him off me; how he swore; how she prayed that never
prayed before; how I cried; how the horses ran away; how her
bridle was burst; how I lost my *crupper*, with many things
worthy of memory which now shall die in oblivion, and thou
return unexperienced to thy grave.

ACT I. SCENE II.

GRU. . . . . . though she may have as many diseases
as two-and-fifty horses: why, nothing comes amiss, so money
comes withal.

PET. . . . . Loud 'larums, *neighing* steeds, and
trumpets clang?

KING LEAR.
ACT III. SCENE VI.

FOOL. He's mad that trusts in the tameness of a wolf, a horse's
health.

ROMEO AND JULIET.
ACT I. SCENE IV.

MER. . . . . This is the very Mab that *plaits the
manes of horses* in the night.

CYMBELINE.
ACT V. SCENE IV.

1ST GAOL. . . . . . . So *graze*, as you find *pasture*.

MIDSUMMER NIGHT'S DREAM.
ACT III. SCENE I.

PUCK. . . . . . Sometime a horse I'll be, sometime a
hound,
A hog, a headless bear, sometimes a fire;
And *neigh*, and bark, and grunt, and roar, and burn,
Like horse, hound, hog, bear, fire, at every turn.

ACT II. SCENE I.

PUCK. When I a fat and *bean-fed* horse beguile,
Neighing in likeness of a *filly foal*.

TAMING OF THE SHREW.
ACT IV. SCENE I.

PET. Where be these knaves? What, no man at door
To hold my *stirrup*, nor to take my horse!
   *   *   *

You lagger-headed and unpolished *grooms!*
   *   *   *

GRU. . . . . . and not presume to touch a hair of my master's horse-tail.

MERCHANT OF VENICE.
ACT V. SCENE I.

LOR. The reason is, your spirits are attentive,
For do but note a wild and wanton herd
Or race of youthful and unhandled colts,
Fetching mad bounds, bellowing, and neighing loud,
Which is the hot condition of their blood.

COMEDY OF ERRORS.
ACT II. SCENE I.

LUC. O, know he is the *bridle* of your will.
ADR. There's none but asses will be *bridled* so.

KING RICHARD II.
ACT III. SCENE II.

K. RICH. Though rebels wound thee with their horses' hoofs.

KING HENRY IV.
FIRST PART. ACT I. SCENE I.

K. HEN. Nor bruise her flowerets with the arméd hoofs
Of hostile paces.
K. HEN. Sir Walter Blunt, *new-lighted from* his horse.

ACT V. SCENE III.
P. HEN. Under the hoofs of vaunting enemies.

HENRY V.

CHOR. Think, when we talk of horses, that you see them
Printing their proud hoofs i' the receiving earth.

ACT V. SCENE II.

K. HEN. If I could win a lady at leapfrog, or by *vaulting* into my *saddle* with my armour on my back.

HENRY IV.
ACT II. SCENE I.

1ST CAR. . . . . . and yet our horse not packed. What, *ostler!*
1ST CAR. I pr'y thee, Tom, beat *Cut's saddle*, put a few *flocks in the point*: the poor jade is *wrung in the withers* out of all cess
2ND CAR. Peas and beans are as dank here as a dog, and that is the next way to give poor jades the *bots*. This house is turned upside down since Robin *ostler* died.

MIDSUMMER NIGHT'S DREAM.
ACT IV. SCENE I.

THES. My love shall hear the music of my hounds,—

KING HENRY VIII.
ACT V. SCENE II.

GAR My noble lords : for those that tame wild horses
Pace them not in their hands to make them gentle,
But stop their mouths with *stubborn bits and spur* them.
GAR. . . . . . . 'tis a cruel'y to load a falling man.

TESTIMONIALS, &c.

EXTRACTS from Opinions of the Press, and Private Testimonials to the Author of the Royal Horse Book "CENTAUR."

OPINIONS OF ENGLISH AND FOREIGN JOURNALS.

THE LONDON GAZETTE.

"Indeed, 'CENTAUR' is one of the most interesting works of its class that has come under our attention, and it should be in the possession of all who have to do with horses, saddlery, vehicles, &c."

PUBLIC OPINION.

"'CENTAUR' is the want of the age."

THE CITY, July, 1882.

Mr. EDWARD W. GOUGH, of Park Hall House, Park Street, Walsall, may be congratulated upon the success which his efforts to relieve the suffering of horses, and to spread general knowledge as to their management have achieved, and also upon the manner in which those efforts are now most deservedly recognized by high and low. At the Exhibition of Means and Appliances for the Protection of Human Life Mr. GOUGH exhibited a special collection of saddlery, comprising the 'humane dock' for harness, the patent saddle bar, a best saddle fitted with bar, a stirrup leather bar to prevent rider being dragged in case of accident, besides copies of his celebrated work 'CENTAUR,' a practical treatise on the humane management of the horse, for the preservation of human life, &c., to which we called attention some time ago, and which is becoming a household word with everybody interested in or connected with horses. A proof of the estimation in which Mr. GOUGH'S inventions and treatise are held is furnished by the award of the jury to him of—

"1. The Highest Award Certificate.

"2. The Silver Medal and Certificate.

"3. The Special Certificate for Distinguished Merit.

"The award was announced to Mr. GOUGH in the following letter from the Secretary :—

[COPY.]

"12, CRANE COURT, FLEET STREET,
"LONDON, E.C.

"E. W. GOUGH, ESQ.

"MY DEAR SIR,

"I have the pleasure to inform you that you are awarded the Highest Prize for your display of Saddlery, and your work "CENTAUR," including Silver Medal and Special Certificate of Distinguished Merit.

"Yours truly,
"LAURENCE SAUNDERS, C.E.,
"*Hon. Sec.*

"We may mention that Mr. GOUGH was selected as one of the deputation to wait upon the Prince and Princess of Teck at Kensington Palace, as well as a member of the Reception Committee for receiving their Royal and Serene Highnesses, Mr. A. B. Burdett-Coutts, the Rajah Rampal Singh, and other distinguished personages, and that such was the feeling amongst the 300 other exhibitors that the announcement of the award to him presented by Prince Teck was received with great and general applause on their part. The inhabitants of Walsall may indeed be proud of their town being so well and successfully represented at this Exhibition in the midst of so many influential London, Provincial, and Foreign exhibits, and there can be no doubt that Walsall must be now considered as the chief place for this class of exhibits. As to Mr. GOUGH'S book, 'CENTAUR' the highest praise is expressed in the words of the judges 'that it was calculated to save more life and limb than all the lifeboats., It may also be stated that gold medals did not apply to the respective section, but that several gentlemen have combined to send one, in addition, to Mr. GOUGH, and that the Prince of Teck complimented him in a special letter. It is hardly necessary for us to report more specially on Mr. GOUGH'S exhibit. Where excellence is so widely appreciated long reviews appear to be superfluous.

"The Royal Horse Book, 'CENTAUR,' has already reached its third (and popular) enlarged edition with an issue of 10,000. The price has been reduced from 21s. to 2s. 6d. per copy, and this excellent work is therefore now within the reach of everybody. It is the intention of the Author to complete it in such a form as to establish it as a standard book of reference for all enquiries or questions as to the horse and its surroundings. Thus, inventors or proprietors of any specialities in connection with or appertaining to the horse, stable, carriage, harness, farm, or any article of recognised value, of whatever class, should communicate their 'notice' or advertisement to the Author for securing an everlasting position in this monster edition, so as not to be omitted from the 'Reference List' and 'Index' in conjunction with the important firms already noted. The perusal of the work itself we recommend to all those who have not yet read it. It reflects the highest credit on the Author's intelligence, thorough knowledge of the subject, and kindness of heart, and deserves the place of honour in the library of sportsmen and owners of horses.

"Mr. EDWARD W. GOUGH'S name ought, in fine, to be written in golden letters in the books of the Royal Society for the Prevention of Cruelty to Animals, of which he is a member. Mr. GOUGH'S achievements in the practical line of saddlery are only second to the success of his book. The articles supplied by him, from harness to mill-banding, from mackintosh coats to sheeting and delivery hose, are all of excellent quality, and bear the stamp of the successful inventor, and we conclude this short report with the wish that Mr. GOUGH may be as well appreciated by his fellow townsmen, and in the narrower limits of the Midland Counties, as he already is in European circles, and by the general public from the prince down to the groom."

THE WALSALL FREE PRESS, July 6th, 1878,

"Many of our readers have had their curiosity excited by seeing on the walls for months past the word 'CENTAUR,' which we understand has been posted in every city, town, and village throughout the kingdom; and inquirers have had their inquisitiveness to some extent gratified by being informed, through the 'Notice to Correspondents' columns in various newspapers, that the word signifies a mythical being, having the head, body, and arms of a man, and the body and limbs of a horse; but although this explained the meaning of the word, it left the mystery pretty much where it was, or rather it made confusion worse confounded, for what could the posting of such a word all over Great Britain mean? Some thought that like the words, 'The Man with the Carpet Bag,' or 'The Ticket of Leave Man,' it referred to some new drama; others thought it referred to some circus that intended visiting the town, and not a few jumped to the conclusion that it was some new machine. But few indeed ever dreamt that it was the title of a book; but such, however is the fact, as will be seen by a notice in our advertising columns. The work, which we perceive is dedicated, by kind permission, to our worthy Member of Parliament, Sir Charles Forster, is a practical treatise upon the horse and his master. The Author is our townsman, Mr. E. W. GOUGH, who is a Member of the Society for the Prevention of Cruelty to Animals, and has often witnessed the unnecessary sufferings to which horses have been put, through the ignorance of inexperienced parties; and the evils resulting therefrom, to both man and animal have frequently impressed him with the idea of preparing and publishing a few simple rules upon the management of horses—a task for which his practical knowledge and long experience pre-eminently qualified him; but, on prosecuting his design, he found, as many others have done, that as he proceeded the work increased, till at length it formed a goodly-sized volume—a specimen copy of which we have been privileged to examine; and, judging from it, we believe the work will prove an exceedingly useful one, for although complete and comprehensive, it is neither cumbrous nor profuse, but such as will enable those entrusted with the care and management of horses and vehicles of every description to avoid many errors and mistakes which arise from lack of that knowledge which the work will impart, and the want of which is productive of much suffering to the animals, and injury to the vehicles; for, as the poet says—

"'Evil is wrought by want of thought,
As well as want of heart.'"

"No pains have been spared to make the book both useful and attractive. It is profusely illustrated with original engravings, specially prepared for the work, which, in order to facilitate and lessen the labours of the inquirer, is divided into chapters, with an appropriate title, or heading, to each, so that time is saved and trouble spared, as every piece of information can be readily found under its proper heading."

STAFFORDSHIRE ADVERTISER, July 6th, 1878.

"Under the title of 'CENTAUR; OR, THE TURN OUT,' Mr. E. W. GOUGH, Saddlery and Harness Manufacturer, of Walsall (who is a Member of the Royal Society for the Prevention of Cruelty to Animals), has just published a Hand-book for the use of all persons who have set up, or about to set up, a 'Turn Out.'

or who may have to deal with Horses, Saddlery, or Harness. In a series of chapters he gives, with *the thoroughness and practical grasp of detail of a man who has mastered his subject by long and careful thought*, very valuable hints and instructions with regard to the selection and classification of Horses, good Grooming, the purchasing or ordering of Harness, Driving, Harnessing, and Unharnessing, and a host of kindred topics, his aim being to ensure *a kindly treatment of the Horse*, and the *comfort and safety* of the *driver or rider*. The instruction is conveyed in a plain, familiar style, and where received and acted upon cannot fail to smooth over many difficulties in the management of 'The Turn Out.' The volume, which, by the way, is profusely illustrated, is, by special permission, dedicated to the Borough Member, Sir CHARLES FORSTER, Bart."

SADDLERS', HARNESS MAKERS', AND CARRIAGE BUILDERS' GAZETTE, London, August, 1878.

"From time to time Walsall has produced numerous books connected with her manufactures, but they have chiefly assumed the form of illustrated catalogues, and purely to promote trade; but one has at last appeared with a much higher and nobler purpose, that is, a humane and intelligent treatment of the horse, and a series of instructions to lighten and make pleasant his often very arduous duties in the service of man. With a personal acquaintance with the Author, Mr. E. W. GOUGH, member of the Royal Humane Society, we can express nothing but the highest satisfaction that such a subject should have occupied his attention and assumed the impress of his intelligent, generous mind. The work is profusely illustrated with subjects of great originality; it is printed in beautifully clear type, and makes an elegant volume of the most interesting and readable matter.

"The seat of the leather trades, in common with the country generally, has recently been greatly exercised in its mind by the appearance upon its walls and in its windows of the word 'CENTAUR; OR, THE TURN OUT,' and which, now that the mystery has been worked up to the top of its bent, we are at liberty to announce, is not that composite order of being met with in Greek and Latin mythology, but the name of an elegant work, in beautiful clear type, profusely illustrated and neatly bound, suitable for study or stable, warehouse, manufactory, or drawing room table.

"The Author, who is known as a gentleman of considerable and varied talent (acquired by both home experience and travel in foreign lands), which he is ever ready to place at the disposal of any good or charitable cause, has been led to write this book from the same kindly feeling which induced him to become a Fellow of the Royal Humane Society, of which he is an unusually active member in his own way. The main scope and object of his work is to induce a treatment of that best friend of man, the horse, which shall be based solely upon kindness and method; the keynote of all, which is struck in one of the early illustrations, representing a hand with corn, placed invitingly under the mouth of a horse. The perusal of this book will teach the reader how he may best carry this thought and tenderness into the harnessing, unharnessing, and, indeed, into every action connected with the horse; until vice or trouble of any kind gives place to a cheerful willingness, which is simply delightful to both. As is natural to a man the business of whose life is to supply vast quantities of saddlery, harness, stable, coach, and colliery requisites, Mr. GOUGH has much to say upon all these things, the perusal of which will repay the time spent.

"To identify his book with his own town, which of all others caters most largely for the horse, Mr. GOUGH has sought for the patronage of the local M.P., Sir Charles Forster, the result being a very prompt and cheerful assent. Under all these favourable auspices, we predict for "CENTAUR" a very successful career, and none the less so that it is published by an enterprising London firm."

The WALSALL OBSERVER, July, 1878.

"'CENTAUR; OR, THE TURN OUT.' By E. W. GOUGH.— This book, whose first title pasted on the walls gave rise to so much enquiry some few months since, is now almost ready to be put into the hands of the public, who will then be able to satisfy their curiosity to the full. The work is described by the author as being 'a practical treatise on the (humane) management of horses, either in harness, saddle, or stable, with hints respecting harness-room, coach-house, &c.' In this brief sentence lies the whole plan of the volume, which differs from any of the standard works upon horses in many particulars—indeed, it may be said to be unique both in design and execution. After a few general remarks, tending to show the advantage to owners of care and tenderness with the horse, the Author proceeds to deal in a plain and practical style with 'The thorough groom,' an official whose value will be enhanced because his character and capabilities will be better known after a perusal of this the opening essay. We say 'essay' advisedly, for the book consists, not of chapters, but of a series of papers upon different subjects connected with the horse and his appurtenances. Next is given some sound advice on selecting the horse, followed by a classification of horses and their standard measure and principal points, and the rules for judging their age. The next essays are devoted to the harness and how to fit it, how to harness and unharness the animal, driving, the vehicle, and riding; while after these come those upon the stable, on various sorts of gears, and some others of less special but more general interest, upon 'The effect of music upon horses,' 'Wonderful horses,' and other matters. Among these miscellaneous articles is one upon 'Horsey phrases,' and a number of hints and recipes. The latter belong to that class of remedy which in the household would be called 'family medicines,' and in no way trench upon the department of the veterinary surgeon. The book is illustrated by a large number of plates, all of which are good, and most of them are excellent in every way. Several are of a special character, and promise to be exceedingly useful. We may specially mention the one showing the anatomy of the horse, which is drawn to scale, and marked in such a clear way that every part of the animal may be technically named with ease. The volume throughout aims to be practical, and, if we may use the term, homely. The minute details on which so much depends, but which are so frequently overlooked, receive full attention, and the advice and information given, while indispensable to the amateur, are not beneath the notice of the most experienced professional. With regard to some things, the latter may perhaps think that prominence is given to 'what everybody knows,' but, unfortunately, it is just those things which are so often forgotten. Throughout there is a vein of kindness which speaks well for the Author's knowledge of, and hence love for, his subject; only in one thing can exception be taken to his remarks. The exception is with regard to the use of the bearing rein, into the discussion on which we must decline to enter, further than to say that Mr. GOUGH certainly gives comprehensible reasons for the position he takes. The book is dedicated to Sir Charles Forster, Bart., M.P., by whom, as the impersonation of the saddlery town of the world, the compliment was well deserved. In his address to the hon. member, Mr. GOUGH justly says that the work 'will be found to contain such instructions as will, if strictly carried out, enable those entrusted with the care of that most useful and faithful companion of man—the horse— to secure its comfort, preserve its health, and prolong its usefulness.' In these days horses, like time, are money; and we have every confidence in recommending this handsome volume to every one who has, or is likely to have, a 'Turn Out.' With 'matter' of so much interest and use, the 'manner' in which it is placed before the public is, perhaps, of little moment; but in this instance the get-up is worthy of its contents, the appearance of the book justifying us in saying that it would grace the shelves of any library. Since the above notice was written, a letter has been received by Mr. GOUGH from Sir Charles Forster, Bart., who says:—'Accept my best thanks for the very handsome edition of your work, which I found awaiting my arrival, at Lysways, on my return. This circumstance will explain why I have not sooner acknowledged its receipt. I have not yet had time to make a complete perusal of the book; but, from what I have read, I am convinced of the necessity of the object which you have in view, and I will not fail to name it among my friends, hoping it may meet with the success it merits. Allow me to congratulate you on the admirable way in which it is got up and illustrated.' This commendation strongly supports our view."

The BRITISH MERCANTILE GAZETTE, London.

"'CENTAUR; OR, THE TURN OUT.' By E. W. GOUGH, M.R.S.P.C.A. This very handsome and thoroughly useful volume reflects the highest credit alike on the head and heart of the Author. The discrimination and thorough knowledge of his subject evinced by Mr. GOUGH is only equalled by the innate love for that noble animal, the horse, which has led him to perform the self-imposed task of compiling such a practical and instructive treatise on all that relates to his equine friend. An excellent portrait of the Author forms the frontispiece, and numerous other highly executed illustrations also adorn the work, the chief aim and object of which is to induce a treatment of the horse which shall be based solely upon kindness and method; the keynote of all, which is struck in one of the early illustrations, representing a hand with corn placed under the horse's mouth, and entitled 'Mutual Feeling.' It also contains valuable information as to stable fittings, and practical hints respecting the harness-room, coach-house, and general saddlery, as used at home and abroad.'

THE STABLE, London, 1st June, 1884.

"Mr. GOUGH'S book is well known as about the best Horse book as well as the undoubted original one, and we are induced to refer to it now partly because a cheap and popular edition is being brought out, and partly because on the occasion of our recent trip to Walsall we fell in with the Author, and were promptly assured from personal conversation that he 'knows about what he writes.' Now-a-days this is *not* a common feature though it is one of sterling merit, *and if some of the impudent pirates who have copied* MR. GOUGH'S *title, stolen his ideas* and ruined them in their adaptation, and generally written heaps of nonsense about horses, had a little of that quality, they would not have misled so many of their unfortunate readers. But no one can ever be misled by Mr. GOUGH'S book, which abounds in illustrations and letter-press of first class value and obvious applicability. Some of the blocks are very high class, and although they have been copied as closely as the copyright laws would allow, the pirates have failed to grasp the ideas, and so far as we have been able to ascertain the blocks of the 'Anatomy of the Horse' the 'Teeth and Feet,' and others stand out alone, and are still unique in the rapidly increasing equine library of the world. That this view is not our own solely is evidenced by the fact that at the Life Saving Exhibition in 1882, the 'CENTAUR' ran away from all competitors, and took the highest award.

"The Author resides at Park Hall House, which might more aptly be called 'The Centaur Hall,' or the 'Perfect Stable,' for Mr. GOUGH'S love of horses, and everything in connection with them, is apparent on every hand. He is one of the largest and oldest established saddlery, harness, mill banding, and horse clothing manufacturers in the trade, and is the inventor, among other things, of the 'Imperial' four-in-hand, the 'Congress' tandem, the 'Royal' pair horse, and the 'CENTAUR' humane harness, so that he speaks with authority on this branch of the subject as well as that which is confined more strictly to the horse itself.

"Referring to this, we may say that the Author is a practical rider and driver, and has made the subject of his work his sole study, his great principle being *humane treatment*. Mr. GOUGH, to thoroughly obtain his end and to master this great question, and illustrate the good results of treating the horse humanely, and so cause him to work better and live longer, was not satisfied with what he saw in his own country, but spent some time abroad, and so saw this noble creature, the horse, under various climes and treatments, and, being a keen observer, [and having one purpose in view, nothing was lost to him which would benefit the horse or his keeper. One of the most important features of the book is its simplicity; every subject is so clearly and fully treated and classified that the dullest reader of its pages could not fail to perceive the Author's object, and after studying the rules and facts laid down, the most ignorant should be able to safely purchase a horse without the least fear of being 'sold.' Mr. GOUGH showed us most flattering testimonials of his work he had received from nearly all the crowned heads of the world, and many hundreds from landed gentry.

"One just received was from His Majesty the King of Siam, thanking Mr. GOUGH cordially for his humane treatment of the horse, and saying, 'it was quite in accordance with the writer's religion.'

"Before taking our leave of Mr. GOUGH he informed us that he was shortly about to publish a cheaper edition of his valuable work, through Messrs. Thacker and Co., of New Street Square, London, E.C., which he hoped to be able to supply at the very low price of 2s. 6d. per copy, so that it would be within the reach of everybody, and we certainly say that *everybody* should possess it. We should strongly advise the trade to stock it as soon as the new edition is ready, and by recommending it to their customers, they will confer a boon upon them, and a still greater one upon the noble subject of the book."

MISCELLANEOUS PRESS OPINIONS.

"The Horse Book of the day."

"It may be said to be unique both in design and execution."

"Undoubtedly written by one thoroughly experienced, and of very kindly feeling."

"Is extremely interesting."

"For all readers."

"The illustrations are specimens of art."

"Is sure to command success."

"The title of this book should be 'The Horse and its True Friend.'"

"Will do honour to the city from which it emanates."

"A most original work, and supplies a real want."

"It is a jewel among books."

"Goes right away at both sides of the question."

"Will become the world's property."

"The success it deserves."

PRIVATE TESTIMONIALS.*

EXTRACTS FROM LETTERS SENT DIRECT TO THE AUTHOR.

THE PRESIDENT OF AMERICA—"'CENTAUR' is a useful and interesting work."

THE KING OF ITALY wrote in the highest terms of "CENTAUR," February 13th, 1882.

---

* The Original of these Testimonials can be seen on application to the Author.

The President of the Council of Ministers of Egypt—"'Centaur' is an inspiration."

The King of Roumania—"I have read the original volume, 'Centaur,' with much pleasure."

The King of Siam, through his Interpreter—"'Centaur' is in harmony with our religion, and is the best book on horses His Majesty has ever seen."

Sir W. V. Harcourt—"'Centaur' is an interesting work."

Lord Northbrook—"'Centaur' is an interesting work on humane treatment."

The Governor of the Tower of London—"'Centaur' contains good practical advice upon the subject."

The Duke of Cambridge—"Received the copy of 'Centaur' with much pleasure."

Sir H. B. W. Brand (late Speaker to the House of Commons)—"'Centaur' is an interesting work on the treatment of the horse."

The Baroness Burdett Coutts—"Shall read 'Centaur' with much pleasure."

Sir Henry Allsopp—"From the perusal of 'Centaur' I derived much pleasure and benefit."

Sir Charles Forster says—of this Work—"I am convinced of the necessity of the object which you have in view, and I will not fail to name it among my friends, hoping it may meet with the success it merits. Allow me to congratulate you on the admirable way in which 'Centaur' is got up and illustrated."

Sir John Morris—"I shall not only read 'Centaur' with very much pleasure, but shall get many of my friends to do so."

J. B. Gough, the American Orator, says:—"I value the book, 'Centaur,' very highly, and shall give it an honoured place in my library at home."

From J. W. Myers, *Proprietor of the largest Hippodrome in the World.*

LONDON, N.,
July 1st, 1882.

E. W. Gough, Esq.,

My Dear Sir,

I am pleased to see that you purpose publishing a popular edition of your very valuable and original Horse Book "Centaur," at 2s. 6d. per copy (enlarged), as the work should certainly reach the hands of all who have to do with horses.

I purchased a copy of the 2nd edition last year at 21s., and consider two of the many illustrations alone to be worth the money. In fact, the book is in constant reference at my Hippodrome, and I would not part with it for any money.

I have the honour to be, Sir,
Yours faithfully,
J. W. MYERS.

HOCHLEY HILL, BIRMINGHAM,
September 11th, 1887.

E. W. GOUGH, Esq., Walsall.

DEAR SIR.

I have been much pleased in reading a copy of your new work named the "CENTAUR."

It contains a large amount of information which cannot help but be very useful. I consider it is carefully written and reflects great credit upon the Author.

I am certainly surprised with your extensive business engagements that you should have been able to give the necessary time and study to get up a work of such magnitude, and in so complete a manner.

I am, Dear Sir,
Yours truly,
FREDERICK RAWLINS.

COOKE'S ROYAL CIRCUS. WALSALL,
July 7th, 1882.

MR. GOUGH.

DEAR SIR,

I am very much pleased indeed with your work entitled "CENTAUR." Having had a life experience with horses, I am quite sure the arguments used by you are in every way correct; in fact, I consider your work a very valuable assistance to any horse proprietor. There is one thing I should strongly suggest, viz., that you should endeavour to make a cheap edition; by so doing, you would bring it under the notice of many who cannot at present avail themselves of so great an assistance; and another thing is, should your work get spread, as it most assuredly will at a cheaper rate among the working classes, I feel confident that much good will arise from it, there will be less cruelty exercised, and more affection shown by the different animals for their masters, thereby rendering a great blessing to the sometimes overworked beast of laden.

I am, yours truly,
ALFRED EUGENE COOKE.

PRINCE OF WALES THEATRE, WOLVERHAMPTON,
July 23rd, 1881.

DEAR SIR,

Mr. Birrell desires me to acknowledge the receipt of your clever work "CENTAUR." He is very much pleased with it, and I know he has been reading it until between three and four in the morning, and desires me to thank you very heartily for the pleasure it has afforded him. To tell you the truth, he has greatly excited my curiosity, and I look forward to much enjoyment in perusing it.

Yours truly,
H. S. SPRINGATE.

E. W. GOUGH, Esq.

The Royal Horse Book "CENTAUR" received the Highest Award (Silver Medal and Special Certificate of Distinguished Merit), at the London Exhibition of Means and Appliances for the Protection and Preservation of Human Life, August, 1882, against world-wide competition.

Testimonials have been received by the Author from all parts of the World.

CONCLUSION: EXPLANATION OF TITLE.

EVERYTHING that has a commencement must have a conclusion, and "CENTAUR" is no exception to the general rule Therefore, as the mythical creature whose name the Author has adopted as the title for his book possesses the head of a man and the extremities of a horse, so this work has its commencement or head, and now comes the conclusion or tail (end). But here the writer, before bringing his work to a close, would add a word or two by way of justification of the peculiar title he has taken for his book.

The "CENTAUR," like most of the ancient legends, had a deep meaning.

Thus—man by his "humane" treatment of the horse imparts to it a portion of his nature, and the animal becomes so wise that it obeys the will of its rider or groom as readily as do the members of the human body the impulse of the brain; and in this sense the horseman and the horse become one, and the brain of the man becomes, as it were, united to and governs the body of the horse.*

The Author wishes it to be clearly and distinctly understood that he makes no pretension to having exhausted the various subjects brought under consideration in this work. To have done so would have necessitated writing a volume

---

* A striking illustration of the power of kindness and companionship upon the horse came under the writers' notice a short time ago. A little boy eight years old was missing from the house of a friend whom the Author was visiting in Warwickshire. Search was made, but the child could not be found; at length he was discovered lying in a field beside a young horse, with his arms round (or upon) the animal's neck. Although the child had only been at the place about three weeks, the horse would follow him like a dog wherever he called it, and when they were lying together, if the horse wanted to get up, it always took care to rouse the child by rubbing its nose against the child's face, nor would it rise until it had seen its young companion at a safe distance first; then the animal would roll over, spring up, and trot to the child's side.

as large as the present upon each subject. What he aimed at was the production of a book containing, in a condensed form, such information as would serve as a guide, and such instruction as would prove practically useful to owners and managers of horses and vehicles, and also to those about to set up a "turn out;" and he hopes the object he had in view has been attained.

He would also express his indebtedness to those gentlemen who have furnished him with information regarding facts which have come under their personal observation; and which have corroborated the Author's experiences and views of the various subjects treated in the "CENTAUR."

As a further explanation of his title, the Author would give the following extract from "Mr. Carrington," a work by Mortimer Collins, published in 1873:—"The rider is of the type of Chiron the Centaur. When he leaps into the saddle it invigorates him; gives him youth again; gives him power. One of those few men is he who make their horse a part of themselves; who, in return for his strength and speed, give the creature they bestride their brain. The meaning of the great Centaur legend lies in this."

A CHAPTER OF SPECIALITIES.

IN placing the following notices of Specialities before the Public, the Author believes that he is not only doing justice to the following well-known firms and to their several inventions and manufactures, but also a duty to the readers of "CENTAUR" in bringing to their notice the several Specialities mentioned in this chapter, each and all of which are to be commended for some special quality. The various opinions have been carefully gone into, and the Author feels that this chapter gives to the reader many things he may desire to know in regard to the numberless inventions appertaining to the Horse, Stable, Harness, &c., and he feels that "CENTAUR" would not have been complete without it.

Messrs. Day, Son & Hewitt.—Day, Son & Hewitt's Horse-keeper's Medicine Chest is one of the articles no horse-keeper should be without; in fact, it is invaluable, and no well-conducted stable is complete without it; for fifty years it has stood the test, it is patronised by royalty, and is used by the principal stock-breeders, horse proprietors, and agriculturalists throughout the British Empire. The advantages of these chests are many, not the least being, that the medicines will keep good for twenty years. The chests not only contain everything necessary for 'doctoring'—but a useful work on "Farriery" is included in each.

James Hanford's Golden Embrocation or "Cure All."—The success which has attended the sale of this Embrocation is a sufficient proof that the Proprietor was warranted in his resolve some years ago to introduce it to the public. That it is a genuine and sure cure for all the ills associated with the keeping and breeding of Horses, Cows and Dogs is fully demonstrated by the large sale it now commands both at home and in the Colonies, and having now stood the test of public opinion for so many years, it deservedly ranks as the best Embrocation ever introduced, not only on account of its cheapness but its curative qualities, which have triumphed over the most obstinate cases. We have read some testimonials of marvellous cures which prove it beyond doubt to be what it professes by name, the "Cure All." One case speaks of a gentleman being thrown off his horse and being cured with using this Embrocation, thus showing it to be good for man as well as beast. One of its special qualities is that it can be used for internal as well as external uses, is always of one standard and therefore a complete medicine chest of itself, and we confidently recommend our readers to give it a trial.

Henry's "Hippacea."—Among the hundred and one specialities in the market as "stable requisites" some have not proved a success, either as "certain cures" or relievers of pain. These, if not gross misrepresentations on the part of the vendors, are, at least, a loss to them, and a vexatious disappointment to the buyer. On the other hand, however, there are genuine inventions of the same class, which have fully justified the claims of their respective inventors, and have accordingly become recognised and recommended as standard value, and a boon alike to suffering horses and anxious owners. Among this last legitimate section we unhesitatingly class the Indian remedy, known to the world as Henry's "Hippacea," manufactured by Mr. F. H. Bowden, in Madras, India, who, to meet the largely increasing European demand for this and other Indian household remedies of his, has recently opened a Central Depot for their supply at 29, Lansdowne Road, Croydon, Surrey. The inventor claims for his "Hippacea," and justly too, judging from the opinions expressed to us by personal friends (to whom samples of this preparation were sent by us for trial and report), and the numerous substantial testimonials of those who have used and keep the preparation in their stables, that this "Hippacea" is simply invaluable, and second to none, for the following troubles and diseases of horses, viz. :—Rheumatism, Wind-stroke, Sprains of all sorts, Sprung Tendons, Sore Throat, Influenza, Stiffness, Bruises, Cuts and Wounds, Broked Knees, Cracked Heels, Over-reaches, Œdema or Swelling of the Legs, Swellings Generally, Sore Shoulders and Backs, Spavins, Heat Lumps, Bites and Stings of flies and noxious insects, Mange and other Skin Diseases and *all* irritable conditions of the skin. For testimonials see Advertisement at end of this work.

Hinkley's Liniment for Horses, Dogs, and Cattle.—The Author has used this embrocation on some horses, and finds it quite as efficacious as stated by the advertisement in our columns. He is of opinion, from economical reasons as well as humane feeling, that no stable should be without it. For curing cracked heels, broken knees, overreaches, sores, cuts, bruises, wounds, insect bites, saddle galls, and splints, it is the best and quickest; as well as for sore throats, influenza, sprains and other complaints. It is used in the Prince of Wales' stables, as well as in many of the nobilities' and gentry's stables throughout Great Britain.

Myers' Royal Cattle Spice.—This spice is patronised by royalty, the nobility and gentry, and is one of the most famed of these introductions. From the results of its use, not only for horses, but also for cattle, sheep, pigs, and even poultry, it will be found to take its stand among all the spices and foods introduced. From the large number of testimonials Mr. Myers has received, it is clearly shown that horses eat better, rest better, are kept in better condition, and will work with more spirit by having "Myers' Spice" mixed with the food, as directed, than if they do not have any at all. The price (which comes to about a halfpenny per horse per day) brings it within the reach of everybody: not only to the owner of horses, but also to breeders of cattle, sheep, pigs, and poultry, this spice will be found invaluable.

Pond's Extract Veterinary Remedy is a very quick and reliable cure for sprains, galls, wounds, swellings, &c., and has this very valuable property, *it will never blemish*. It can be applied freely, and a bandage bound on continuously for days and nights together, keeping it wet through with the liquid, and yet no mark will be left in any case. This makes it much superior to oils or compounds containing turpentine, which often burn the hair off if left on many hours together. The effect of the application is *cooling*, it reduces inflammation and swelling, and heals raw spots and galls very quickly. The manufacturers in their advertisement offer to send a sample bottle free to any readers of this book.

Roper, Son & Co.—This firm, the manufacturers of "Jem Cook's Alterative and Condition Powders," may be said to be one of the most successful firms, for this particular kind of horse medicine: from the large number of testimonials received, it stands very high amongst its compeers. They keep horses in perfect health and prime condition, and free from the various complaints incidental to horses. It is recommended by a large number of veterinary surgeons, and is used by many large owners of horses.

Spratt's "Forage Biscuits" and "Locurium" are two articles which have been favourably received by the public. The "Biscuits" are useful to hunters, and occasionally given for mid-day meal instead of oats, produce a beneficial effect. "Locurium," a patent vegetable oil, is an extraordinary cure for all sorts of wounds, cuts, bruises and burns, and the numerous ills to which horses are subject.

Messrs. Atkinson & Philipson.—The health and general well-being of the horse are not only governed by good feeding and grooming. They are very often influenced by the character of the vehicle to which he is attached, and before his owner can be able to decide whether his animal is striving to perform a task beyond his powers, he must possess a knowledge of the manner in which his strength can be applied with the greatest effect. It is only in recent years that this subject has received the attention it demands, but it is encouraging to find that it has been taken up by eminent coachbuilders duly qualified to deal with it. We may therefore anticipate that a new era has set in, and that the near future will see carriages of every kind constructed not only of a size and weight commensurate with the carrying capacity, but with the power of the horse or horses by which they are to be drawn. In "Harness as it has been, as it is, and as it should be," written three years ago by Mr. John Philipson of the firm of Atkinson & Philipson, Coachbuilders, of Newcastle-on-Tyne, the horse-owning and carriage using community, in addition to being treated to an interesting historical sketch of harness and its uses, gained a general knowledge of the horse and his trappings that could not fail to be valuable. In making public his ideas, Mr. Philipson was endeavouring to make known the advantages to be gained by such methods of driving as that practised in South Africa, and some parts of India, where two-wheeled vehicles are used with a pair of horses running abreast as was the case in the old English curricle, but without the serious disadvantage of one horse bringing down another when he falls. Messrs. Atkinson & Philipson have now constructed a large number of English dogcarts on this system, but by an ingenious arrangement, they are made so that they may be used with shafts alone. We are glad to find that this plan, which until recently was little understood in this country, has met with much encouragement from country gentlemen. The question of draught is another subject that is engaging the attention of the builders we have mentioned. Mr. Wm. Philipson, the eldest son of Mr. John Philipson, and junior partner in the firm, has succeeded in gaining the Worshipful Company of Coachmakers' first prize for an essay on the subject. He deals exhaustively with the question in all its bearings, and successfully explodes many old fashioned notions and prejudices about horses and carriages. In building their celebrated Tilburys, Cape carts, Whitechapels, and gigs, as well as the larger four-wheel carriages such as landaus, broughams, char-a-bancs, and private omnibusses, Messrs. Atkinson and

Philipson do not conform altogether to popular usage. The purchaser of one of their soundly-built and thoroughly finished carriages, usually finds that it runs with a degree of smoothness and comfort and with less distress to the horse than he had previously thought possible.

Mr. J. A. Barnsby, of Walsall, manufacturer of every kind of ladies and gentlemen's saddles, has a world-wide fame for being one of the most notable saddle makers in England. He not only manufactures one or two, or a dozen different kinds and patterns of saddles, but the variety can be counted by hundreds; if we mistake not, he has a larger number of patterns than any other house in the trade. The various descriptions of saddles are legion; not only are they made for home, but every kind suitable for the continental, South American, China, Japan, East and West Indian, Australian and Canadian Markets are to be found at his establishment in Lichfield Street, Walsall. The workmanship shown in every saddle turned out by Mr. Barnsby, is excellent in the extreme, some are most chaste and elegant in design, while others are good and plain, but all bear the stamp of care and good material in their manufacture; among some of the hundreds of patterns, may be mentioned those for ladies and children, which are inlaid with beautiful designs. The new British Army Regulation Staff-officer's saddle, all-over hogskin with basil lining. The Cape Police officers and travelling saddle, particularly suitable for long riding and a special ladies saddle, fitted with lever spring top safe. In the advertisement at end of this chapter, some of the most popular designs of saddles may be seen, and we may mention that numbers 179, 130, 62, 213, 244, and others, are some of the best. Mr. Barnsby being solely a manufacturer of horse trappings, is enabled to submit to his customers a larger variety of designs than he otherwise would, if he laid himself out to supply other goods as well, and we would recommend any of our readers, before ordering elsewhere, to send for his illustrated catalogue of designs. Mr. Barnsby has also patented a stirrup-leather bar, to prevent the rider being dragged in case of accident. This bar possesses several advantages over the ordinary bar, it is very simple in its mechanism, and most effective in its action, in an instant the rider's foot is released from the saddle, and so prevents him being dragged by the horse; by an ingenious arrangement the lever is prevented from being wrenched off by a side strain; it is made with or without spring, and in various kinds of metal and sizes. The price is very moderate, being but little more than the old common pattern, and not only forms a most useful, but an ornamental part to the saddle. This bar has been in use several years and has gained a high name among horsemen who are exposed to accidents. An illustration of this most useful bar is given in Mr. Barnsby's advertisement.

Joseph Clare.—Turning for the moment from the consideration of bits, snaffle, &c., we would draw our readers attention to the well-known wares of Mr. Joseph Clare, of Lower Forster Street, Walsall. Curriers are dressers of leather after the hides are tanned, the hides are cut up to suit the different purposes for which they are required. They have to undergo many processes before they are ready for the "Turn-out" such as tallowing, blacking or staining, enamelling and japanning in many different colours. This latter art may be said to have attained almost complete perfection, as a glance at the many really splendid specimens of well-prepared hides shown by this firm will prove.

J. Tonks & Co.'s Specialities are Saddle leather. Hogskins, skirt hides, backs, middlings and shoulders, &c. Harness leather. Black and brown hides and backs for stout and light straps. Belt leather, &c. Bridle leather, flat rein backs, bridle and collar rein backs, bridle butts and stirrup butts, &c., all qualities. Patent leather. Horse hides, horse fronts, flap, winker and border middlings, enamelled hides, coach backs, splits, seals, &c.

Messrs. Urch & Company.—The proprietors of three distinct establishments for the manufacturing of Harness, Saddles, Saddle-trees, Bits, Bridles, and all the paraphernalia belonging to the equipment of horses for the stable, carriage, and field. Messrs. Urch, of Long Acre, London, are to be reckoned among the great manufacturers of London. The British public are as fond of horses as any nation in the world, and in no country does the hunting field present a nobler aspect than in England. Messrs Urch's hunting saddles are those adopted by our first-class sportsmen, and it is an interesting fact in connection with this establishment that from the tree, the web, the iron, and steel to the "pig-skin," all is of their own manufacture and preparation. So, also, with their harness, every set is made on the premises, from the rough material to its complete perfection; and in no city, town, or province, is fashion more correctly studied, or harness, whether for the tilbury or dog-cart, the state carriage or the brougham, the four-horse drag or the barouche, better "turned out" in all the details which are met for attraction, as well as for thorough service. This firm has also invented a new style for ladies' side-saddles, which, by a flexibility in the seat and a special adaption of the crutches, enables the rider to feel at ease and actually enjoy rest from that fatigue which on the old-fashioned side saddle is inseparable from a long experiment of horse exercise. Nor is their attention solely devoted to harness, or to saddles and bridles, but horse clothing in every variety is found at their establishment, so that in a business which in the ordinary nomenclature of a trade is styled a harness factory, there is not an article connected with horse fittings that is omitted from their catalogue. It is important to buyers and dealers to know that this old-established house are saddlers to the Queen and Royal Family, also H.M. the Viceroy of Egypt and H.M. Government of India. They manufacture the finest kinds of single, double pair-horse, tandem, and four-in-hand harness; also saddles and horse clothing of every description and style, of the best materials and workmanship; no machine work is allowed. Urch's Patent Double Spring Bar for releasing the stirrup leather when the rider is thrown, should be attached to every saddle. Gentlemen ordering private outfits in England; also exporters of English horse goods, are recommended to communicate with Messrs. Urch & Co., as the prices will be found moderate, considering the quality of their manufactures.

Messrs. Doulton & Co.—Among the most important things in the construction of a stable is the impervious nature of the materials with which it is lined, preventing the absorption of all moisture, which is sure to be given out again under certain conditions. The lining of the walls with glazed tiles is an advantage, but better still is the use of the blue Staffordshire brick for the paving. A large proportion of iron is found in the clay with which this class of ware is made, and hence its great strength. In stable pavings there should be no porosity, they should be hard to resist the constant wear and tear of horses' hoofs, and they should never wear slippery. The blue Staffordshire stable paving answers all these purposes, it is quite impervious to any moisture, and when laid to a proper fall, all wet at once runs off into the drain provided, leaving the stable comparatively dry. The clay is so close in texture as to be of immense strength, and the paving is made with deep grooves to form a firm foothold, which never wears slippery. It is made in various patterns. The same material is also used for coach-houses, yards for washing carriages, and often times for public pavements. Being so strong, and cleanly, and never liable to rust, mangers are formed with them. Outside plinths and quoins to buildings are carried up in these blue bricks, and, in fact, any position requiring extra strength in a building is often made of this excellent material.

Hamblet's Terra-Metallic Pavings.—These pavings are used in a large number of stables of the nobility and gentry throughout Great Britain, and wherever they are laid they give every satisfaction; they are almost everlasting in wear, their hardness causing them to be specially suitable for this purpose. It is not too much to say of these celebrated pavings that they are considered to be some of the best manufactured. These pavings are made in blocks varying in length from 6in. to 12in., and in width from $1\frac{3}{4}$in. to 6in., and in depth from $2\frac{1}{2}$in. to $4\frac{1}{2}$in., and are manufactured in a variety of patterns (some of

P

which are shown on the back cover of this work). All the blocks being made so as to join together to suit any sized stable, they can be laid by any ordinary workman in London or country without the aid of a skilled artizan. They are made from the best selected marls and rocks of the celebrated South Staffordshire marl deposits. Under the action of intense heat they vitrify throughout, and are thus impervious to moisture, while not being of a slippery nature like some of the buff vitrified kinds; this is a desideratum which will be found really necessary for the cleanliness and healthiness of a stable. They will wear longer than any other kind, and are growing largely into favour. In cases where required the sharp edges of these pavings are rounded so as to avoid any chance of cutting. Being of a dark slate colour they do not wear dirty-looking, and are easily kept clean. Catalogues, prices, and all particulars, can be obtained from Joseph Hamblet, Piercy Blue Brick, Tile and Pipe Works, West Bromwich.

W. B. Wilkinson & Co., of Newcastle-on-Tyne, and 13a, Great George Street, S.W., London, lay a granite concrete that is a most suitable material for floors. It is laid with crushed granite and special quality Portland cement on a foundation of hard broken stones or bricks in a soft state to any falls required. For stables it is grooved to prevent the horses slipping, and channelled for drainage. It is very durable, jointless, impervious to moisture and reasonable in price. Dr. Ballard, in his report to the Local Government Board as to effluvium nuisances, speaks of it "as the most perfect flooring he had seen for stables," and "as perfect a floor for a slaughterhouse as could be devised," and the way in which the public patronize it for footpaths, station platforms, warehouses, &c., as well as for stables, yards, roadways, &c., seems to justify so high a eulogy.

Messrs. Hassall and Singleton.—As will be seen from our pages, this firm manufacture Stable Fittings of the most varied kinds, which are considered to be some of the finest and most perfect in the world They are referred to in the Chapter on Stables and Stable Fittings, where a full description of them is given, and being illustrated by some excellent engravings, the reader will be able to judge of their perfection.

Bown's Newmarket Clipper is well known as being a very superior article, one Clipper having done service for over 200 horses. This Clipper has received many unsolicited testimonials. It is the most endurable of any manufactured, and is very easy to work, one being known to clip 89 horses without re-sharpening. It is one of the handiest machines manufactured.

Plant's Patent Horse Clippers are manufactured of the very best material, and are the best possible value; there is no friction or noise, they work easily and effectively, and are considered to be as good as any in the market. Their low price brings them within the reach of all.

Messrs. Benjamin Bunch & Sons.—This first-class Staffordshire Firm, of Walsall, manufacture iron and steel specially adapted for making tyres, hames and horse shoes, and the quality and finish of their goods is unsurpassed in Staffordshire.

F. Eglington of Walsall, manufacturer of bits, snaffles, spurs, stirrups, lasso rings, slides and bombillas, is the only maker of that name in England, and is the very oldest manufacturer in the trade, being established since 1834; he is also maker of breast buckles for carriage and van harness. F. Eglington manufactures the above for the Home, South American, West Indian, Australian, and South African Markets.

Mr. George Eld.—It will be seen that Mr. Eld, of 21, Navigation Street, Walsall, is the maker of every kind of brass and iron cased all over and half-cased cart hames, traces, manger chains, back bands, gear buckles, and cart gear furniture in general; cart hames suitable for York, Lincoln, and all the English Markets, as well as for the Welsh, Scotch, and Irish Markets. He also makes and supplies every kind of hames suitable for the Australian and New Zealand, Cape, Canadian, Grecian, and West Indian Markets, making a special line of those for Australia, New Zealand, and the Cape.

Messrs. Hawkins & Co.—For bits, spurs, stirrups, harness furniture, and every description of steel goods, we would refer our readers to the advertisement showing that Messrs. J. H. Hawkins & Co., of 16, Station Street, Walsall, can not only execute orders in detail to any extent, but they are one of the oldest established and largest actual manufacturers in their special line. In the seat of the leather trades they are the possessors of numerous Prize Medals awarded in different parts of the world, and dating back as far as 1796, which, together with the fact that they are constantly engaged upon Government contracts, fully endorses and justifies direct recommendation.

Thomas Venable's Harness Furniture.—We will now take the opportunity of mentioning that, to insure the success of obtaining a good set of harness is to have the mountings of the most substantial make, for if a tongue, a buckle, or one of the hames should break there is no knowing what the result may be. Some people have different opinions on the material of the mountings, for instance, a great many have silver or German mountings, others have brass (which looks exceedingly well when made of the best quality) and again, others prefer a metal called nickel silver or white metal, the latter is extensively used abroad ; the old established firm of Thomas Venables, (late Harvey) Bradford Works, Walsall, have at the present time a large order for the latter material on hand for Australia. As an improvement to the looks of the harness we should advise the use of ornaments or, what are now more fashionable, monograms or initials, which can be made easily by giving the first letter of christian and surname, they look neat and are easier cleaned.

Dawes' Horse Cloths, Halter Webs, Nets, Oilcloth, Cart, Waggon, and Rick Sheets are considered superior in every respect to anything in the market. Mr. Dawes manufactures all kinds of twines, packing, &c., while all descriptions of cotton waste, flax, hemp, tar, shoe threads, &c., are always kept in stock by him in large quantities.

Mr. Arthur Hart's Saddlery Webs, of every description, are manufactured in wool, union, linen, cotton, and jute, and are considered the best in the market. Mr. Hart has also patented some Braces, specially adapted for cavalry use, the sword belt being suspended from the Braces the weight on the belt is distributed over the body, and there is no possibility of the belt appearing below the shell jacket.

Brecknell's Saddle Soap.—This article being now so extensively used our readers will scarcely need to be informed that it stands generally so high in favour for its merits. It is only necessary for us to say that it is without question unequalled for cleaning saddles, and that it helps to preserve the leather, at the same time giving to it a nice appearance. The fact that it is used in royal and hunting stables, as well as by the Army, speaks for its excellence.

Jamieson & Co's Harness Composition is one of the best known in the trade. It produces a brilliant black polish on every description of leather, instead of, as with some polishes for harness which produce a black polish, destroy the leather, through having some deleterious acid in their manufacture. This celebrated composition is very nutritious to the leather, and, in addition, renders it waterproof, which is a desideratum. The Author has known this composition for many years, and can recommend it as the best he has ever used.

R. A. Lister & Company.—The new double roller "Beaufort Hunt" corn crusher, at 52s. 6d. is a leading speciality of this well-known firm of Dursley, Gloucestershire. It can be adjusted to simply crack beans in half or to crush oats perfectly, the makers send them on a month's trial to any respectable horse keeper. These mills have been recently approved of by the Indian cavalry officers for crushing grain for horses. This firm also make a speciality of their chaff cutters, a handy little machine being sold as low as 37s. 6d.

The London Rubber Co's Specialities.—In waterproof and india-rubber goods. Particularly worthy of note are the reliable garments specially manufactured and supplied by The London Rubber Company, comprising driving and riding coats and cloaks for ladies and gentlemen and coachmen. Some of their special registered shapes for ladies, are, for elegance and convenience, far in advance of anything hitherto produced, combining graceful appearance with perfect freedom for the arms, and, while particularly useful for riding or driving, form very desirable garments for walking, being made in choice colours and beautiful patterns. Mandleberg's Patent Ventilator, as applied to any garment desired, is the most perfect of ventilation, favourably noticed by the "Lancet" and other scientific and hygienic mediums. The superiority of this firm's manufactures obtained for them the highest award (Gold Medal) at the International Health Exhibition. Every horse owner should use their rubber horse-Shoe pads, which are a great protection to tender footed animals, and prevent stones from getting into the hoof.

Swinden's Watches.—We notice that hunting, driving, and shooting watches are now specially made with stronger cases, and also with movements that are better able to contend with the extra wear and tear to which they are subjected. The watches manufactured by Messrs. Swinden & Sons, of Birmingham, are of this class, being made extra strong with a view to the uses to which they are likely to be put.

The London and Provincial Horse and Carriage Insurance Company insures Horses, Carriages, and Cattle. All particulars can be obtained of Mr. A. Waters, Secretary,

The "Humber" Cycles.—A wonderful advance has been made during the past few years in the construction of bicycles and tricycles. Some of the cycle manufacturers, particularly Messrs. Humber & Co., have brought out and patented some most useful novelties in the shape of a safety bicycle with the little wheel in front, so that it is impossible to have a header from it; a tandem tricycle, and a new kind of machine, with the handles and small wheel in front, and called the Humber Automatic Tricycle. A lady or gentleman can ride this machine. Only recently a Birmingham lady rode 200 miles in one day on this new and very popular machine. It is rather remarkable that all the tricycle championships of the United Kingdom have been won on machines made by Humber & Co., of Corporation Street, Birmingham. Cycling is now firmly established and recognised as one of our national institutions, and has overcome the antipathy usually bestowed on new inventions. Amongst the votaries of the cycle are our princes and princesses, noblemen and noblewomen, &c. The healthfulness of cycling is admitted and recommended by the medical fraternity because it provides the necessary exercise for the body in such a way that it is available at all time.

ADVERTISEMENTS.

J. A. BARNSBY,
WALSALL, STAFFORDSHIRE,

Manufacturer of Ladies and Gentlemen's Saddles of every description, for the Home, Continental, South American, China, Japan, East and West Indian, African, Australian, and Canadian Markets.

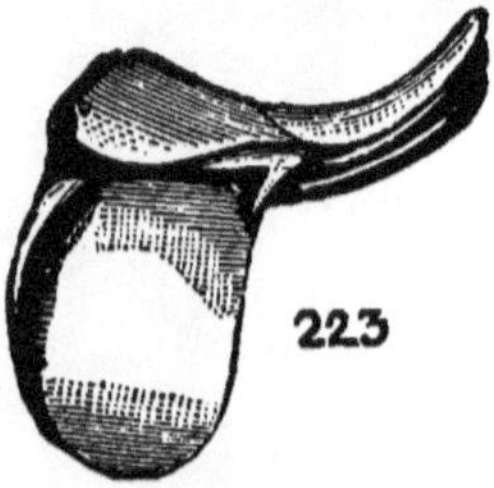

223

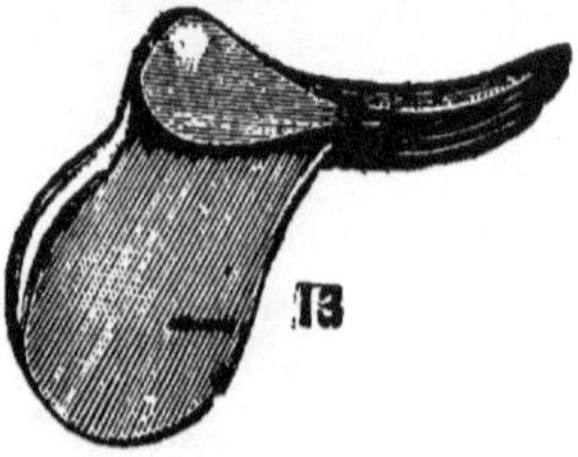

13

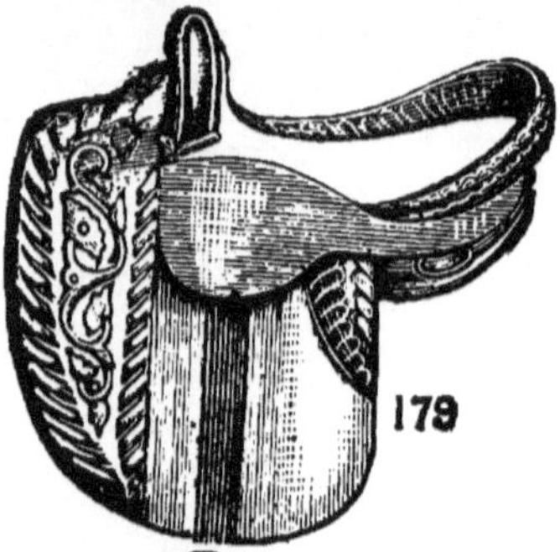

179

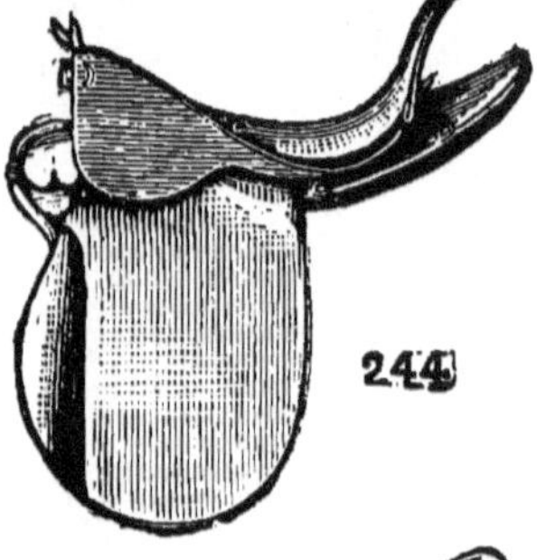

244

130

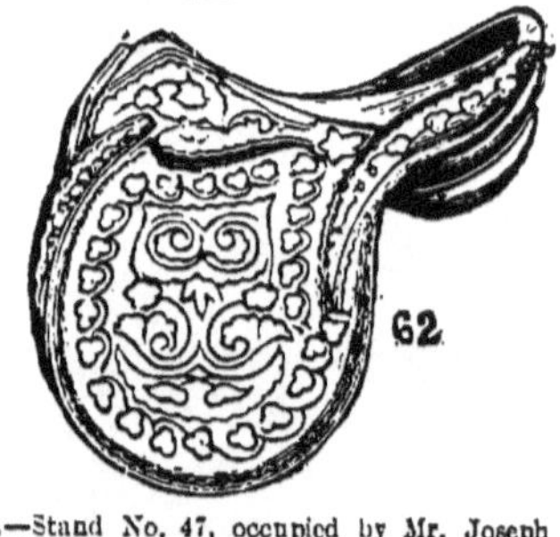

62

EXHIBITION, BINGLEY HALL, BIRMINGHAM.—Stand No. 47, occupied by Mr. Joseph A. Barnsby, 136, Lichfield Street, Walsall, is a worthy representative of the far-famed saddle-making town. Absolutely confined to Horse trappings, Mr. Barnsby has contrived, not by articles manufactured specially for exhibition, but merely by the showing of specimens of his ordinary manufacture, to make his stand one of the most attractive in the Hall. On it are to be found saddles of every description. The whole of the exhibits are made in a way that shows the excellency of the workmanship, and several are most ornate and tasteful, and have been highly commended by makers in the trade. The hogskin saddles and pilches in particular, for ladies and juveniles, are inlaid with beautiful patterns, while those for more arduous work are compact and neat. Among the special saddles of the stand are the new British army regulation infantry staff officer's saddle, all-over hogskin, with basil lining; the Cape police officer's and travelling saddle, specially adapted for lengthened riding; and the ladies' saddle, fitted with lever-spring top safe. Another exhibit is Barnsby's patent stirrup-leather bar. This, although simple in its mechanism, is most effective in its action. In case of accident the rider's foot is instantly released from the saddle, and he is thus prevented being dragged by the horse. This bar has been in use for several years, and has gained for itself a high name among horsemen who are exposed to accidents.

J. A. BARNSBY, 136, Lichfield Street, Walsall, Staffordshire.

ADVERTISEMENTS.

BARNSBY'S PATENT STIRRUP-LEATHER BAR,
To prevent Rider being dragged in case of accident.

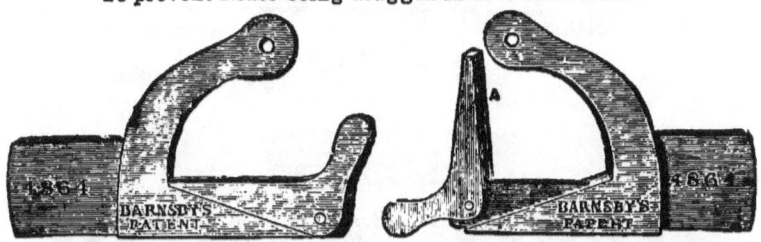

The above illustration shews to the reader the utility of this Bar, which possesses several advantages over the ordinary Bar. Although simple in its mechanism, it is most effective in its action, and in case of accident the rider's foot is instantaneously released from the saddle, and so prevents his being dragged by the horse, as in the case of most accidents.

It will be noticed in the drawing that the groove lettered A when closed fits securely over the stay marked B, which gives it additional strength, and prevents the lever from being wrenched off by a side strain.

It can be made with or without spring, and in various kinds of metal and sizes. The price is far from expensive, being but little more than the old common pattern, and not only forms a most useful but an ornamental part to the saddle.

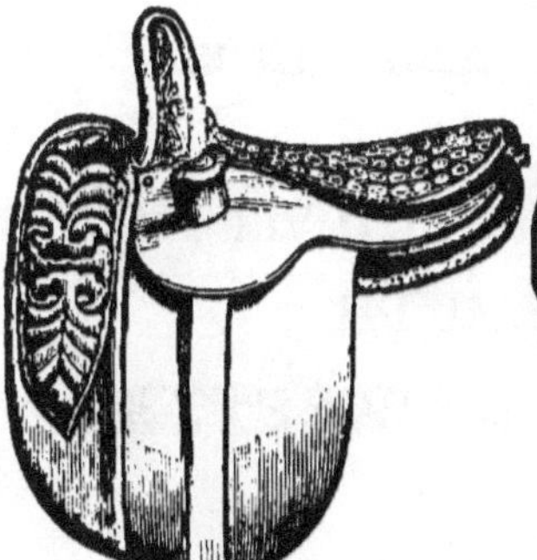

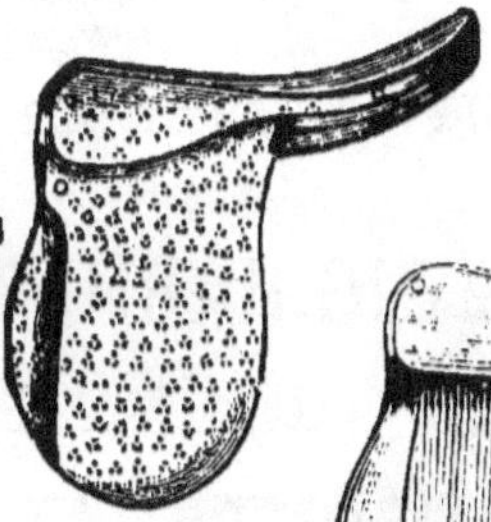

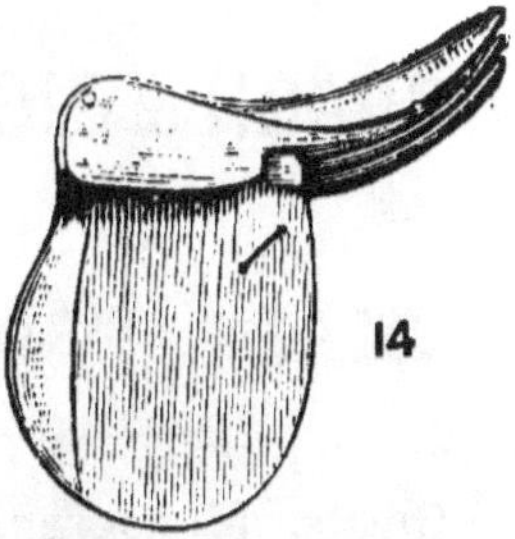

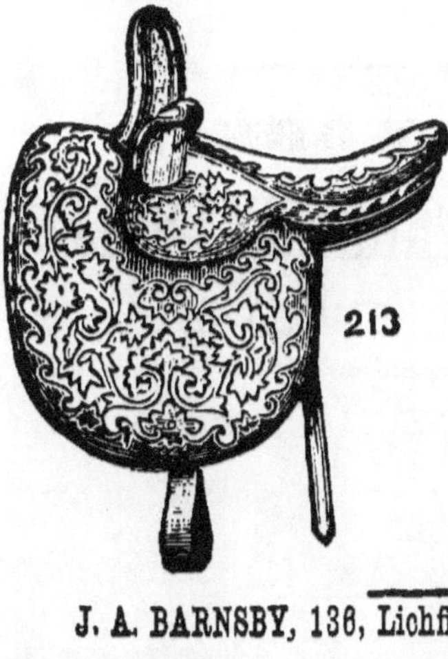

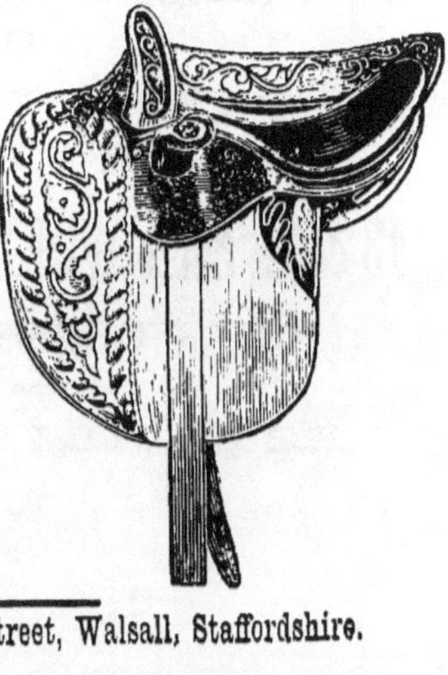

J. A. BARNSBY, 136, Lichfield Street, Walsall, Staffordshire.

ADVERTISEMENTS.

ESTABLISHED 1849. ESTABLISHED 1849.

THOMAS VENABLES,
(Late THOMAS HARVEY),

Brass Founder, Silver Plater,

AND

MANUFACTURER OF ALL KINDS

OF

COACH & GIG HARNESS FURNITURE,

SPURS, STIRRUPS,

CHAIN FRONTS AND ROSETTES.

Crests, Monograms, &c., from any drawing, seal, or description.

BRADFORD WORKS,

13 & 14, BRADFORD STREET, WALSALL,

STAFFORDSHIRE, ENGLAND.

ESTABLISHED 1849.

ADVERTISEMENTS.

JAMIESON & CO.'S HARNESS COMPOSITION

Produces a **Brilliant Black Polish** on every description of Leather, also renders it **Waterproof**. This Composition is very **nutritious to the Leather**.

PLATE POWDER.

This Powder is highly recommended for giving a Splendid Polish to Gold, Silver, and Plated Goods. Warranted free from Mercury or any injurious ingredients.

Polishing Paste.

Polishes quick, and leaves a Fine **Bright Lustre**, on Brass, Copper, Glass, &c.

Sold by all the principal Saddlers, Ironmongers, &c., throughout the Kingdom and Colonies.

		SIZES.		
In Boxes—Harness Compo.	— —	1/-	1/6	3/-
,, ,, Plate Powder	... ...	-/3	-/6	1/-
,, ,, Polishing Paste	... ...	-/1	-/3	-/6

J. and Co. would call the attention of the Public **to beware of Spurious Imitations** of their Goods.

WORKS—86, Spring Garden, Aberdeen.

HOME AND EXPORT.

ADVERTISEMENTS.

THE NEW CHEMICAL INK!
MADE ON A PRINCIPLE NEVER BEFORE ATTEMPTED.

FAC-SIMILIE OF LABEL ON EACH BOTTLE.

ALL LABELS ARE IN BLACK ON A LAVENDER GROUND.

THIS NEW CHEMICAL INK is considered the best Ink that can be manufactured. It is made of PURE CHEMICALS which have a LASTING PERFUME, while the COLOUR is a beautiful PURPLE when written, drying a DEEP BLACK.

It does not corrode nor rust on the Pen, and does not get thick, sticky, nor greasy. It is Indelible, never fades, but gets darker by age. It is cheaper than the Iron Inks, as it does not waste. It is not affected by weather nor climate, and has no sediment. It never smears the paper, but dries rapidly, and is the best Black Ink, that is pleasant to write with, and suitable for every person's use.

In Capsuled Bottles, at 6d., 1s., and 2s. each.

HENRY THACKER & Co.,
MANUFACTURERS,
NEW STREET SQUARE, LONDON, E.C.

HINKLEY'S LINIMENT

THE BEST & QUICKEST CURE FOR

SORE THROATS,
INFLUENZA,
CURBS, SPRAINS,
SPRUNG SINEWS,
SWOLLEN LEGS,
SURFEIT,
THE ITCH,
WINDGALLS,
LAMENESS, &c.

AS USED IN THE PRINCE OF WALES' STABLES.

SOLE MANUFACTURERS,

Hinkley, Walters, & Co.,
48a, *GLOUCESTER PLACE,*
PORTMAN SQUARE,
LONDON.

THE BEST & QUICKEST CURE FOR

CRACKED HEELS,
BROKEN KNEES,
OVER-REACHES,
SORES, CUTS,
BRUISES,
WOUNDS,
INSECT BITES,
SADDLE GALLS,
SPLINTS.

SOLD BY ALL SADDLERS, CHEMISTS & CORN MERCHANTS

PRICE PER BOTTLE

1/- 1/6 and 2/6

☞ NO STABLE SHOULD BE WITHOUT IT ☜

ADVERTISEMENTS.

ESTABLISHED NEARLY HALF A CENTURY.

GOUGH & CO.

PARK ST., WALSALL,

ENGLAND,

SADDLERY, HARNESS,

MILL BANDING,

AND

HORSE CLOTHING MANUFACTURERS.

First Prize Medal and Special Certificate of Distinguished Merit, London, 1882.

GOUGH & CO., are the Inventors and Manufacturers of
The "IMPERIAL," Four-in-hand Harness.
    The "CONGRESS," Tandem Harness.
        The "ROYAL," Pair Horse Harness.
            The "CENTAUR," Humane Harness.

Testimonials from most of the Crowned Heads of Europe, can be seen on application.

ADVERTISEMENTS.

THE "CENTAUR" WEB HARNESS.

Invented by E. W. GOUGH.

STRONG,
HANDY,
CHEAP, AND
HUMANE.

Sore Shoulders and Backs cured, and Jibbing prevented.

No furniture to clean, and no heavy weight to lift on and off the horse.

The above invention is particularly suitable for Invalids, Convalescent Homes, Hospitals, &c., &c.

Send size of Horse and kind of Vehicle to the
SOLE MANUFACTURERS:—

GOUGH & CO., WALSALL.

ADVERTISEMENTS.

IMPORTANT TO OWNERS OF HORSES.
JEM COOK'S ALTERATIVE
AND

In 1lb. tins only,   1s. 4d. each.

CONDITION POWDERS

WILL KEEP YOUR HORSE IN PERFECT HEALTH AND PRIME CONDITION, AND FREE FROM PINK EYE, INFLUENZA, COLDS, ASTHMA, SCAB, COLIC, AND OTHER DISEASES PREVALENT AT ALL SEASONS OF THE YEAR.

TESTIMONIALS.

Messrs. R. Roper, Son & Co.   February 27th, 1883.

GENTLEMEN,—In the course of my practice I have found that "Jem Cook's Horse Powders" have been extensively used, and, from enquiries I have made, with very good results.   WILLIAM JACKSON, M.R.C.V.S.
(Veterinary Inspector for the Borough of Sheffield).

Owlerton Brewery, Sheffield, March 9th, 1883.

Messrs. R. Roper, Sons & Co.

GENTLEMEN,—We shall always have pleasure in showing your friends the condition of our horses by the use of "Jem Cook's Alterative and Condition Powders."   Yours truly, J. L. COCKAYNE & SONS.

Sold retail at 1s. 4d. per lb. tin, by all Saddlers and Corn Factors throughout the World. Wholesale of Saddlers' Ironmongers, or the Proprietors,

R. ROPER, SON & Co., Broad Street, Sheffield.

BENJAMIN BUNCH & SONS,
Staffordshire Iron Works, Walsall,
MANUFACTURERS OF

BEST BARS  **BEST BARS**

OF ALL KINDS.

TYRE BARS, HAME AND HORSE-SHOE IRON, SMALL ROUND AND SQUARES, MERCHANT HOOPS, HAME HOOPS, &c., &c.

TESTIMONIALS

As to the SUPERIORITY of

THE "NEWMARKET" CLIPPER,

In addition to many others unsolicited.

GREAT WESTERN RAILWAY
From COLONEL MILNE,
HORSE SUPERINTENDENT'S OFFICE,
PADDINGTON,
17th Jan., 1883.

Sir,—At your request, I beg to say that the "Newmarket" Horse-Clipping Machine, patented by you, has been in use in our stables for some time, and has given satisfaction.

MR. W. BOWN.

FINCH ROAD TRAMWAY STABLES,
Oct. 21, 1882.

MR. W. BOWN.

Sir,—Will you kindly get this machine sharpened as early as possible. We have clipped over 50 horses with the two machines. The other still goes all right. I will send for this one this afternoon.

I am, yours truly,
J. JEANS,
Foreman Birmingham Tramway & Omnibus Co.

THE JOHNSON HOUSE,
HAYTS CORNERS, N.Y.
SHERIDAN & SON, PROPRIETORS.

P. HAYDEN, Newark, N.J.

Have used this same machine (the "Newmarket") ever since Nov. 30, 1880, and clipped 57 head of horses, besides legs of any number, and it is as good as ever, and I think it will never let up. Have never changed the set screw the least particle. Have not used the new one much yet, but works well, and the old machine has been the means of selling a great many machines ("Newmarkets") around and about here.

Yours, &c.,
A. H. SHERIDAN.

EXTRACT FROM *THE SPIRIT OF THE TIMES.*

THE NEWMARKET CLIPPER.—Of all clipping machines for sale in this country, we think there is none better than Bown's celebrated Horse and Toilet Machine. There is a perfectness about it that experienced operators tell us they can rarely find equalled. It has a record of clipping eighty-nine horses without resharpening. Each clipper is put up in perfect order, in a leather pocket, and duplicates for repairs are always on hand. P. Hayden, Newark N.J., sole agent for the United States.

DUNBAR, 23rd Nov., 1881.

MR. WM. BOWN, Birmingham.

Dear Sir,—I sent yesterday, per railway company, two Newmarket Clippers to sharpen. Please return at earliest. One has clipped 32 horses (cart horses), some very rough coats. Your esteemed attention will greatly oblige.

Yours truly,
GEO. GRAHAME, JUN.

BARK STREET, BOLTON,
July 28, 1881.

To W. Bown, Esq

Dear Sir,—In ordering my clippers for the coming season, I feel it only due to you to say that after having tried the Newmarket Clipper for several seasons, I am convinced that it is "the Clipper of the Future" having sold it in large quantities and in every case with entire satisfaction,

I am, Sir,
Yours truly,
ABRAHAM ENTWISTLE.

I have much pleasure in recommending your Newmarket Clipper. Professionally I have clipped numerous horses, and have engaged other men to do so. Have always used the Newmarket Clipper in preference to any other. As a proof of its superiority, I have a Clipper which has clipped upwards of 200 horses. I strongly recommend your Clipper wherever I go to.

J. EDWARDS, Horsebreaker.
67, Hingeston St., Birmingham.

SANDY LANE, SKELMERSDALE,
Sept. 22, 1880.

MR. WM. BOWN.

Dear Sir,—I have sent off to-day two pairs of clippers for repairs—one pair Clarke's, and one pair Newmarket. I have clipped nearly 200 horses and ponies with the Newmarket during the last two years; and but for breaking out the teeth through a fall, it looked like clipping twice that number.

Yours truly,
G. R. WANTY.

WALNUT HOUSE, WORCESTER.

I have thoroughly tested the Newmarket Clipper during two seasons; and I am so satisfied with them that I have requested my own servant as well as the firm's, to use no other. The men regulate this single-screw machine so much easier than those with two or three screws.

Yours truly,
GEORGE CARLESS, M.R.C.V.Sh.,
Pro PERRINS & CARLESS.

LICHFIELD,

I beg to say that I like the Newmarket Clipper that I had from you better than any other I have had used. The work done by it is certainly equal to any other machine. I find it is more endurable than others, and my grooms say it is easier to work than any they have used.

I remain, yours, &c.,
R. T. COOPER.

To be obtained Wholesale of all Saddlers, Ironmongers, Merchants, and Factors; and Retail of all Saddlers and Ironmongers throughout the Kingdom.

N.B.—CLIPPER REPAIRS OF ALL MAKERS PROMPTLY EXECUTED

ADVERTISEMENTS.

THE "BEAUFORT HUNT" MILL
FOR CRUSHING OATS, BEANS, PEAS, MAIZE, RICE, &c.
A Boy can crush Four Bushels per hour.
PRICE £2:2:0, CARRIAGE PAID.
5,000 SOLD IN 1831.

COPY OF ORDER.
Stables, Marlborough House, Pall Mall, S.W.
1 Dec., 1881.
Dear Sir,—Please send one of your Oat and Bean Crushing Machines, the same as I have had lately from you for my nag stable at Kingscote, for the use of the stables at Sandringham. It must be directed to H.R.H. The Prince of Wales, Sandringham, Wolferton Station, G.E.R., and in the corner to the care Mr. Westoner, the Stables. Yours faithfully,
NIGEL KINGSCOTE.
To Mr. Lister, Victoria Iron Works, Dursley.

R. A. LISTER & Co., are also Patentees and Manufacturers of Chaff Cutters, Land Rollers, Cheese Presses, Cream Separators, and Machinery in general, for the Farm, Garden, or Estate. Prices and full particulars from
R. A. LISTER & Co, Dursley, England.

PRIZE MEDAL, CALCUTTA EXHIBITION, 1883-4.

BRECKNELL'S
SADDLE
Used in the Royal Stables,
by Her Majesty's Cavalry,
and in Hunting Establishments.
SOAP.

THE BEST THING MADE FOR CLEANING SADDLES.

Brecknell, Turner & Sons, to Her Majesty, Haymarket, London.

J. TONKS & CO.,
(LATE TONKS & CLARE)
COACH, SADDLE, & HARNESS CURRIERS,
MANUFACTURERS OF
JAPANNED AND ENAMELLED LEATHERS,
GOODHALL STREET,
WALSALL, ENGLAND.

JOSEPH CLARE,
(LATE TONKS & CLARE)
COACH, SADDLE, & HARNESS CURRIER,
MANUFACTURER OF
JAPANNED AND ENAMELLED LEATHERS,
48, LOWER FORSTER STREET,
WALSALL, ENGLAND.

ADVERTISEMENTS.

The Perfection of Steel Pens.

THE PEN OF PENS

REGISTERED.

MANUFACTURED WITH FINE, MEDIUM AND BROAD POINTS.

In introducing The Pen of Pens, HENRY THACKER & Co. have borne in mind the one necessity of having a pen to suit every style of writing, as well as every taste; a pen with a fine hard point, yet having the flexibility, freedom, smoothness, and softness of a Gold or a Quill Pen.

The peculiarities and advantages of this Pen over all other kinds, is the shape, which will hold a sufficient quantity of ink to write an ordinary letter, and the spring, which makes the pen suitable for fine, free, or large hand writing. For Bankers, Merchants, Insurance Offices, Solicitors, Clergymen, Authors, Ladies, College, School, Office, Public and Private Use, it will be found The Pen of Pens.

Being manufactured for every purpose, it is the most perfect steel pen ever introduced. The fine point is unsurpassed for fine and rapid writing, while the Medium and Broad Points are the nearest approach to Gold or Quill Pens, both as regards durability, smoothness, and flexibility, suiting the requirements of every hand.

HENRY THACKER & Co., believing that the best Pen is the cheapest, have made arrangements with SIR JOSIAH MASON, of BIRMINGHAM, to manufacture them out of the finest quality steel, and feel assured that the name of this celebrated maker, will be a sufficient guarantee of quality, strength, and durability.

PRICES:

REGISTERED BOX CONTAINING	REGISTERED BOX CONTAINING	SAMPLE BOX CONTAINING
One Gross 2/6	Four Dozen 1/-	1½ Dozen 6d.

HENRY THACKER & CO.,
Sole Proprietors,

Manufacturers of "THE INK OF INKS" for Writing and Copying,

NEW STREET SQUARE, LONDON, E.C.

And of EVERY STATIONER throughout the WORLD.

ADVERTISEMENTS.

THE GOLDEN EMBROCATION,
OR
"CURE ALL,"
FOR
HORSES, CATTLE, AND DOGS.

A CERTAIN CURE
FOR
Cuts, Sore Backs, Sore Shoulders, Bruises, Warbles, Wounds, Broken Knees, Sprains, Splints, Curbs, Chapped Heels, Over-reaches, Wind Galls, Sprung Sinews, Rheumatism, Lameness, Sore Throats, Sore Mouths in Sheep and Lambs, Fly Galls, Sore Udders, Sheep Scab, Foot Rot, and Inflammation of the Bowels, &c., &c.

This Embrocation is prepared from an old and valuable recipe, and has been used many years in private practice; and in consequence of the numerous and unsolicited testimonials received, the proprietor, some years ago, resolved to bring it before the public. The enormous sale it has had since then, and the wonderful cures it has effected, has proved it to be the best, quickest, most reliable, and cheapest preparation ever offered to owners of horses, cattle, and dogs.

Its effects, when applied to Horses or Cattle which are suffering from deep-seated sprains, are truly surprising. It gives immediate relief from the most agonising pain, it cleans and soundly heals all cuts and sores, and causes the hair to grow quickly over the healed skin.

It may be used internally for the following diseases :—Windy Colic, Stoppage of Urine, Disease of the Kidneys, Bloody Urine, Worms, Bronchitis, and most diseases to which Horses and Cattle are subject. Given in two tablespoonful doses in warm gruel.

A supply should be kept ready for immediate use in every Stable, Cow House, Cattle Shed, and Farm House.

SOLD BY
SADDLE & HARNESS MAKERS; CHEMISTS AND DRUGGISTS; AND HAY AND CORN DEALERS.

Wholesale Agents and Sole Consignees for South Australia:
J. C. Genders & Co., Wholesale Saddlers, Adelaide.

SHIPPING AGENTS :
Messrs. FILBEY & KEMP, 32, Great St. Helens, London, E.C.

SOLD IN BOTTLES AT 1S. 9D. EACH. FULL DIRECTIONS WITH EACH BOTTLE.
N.B.—Be sure to ask for the Golden Embrocation, or "Cure All."

Sole Proprietor: **JAMES HANFORD, 8, Strawberry Road, Armley, Leeds.**

From J. C. GENDERS & CO., Wholesale Saddlers, Adelaide.
MR. J. HANFORD, LEEDS.—Dear Sir,—The efficiency of this valuable preparation is now proved beyond doubt by a large number of people who have used it in South Australia; without exception all speak of it in terms of highest praise, and its popularity is now well established. One trial will convince. We remain, yours truly,
Adelaide, 28th April, 1883. J. C. GENDERS & CO.

CROWN POINT, LEEDS, *Nov. 8th*, 1884.
Mr. JAMES HANFORD,—Dear Sir,—Having now used your "Golden Embrocation, or Cure all," for over five years, and marked the speedy cures effected upon my horses, I can confidently say, after having tried every Embrocation of note, that your "Cure All" has proved the most effective and successful.

I may add, that being a proprietor of between 60 and 70 horses, and having proved the special qualities of your preparation, it gives me great pleasure in adding my testimony to its efficiency, and for the future my stables will not be without a supply.
I am, Sir, yours respectfully,
JOHN TURTON.

P.S.—If you think the above will be of any service to you, make what use of it you like, as I think every owner of horses and cattle should give it a trial.

ADVERTISEMENTS.

HASSALL & SINGLETON,

MANUFACTURERS

OF

WROUGHT & CAST IRON

STABLE FITTINGS

Of the most Improved Designs.

FOR A SELECTION
SEE PAGES 101 TO 108.

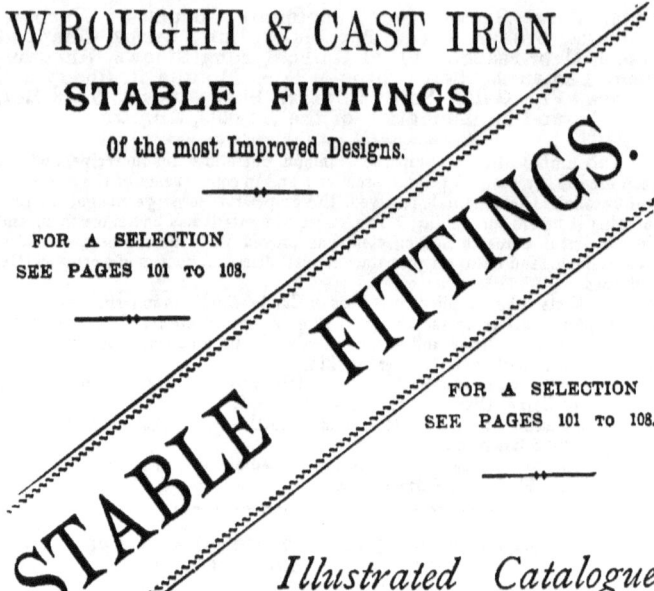

FOR A SELECTION
SEE PAGES 101 TO 108.

Illustrated Catalogue

on Application.

HASSALL & SINGLETON,
PHŒNIX FOUNDRY,
BIRMINGHAM.

ADVERTISEMENTS.

ESTABLISHED 1834.

F. EGLINGTON,

MANUFACTURER OF

Bits, Snaffles, Spurs, Stirrups,

LASSO RINGS,

SLIDES & BOMBILLAS,

FOR

SOUTH AMERICA, WEST INDIES, AUSTRALIA, SOUTH AFRICA, AND THE HOME MARKETS;

ALSO MAKER OF

BREAST BUCKLES,

FOR CARRIAGE & VAN HARNESS,

PARK STREET,

WALSALL, ENGLAND.

ADVERTISEMENTS.

FOR THE PRESERVATION OF HUMAN LIFE.

INVENTIONS
FOR
RIDING AND DRIVING.
By E. W. GOUGH.

"*Not for a day but for all time.*"

AT LAST!!!—A TOTAL DEPARTURE FROM ALL EXISTING SADDLE BARS.

SADDLE BAR.
Patent,
No. 4374.
Price
2/6 per pr.

The "Centaur Saddle Bar" is an automatic invention for instantaneously releasing the rider in case of accident. It is entirely free from complication, the bearing is direct, it cannot get out of order, or refuse to act, either from rust, grit, grease, or perspiration of the horse, and is pronounced by practical authorities to be the simplest, safest, and cheapest stirrup bar in the market. It can be fitted to any saddle, and all sizes, old and new. To be had of all Saddlers and Harness Makers, or direct from GOUGH & Co., the "Centaur" Saddlery Works, Walsall.

Read the unsolicited testimony on next page.

"*Is simplicity itself.*"

REIN Billet,
Patents,
Nos.
4538 and 5070.
Price from
6d. each.

The "Centaur Rein Billet" (or Billetless Rein), for driving, riding, pillar reins, and suitable for coupling reins, dog leads, and other analogous purposes. This invention dispenses with the buckle, tong, punch-holes, crue-holes, loop and billet-strap, thus ensuring less weight, less cost, and absolute safety, the substance of the leather being considerably strengthened (instead of weakened as in the old billets) in the process of manufacture. To be had of all Saddlers, Harness Makers, and Leather Workers, or direct from GOUGH & Co., the "Centaur" Saddlery Works, Walsall.

"*Will last a lifetime.*"

LIFE Belt.
For daily wear
Price from
3/6 each.

The "Centaur Ventilated Body Belt," for Horsemen, Cricketers, Football Players, Pedestrians, Athletes, Bicyclists, and general wear, is a healthy and permanent support back and front, bracing and strengthening, is very neat and durable, less cost and weight than electropathic, chain, or galvanic complications, and can be worn by all ages at all times. Send measurement to the Sole Manufacturers, GOUGH & Co., the "**Centaur**" Saddlery Works, Walsall.

A LIFE-SAVING SADDLE BAR.

May 1st, 1885.

GENTLEMEN,
Notwithstanding the many efforts on the part of inventors and the trade generally to produce a reliable Saddle Bar, the complication of construction and consequent high price of most of them, coupled with the non-reliability of any, creates a want which it has long been my desire to supply.

The greatest danger to which horsemen are liable in cases of accident is that of being dragged after being thrown, from the fact of their inability to release the stirrup leathers from the saddle bars. Patents in Spring Stirrup Irons are proved to be at the *wrong end of the strap* at the critical moment.

Scarcely a hunting season closes without leaving numerous records of serious and fatal accidents, and anything which has the humane object of saving life under any and all circumstances, either in the field or upon the road, cannot be too much valued by all who ride horses.

I have taken out a Patent for my invention, the "CENTAUR" Safety Saddle Bars, which will render accidents of the above kind, to those who use them, simply impossible, as in case the rider be thrown in any conceivable way, either backward, forward, or sideways, the stirrup leathers are instantly disengaged from the bars upon which they are suspended.

This invention possesses three very essential features, namely: simplicity, effectiveness, and cheapness, and will, it is hoped, recommend itself to every horseman throughout the land.

Your obedient Servant,
E. W. GOUGH, Inventor.

[COPY.]

To MR. E. W. GOUGH.   LONDON, *April 8th,* 1885.

DEAR SIR,
I have this day forwarded your declaration and provisional specification for "Improvements in Safety Bars" to the proper authorities, and in course of post expect acknowledgment of same, which I will despatch to you immediately.

By sensitive men like yourself, encomiums are generally looked upon as flattery, but I hope you will do me the justice of disabusing your mind as to my being actuated by any motive of that kind in giving expression to my unbiassed and candid opinion of your invention.

I have been an inventor and patentee for over twenty years, and having paid considerable attention to the construction of Saddle Bars, I am tolerably well acquainted with most of those now in use.

Notwithstanding that I have patented one myself, I assure you that so far as simplicity of construction, general effectiveness, and the moderate price which it appears to me capable of being produced at, yours is infinitely superior to anything which has previously come under my notice, and I sincerely hope your very meritorious and humane achievement may meet with that acknowledgment and appreciation which it so deservedly merits.

I am, dear Sir,
Yours truly,
W. H. ST. AUBIN,
Mechanician and Patent Agent.

ADVERTISEMENTS.

SPRATTS PATENT
MEAT "FIBRINE" VEGETABLE
DOG CAKES.
(WITH BEETROOT.)

FORAGE BISCUITS.

One Biscuit taken with the rider and given during a long day's hunting will frequently cause an otherwise bad feeder to readily take to his food on his return home. Given occasionally instead of the mid-day feed of Oats, they produce an extremely beneficial effect upon the health and appearance of a horse.

Mr. FRANK GOODALL, the QUEEN'S HUNTSMAN, says of
"LOCURIUM."

"I find it better than anything I have ever used for Cuts, Bites, and Wounds."

This PATENT VEGETABLE OIL is an extraordinary Cure for all sorts of Wounds, Cuts, Bruises, and Burns, in Man or Animals. Invaluable for Cracked Heels, Broken Knees, Overreaches, Sore Backs in Horses, and for Sore Feet in Hounds or Sporting Dogs. Fresh Wounds heal up quickly with no trace of inflammation or proud flesh.—*For Animal Use, 2/- per Bottle; for Human Use, 2/3 per Bottle.*

"Home for Lost Dogs, London, S.W.—LOCURIUM is a capital lotion for Cuts and Bites. Where dogs have been bitten I have found it to possess very considerable healing qualities.—J. CHARLES COLAM, Secretary."

"Eltham.—In injuries to Mares, from Kicks, Cuts, and other accidental Wounds, I find the healing properties of LOCURIUM very remarkable; I strongly recommend it for Broken Knees.—WILLIAM BLENKIRON."

"I find LOCURIUM most useful.—T. PRITCHARD, M.R.C.V.S.L., Hereford."

"Please send a gallon of LOCURIUM. I found it answer very well last winter.—EDWIN JOHNS, Stud Groom, The Kennels, Kenilworth."

Spratts Patent, S.E.

THE LONDON RUBBER COY.'S
Specialities in Ladies and Gentlemens
WATERPROOF CLOAKS, COATS, AND CAPES
FOR
DRIVING AND RIDING,
EVERY GARMENT WARRANTED.
AT MANUFACTURERS PRICES.

Coachmen's Waterproof Coats & Capes, Waterproof Driving Aprons.
RUBBER MATS FOR CARRIAGES AND DOORWAYS.
WATER TUBING FOR CARRIAGE HOSE,
RUBBER PADS, (A great saving to the horses foot).

Price List and Patterns on application to

The LONDON RUBBER CO., North Western Arcade, Corporation Street, Birmingham.
THE LONDON RUBBER CO., 76, STRAND, LONDON,
MANCHESTER RUBBER CO., 95, MARKET STREET, MANCHESTER.

INSURE YOUR HORSES AND CARRIAGES WITH
THE LONDON & PROVINCIAL HORSE & CARRIAGE INSURANCE CO., LIMITED,
CHIEF OFFICE: 17, QUEEN VICTORIA STREET, LONDON, E.C

The oldest Office in the United Kingdom for the Insurance of Horses, Carriages, and Cattle.

A. WATERS, *Secretary*

ADVERTISEMENTS.

ATKINSON & PHILIPSON,
(ESTABLISHED 1794)

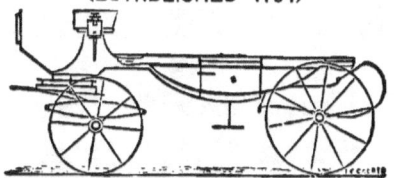

Carriage and Harness Manufacturers.

Prize Medallists and sole makers of Landaus and Victoria Phaetons, fitted with **PHILIPSON'S WHIP CEE SPRINGS**; Inventors of the registered Castlereagh and Ravensworth Cars, and several other light, elegant, and useful Carriages.

Messrs. A. & P.'s numerous Showrooms contain SEVERAL HUNDRED CARRIAGES, comprising Landaus, Broughams, Phaetons, Dog Carts, &c., all constructed on soundly scientific principles, and fitted with every modern accessory, calculated to enhance the pleasure and safety of driving.

THE DESIDERATA HARNESS was introduced by Messrs. A. & P., as the only humane method of harnessing a horse, to ensure the ease and comfort of the horse and the safety of the driver.

ILLUSTRATED CATALOGUES FREE ON APPLICATION.

Northumberland Carriage and Harness Manufactory,
27, PILGRIM STREET,
NEWCASTLE-ON-TYNE.

MYERS' ROYAL CATTLE SPICE
For Horses, Cattle, Sheep, Pigs, Poultry, and Game.

PATRONS:—
HER MOST GRACIOUS MAJESTY THE QUEEN.
His Royal Highness the PRINCE OF WALES.
His Royal Highness the DUKE OF CONNAUGHT.

HIS MAJESTY THE KING OF HOLLAND.	THE RIGHT HON. THE EARL OF ZETLAND.
THE KING OF BELGIUM.	THE RIGHT HON. LORD FITZHARDINGE.
HIS GRACE THE DUKE OF BUCCLEUGH.	THE LATE SIR WALTER C. TREVELYAN, BART.
HIS GRACE THE DUKE OF SUTHERLAND.	SIR HUGH CHOLMLEY.
THE MOST NOBLE THE MARQUIS OF LONDONDERRY.	W. MCCOMBIE, ESQ., M.P.
THE RIGHT HON. THE EARL OF COVENTRY.	JAMES REID, ESQ. H. ADAMSON, ESQ.

The LEADING EXHIBITORS and PRIZE TAKERS at all the PRINCIPAL CATTLE SHOWS, etc.

MARK THESE RESULTS, IF USED AS DIRECTED, THAT

HORSES eat better, rest better, work with more spirit, and are kept in better condition.
COWS (MILCH) yield a larger quantity and a better kind of milk.
COWS (FEEDING) fatten more rapidly, and the meat is better in quality.
SHEEP are kept free from disease, and a better quality of wool and mutton is produced.
PIGS feed quickly, at small cost, and firm and sweet mellow bacon is obtained.
POULTRY thrive and do well upon it, its use ensuring a larger quantity of eggs the year around.

The manufacturer particularly desires that you will use the spice regularly two or three times a day. By giving it to your animals at intervals no good will result; it is the regularity of its use that ensures success. At a cost of about one halfpenny per head per day, you may keep your cattle in perfect health, and fatten them in half the time.

T. MYERS, Steam Spice Mills, York, Hull, and London.
Sold in 1 cwt. and ½ cwt. Bags, at 34s per cwt.

ADVERTISEMENTS.

UNE OF THE OLDEST HOUSES IN THE TRADE.—ESTABLISHED 50 YEARS.

16, STATION STREET,
AND
NAVIGATION STREET,
WALSALL, Eng.

PRIZE MEDALS—
LONDON, 1851.   PHILADELPHIA, 1876.   LONDON, 1862.

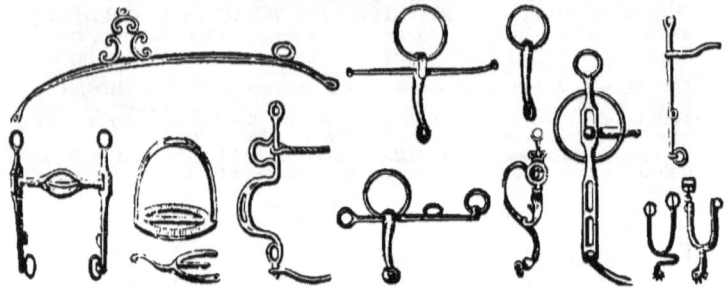

J. H. HAWKINS & CO.,

WHOLESALE MANUFACTURERS OF

BRIDLE-BITS, STIRRUPS, SPURS, CHAINS, CURBS, SADDLE-BARS,
CHAIN BURNISHERS,
HAMES AND HARNESS FURNITURE.

Every description of SADDLERY HARDWARE for Home and Foreign Markets.

GOVERNMENT AND RAILWAY CONTRACTORS, &c.

☞ A LARGE STOCK ALWAYS KEPT. ☜

ILLUSTRATED CATALOGUES AND PRICES ON APPLICATION

ADVERTISEMENTS.

HENRY'S GREAT INDIAN REMEDIES.

THE STABLE REQUISITE.

MANUFACTORY:  MADRAS, INDIA.

TRADE MARK.

THE CURE FOR

Rheumatism
Wind-stroke
Sprains of all Sorts
Sprung Tendons
Sore Throat
Influenza
Stiffness
Cuts and Wounds
Broken Knees and Bruises.
Cracked Heels

Over-reaches
Œdema, or Swelling of the Legs
Swellings generally
Sore Shoulders and Backs
Spavins
Heat Lumps.
Bites and Stings of Flies and Noxious Insects.
Mange

and other **Skin Diseases** and all irritable conditions of the Skin.

PRICE 2/6, 5/-, & 10/- PER TIN.

A FEW OF MANY TESTIMONIALS.

I tried your "Hippacea" on the throat of a young mare suffering from **Influenza.** She was well in three days. Her companion caught the same complaint, and I left it to nature, in order to prove the remedy, and she has been coughing and running at the nose for a fortnight. Please send me another tin of "Hippacea," as I do not want to be without it in my stable.

ROYAL CRESCENT MEWS, BATH,   JOHN TALL.
29th November, 1884,   *Livery Stable Keeper.*

I tried your sample of "Hippacea" on one of my horses with a sore back. It was a very severe case caused by a side saddle when hunting in a hilly country. I found it **heal the wound and also encourage the growth of the hair** more quickly and better than any remedy I have ever yet tried. And in a slight case it was really wonderful. Being the hunting season, and my horses so liable to hurt, I sent at once for more "Hippacea," not caring to be without it in my stable; having found its really excellent virtues.

MONTPELIER RIDING SCHOOL, BATH,   JAMES ROBERTS.
25th November, 1884.   *Riding Master.*

I have used "Hippacea" for some months, and have found it most beneficial for **cuts, bruises, and sore hoofs** among my horses. Any wound it heals very quickly.

MADRAS, *21st May, 1884.*   J. H. PEEBLES.

I have tried Henry's "Hippacea" on an **enlargement** on a horse's hock and it entirely removed it after two or three applications. I think it a very useful stable requisite, and should always be kept at hand. In fact, I can strongly recommend it.

CROSSCANNONBY, MARYPORT,   ROBERT ELLWOOD.
November 20th, 1884.

Central Depôt for Europe—

F. H. BOWDEN,
29, LANSDOWNE RD., CROYDON, SURREY.

ADVERTISEMENTS.

Established 1825.   Established 1825.

SWINDEN & SONS,

MANUFACTURERS OF

WATCHES,

SPECIALLY STRONG AND SUITABLE FOR

✣ HUNTING, ✣

DRIVING, SHOOTING, &c.

CLOCKS

OF EVERY DESCRIPTION.

27, 28, & 29, TEMPLE STREET, BIRMINGHAM.

WATCHES, CLOCKS, &C., REPAIRED BY EFFICIENT WORKMEN.

ADVERTISEMENTS.

STABLE FLOORS, STABLE YARDS, COACH HOUSES, &c.

IT is of great importance to have the Floor of a Stable impervious to damp and urine and without joints; to have smooth open channels, and, where it can be arranged, to have no communication with underground drains inside. Various materials are used, but none are better and few equal to **Wilkinson's Granite Concrete**, which is laid down soft and grooved or indented to give a foot-hold; channels are also formed in the same material: it is no new invention; it has been tried and extensively used for over thirty years. The cost compares favorably with other modes of paving. It is extensively used by Her Majesty's Government, and patronized by a large number of the nobility; by Railway Companies; large mercantile firms, such as Crosse & Blackwell, Pears & Co., Pink & Co., and many others.

Several thousand references, prices, and full particulars on application to

W. B. WILKINSON & Co., 27, Great George Street, Westminster; or to

The Works, Newcastle-on-Tyne.

W. & J. PLANT,
PATENTEES & MANUFACTURERS OF HORSE CLIPPERS,
105, POOL STREET, WOLVERHAMPTON.

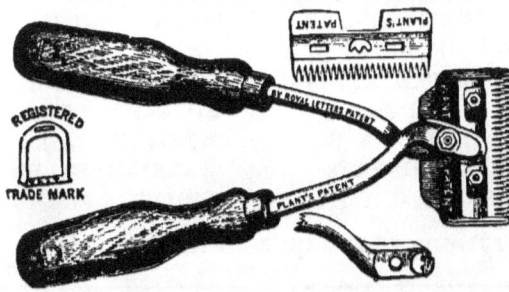

These Machines are of the best material and workmanship.

No Friction nor noise.

Makers of other pattern Clippers.

Clippers of all kinds repaired.

Can be had of all Saddlers and Ironmongers.

GEORGE ELD,
21, NAVIGATION STREET, WALSALL, STAFFORDSHIRE, ENGLAND.

MANUFACTURER OF ALL KINDS OF

Iron and Brass Cased Cart Hames, Traces, Manger Chains, Back Bands, Cart Gear Furniture, Buckles, Rings, etc.

FOR HOME AND EXPORT.

ADVERTISEMENTS.

SAVE THE PIECES !   COPYRIGHT REGISTERED !

GLU-ENE

A COMPOUND WATER-PROOF CEMENT

FOR MENDING EVERYTHING.

Transparent !   Colourless !   Adhesive !
Resisting !   Durable !   Tenacious !

GLU-ENE

REPAIRS, UNITES, FIXES and JOINS

AMBER	VASES	MEERSCHAUM	STATUARY
STONE	WHIPS	CARDBOARD	CARD CASES
GLASS	IVORY	JEWELLERY	WORK BOXES
WOOD	SHELLS	FURNITURE	INLAID WORK
CHINA	PARIAN	CROCKERY	PAPIER MACHE
SLATE	FOSSILS	MINERALS	BILLIARD CUES
BONE	VENEER	CABINETS	WRITING CASES
TOYS	MARBLE	TRINKETS	WALKING STICKS
JET	PLASTER	LEATHER	PICTURE FRAMES

And everything that requires mending.

DIRECTIONS FOR USE.

Place the bottle in hot water, or before the fire to liquify the GLU-ENE. Well cleanse the parts to be joined, then dry and warm the article before applying the Glu-ne. Apply with a camel's hair brush, and press the parts firmly together, squeezing out as much of the Glu-ene as possible, and place it in a dry place for 48 hours.

For porous substances apply one or two coats, as it is absorbed by the article, but for ordinary use one application is sufficient.

⁎ All articles should be thoroughly free from grease, and after being joined with Glu-ene should not be washed in soda and water; but may be washed and cleaned in the ordinary way, without any fear of separating.

In bottles 6d. and 1s. each.

HENRY THACKER & CO.,
Ink Manufacturers and Stationers,
NEW STREET SQUARE, LONDON, E.C.

ADVERTISEMENTS.

GLUXINE,

THE PATENT HOLDFAST PASTE.

A PERFECT SUBSTITUTE FOR

PASTE, GUM, STARCH, SIZE AND DEXTRINE,

FOR IT WILL STICK.

In large-mouthed Glass Bottles with Cap and Brush complete,

Price 6d. and 1s. each.

- **GLUXINE** is a Semi-Transparent Liquid, forming a cheap and perfect substitute for Paste, Gum, Starch, Size, Dextrine and other adhesive substances.
- **GLUXINE** is quite free from smell, and does not spoil. It never gets mouldy nor sour by keeping, like all Pastes. It contains no lumps nor grit, but is perfectly free and smooth.
- **GLUXINE** does not stain nor injure any article. It dries quickly, brushes smooth, and does not cause bubbles like Paste or Glue.
- **GLUXINE** is always ready for use, and can be thinned instantly with either cold or hot water, when needed.
- **GLUXINE** is cheaper than Gum or Paste, lasting longer, and not wasting by evaporation, as it does not dry up when kept covered.
- **GLUXINE** is suitable for Office or Library use in the place of Gum, and for Home use in the place of Gum or Paste.
- **GLUXINE** is more suitable for mounting Photographs, Engravings, &c., than Starch, Gum, Paste, or Dextrine; it is easier in use, always ready, and its adhesive qualities are superior to any other known article.
- **GLUXINE** is the best for every purpose wherever Gum, Starch, or Paste is used, AND WHEN ONCE TRIED WILL ALWAYS BE USED.

HENRY THACKER & CO.,

MANUFACTURERS,

NEW STREET SQUARE, LONDON, E.C.

ADVERTISEMENTS.

GOUGH & CO.'S
CELEBRATED 3 GUINEA
GENTLEMENS'
RIDING SADDLES

Are manufactured of real Hogskin and forwarded complete, with Girths, Leathers, and Stirrups, Suitable for Hunting and all Hackney purposes.

	Each.
Every description of SADDLE made to order and measure from	£3 3 0
Ladies' Saddle ,,	4 10 0
Youths' Saddle ,,	2 10 0
Boys' Pilch ,,	1 10 0
Boys' and Girls' combined Pilch ,,	2 2 0
Weymouth Hunting Bridles (Double Rein and Double Bits) complete ,,	1 1 0
Pelham's Bridles (Double Rein and Single Bit) complete ,,	0 12 6
Snaffle Bridle, with Bit, complete ,,	0 7 6

HARNESS

Of every description manufactured by

GOUGH & CO.,
PARK STREET, WALSALL, ENGLAND.

ADVERTISEMENTS.

HARNESS.

SADDLERY, HORSE CLOTHING, FARM GEARS, COLLIERY TACKLE,

AND

MILL BANDING,

MANUFACTURED BY

GOUGH & CO.,

PARK STREET, WALSALL, ENGLAND.

Thoroughly practical Workmen sent any distance to execute Repairs, &c., by Contract or otherwise.

Every article in the Saddlery Trade kept in Stock.

ADVERTISEMENTS.

F. DAWES,

The Butts Ropery, & 18, Stafford Street,

WALSALL, ENGLAND,

MANUFACTURER OF ALL KINDS OF

Ropes, Cordage, Lines, Twines, Engine Packing, Halter Webs, Whip Cords,

HORSE CLOTHS, NETS, HALTER WEBS, OILCLOTH, CART, WAGON, AND RICK SHEETS.

All descriptions of Cotton Cleaning Waste, Flax, Hemp, Tar, Shoe Threads, Saddlers' Threads and Checks, Roofing Felt, Brushes, &c., always in Stock.

ESTABLISHED 1796.

CHARLES & CO.,

Steam and General Printers,

GREYSTOKE PLACE, FETTER LANE,

LONDON, E.C.

Printers of the 3rd Edition of "Centaur."

ESTIMATES OF ANY MAGNITUDE SUBMITTED.

ADVERTISEMENTS.

"TRY IT ONCE, AND YOU WILL NEVER USE ANY OTHER!"
(EXTRACT FROM A LETTER.)

THE INK OF INKS!

THACKER'S VIOLET-BLACK INK,
IS THE ONLY INK TO SUIT

EVERY USE, BODY, TRADE, WEATHER, PROFESSION.

VIOLET-BLACK WRITING INK } Writes a bright dark colour turning to a deep Purple Black.

Does not RUST or CLOG the PEN, never THICKENS, always FLUID and FREE from SEDIMENT.

In Bottles, 8/- 4/- 2/- 1/- and 6d. each.

VIOLET-BLACK COPYING INK } Writes a beautiful bright colour turning (in Copy and Letter) to a deep Purple Black.

Gives at once a LEGIBLE and DARK COPY, several COPIES can be TAKEN. COPIES after SIX MONTHS; never gets THICK or STICKY.

In Bottles, 12/- 6/- 3/- 1/6 and 9d. each.

(Copy of one Testimonial out of Hundreds received).

Messrs. HENRY THACKER & CO.

    Gentlemen,

        As we copy all our letters, it is of importance to us to have good ink; during the last 25 or 30 years, we have had a great variety of different sorts; but we have no hesitation in stating that we have met with none that will for a moment bear comparison with yours, it not only flows freely from the pen, but the copies retain their bright and clean colour for years.

        Signed for NASMYTH, WILSON, & CO., Bridgwater Foundry,
                Patricroft, Near Manchester.
                          4th November, 1870.

HENRY THACKER & CO., MANUFACTURERS,
NEW STREET SQUARE, LONDON, E.C.

ADVERTISEMENTS.

THE WONDERFUL MARKING INK!

PERGAMENA.

NO KNOWN CHEMICAL CAN TAKE IT OUT.

NO HEATING! NO PREPARATION!

WRITES BLACK and EVERLASTINGLY KEEPS BLACK.

Price SIXPENCE per Bottle.

BOTTLES CONTAIN FOUR TIMES THE QUANTITY OF ORDINARY MARKING INKS.

EVERY BOTTLE GUARANTEED.

This wonderful Marking Ink, discovered by an INDIAN CHEMIST, from whom the Proprietors have purchased the secret and sole right of manufacture, contains the following **TWENTY-FIVE QUALITIES**, possessed by no other Ink in the world :—

1. Writes Black and remains everlastingly Black.
2. No preparation of any kind required.
3. No heating or hot iron necessary.
4. No chance of burning the cloth.
5. No scorching or iron mould possible.
6. No chemical solution can take it out.
7. Will stand any amount of boiling.
8. Will never turn brown or rusty.
9. Will not injure the finest material.
10. Can be used with steel or quill pens.
11. Will flow like ordinary Ink from the pen.
12. Can be used with stencil plates.
13. The best Ink for rubber stamps.
14. Can be used for ornamenting toilet mats, and hundreds of other articles of cloth, silk, and linen.
15. Like the Ink of the Ancients, it is imperishable.
16. Is the Blackest Marking Ink at the time of writing.
17. No caustic alkalies or other chemical can remove it.
18. The more it is washed or boiled the brighter and more intense the Black.
19. It is not an ordinary marking Ink.
20. For Manufacturers of Linen articles it is the best Ink for Stamping or Marking.
21. For hotel, hospital, and general use, it is the cheapest and best.
22. It is not a dye, but a Chemical Marking Ink.
23. It will not corrode or eat away steel pens.
24. It does not spoil by age, like ordinary marking Inks.
25. It will last longer than any fabric it is written on.

CAN BE HAD OF EVERY CHEMIST AND STATIONER IN THE KNOWN WORLD.

Also in Bottles for large users at 1/-, 2/6, 5/-, 10/- & 20/- each.

HENRY THACKER & CO.,
MANUFACTURERS AND SOLE PROPRIETORS,
NEW STREET SQUARE, LONDON, E.C.

ADVERTISEMENTS.

THE "GENUINE HUMBER"

BICYCLES AND TRICYCLES

DEPOT, CORPORATION STREET, BIRMINGHAM.

PRICE LISTS FREE.

CHARLES AND CO., STEAM PRINTERS, GREYSTOKE PLACE, FETTER LANE, E.C.

HORSE, CATTLE, & SHEEP MEDICINES.

By Royal Appointment.

DAY, SON & HEWITT,

INVENTORS AND ONLY PROPRIETORS OF THE
"ORIGINAL"

HORSE KEEPER'S MEDICINE CHEST,
For all Disorders in Horses.

Patronised by Royalty, and used for Fifty years by the principal Stock-Breeders, Horse Proprietors, and Agriculturists of the British Empire.

Price Complete, 57s. 6d.
Keep good 20 years.
Carriage paid to any Port or Railway Station.

The No. 4 CHEST contains the following Matchless Preparations :—

The CHEMICAL EXTRACT, for Kicks, Cuts, Wounds, Bruises, Saddle-galls, &c.
The GASEOUS FLUID, for Fret, Colic, or Gripes in Horses, and Debility.
The RED PASTE BALLS, for Conditioning Horses, and imparting a mole-like Sleekness of Coat.
The RED CONDITION POWDERS, for Coughs, Colds, Staring Coat, &c.
The BLACK PHYSIC BALLS, for Worms in Horses, and warding off Disease.
The BLISTER OINTMENT, for Old Strains, Swelling of the Joints and Tendons.
The "GASEODYNE," for Heaving and Paining; "Alcoholic Ether," for Chills, &c.

Horsekeeper's Chest, No. 4, including "Key to Farriery," £2. 17s. 6d.
Complete Stock-Breeder's Medicine Chest, No. 1, with "Key to Farriery," £6. 6s. 0d.
Stock-Breeder's Medicine Chest No. 2, including "Key to Farriery," £2. 16s. 6d.

Each Article can be had separately in Boxes.

PRIZE MEDALS AWARDED IN ENGLAND AND THE COLONIES.

CAUTION.—Beware of IMITATIONS, and see that the Name of DAY, SON & HEWITT is on all Bottles and Packets.

—o—

DAY, SON and HEWITT,
22, Dorset St., Baker St., London, W.; & Wantage, Berks.

ESTABLISHED 1833.

ESTABLISHED 1789.

ARTHUR HART,
VINEY BRIDGE MILLS,
CREWKERNE, ENGLAND,

MANUFACTURER OF

SADDLERY WEBS

Of every description,

FOR THE ENGLISH & FOREIGN MARKETS,

BY HAND AND POWER.

Girth, Roller, Brace, Body-Belt, Straining, Rein, Halter, Tray, Pack, Circular, Elevator, &c., Webs,

IN

WOOL, UNION, LINEN, COTTON, & JUTE.

UPHOLSTERY WEBS & TWINES.

Samples and Prices free on application.

HART'S PATENT BRACES,

SPECIALLY ADAPTED FOR

CAVALRY

Use. The sword belt being suspended from the Braces the weight on the belt is distributed over the body, and there is no possibility of the belt appearing below the shell jacket.

GIRTHS, ROLLERS, SURCINGLES, HALTERS, BODY-BELTS, GROOMS'-BELTS, ATHLETIC-BELTS, &c., &c.

Super Seamless Flax Hose Web.

NO INFERIOR QUALITIES MADE.

ARTHUR HART,

VINEY BRIDGE MILLS,
CREWKERNE, ENGLAND.

Contractor to the Government.

www.ingramcontent.com/pod-product-compliance
Lightning Source LLC
Chambersburg PA
CBHW031331230426
43670CB00006B/304